Global Issues Series

General Editor: **Jim Whitman**

This exciting new series encompasses three principal themes: the interaction of human and natural systems; cooperation and conflict; and the enactment of values. The series as a whole places an emphasis on the examination of complex systems and causal relations in political decision-making; problems of knowledge; authority, control and accountability in issues of scale; and the reconciliation of conflicting values and competing claims. Throughout the series the concentration is on an integration of existing disciplines towards the clarification of political possibility as well as impending crises.

Titles include:

Berhanykun Andemicael and John Mathiason
ELIMINATING WEAPONS OF MASS DESTRUCTION
Prospects for Effective International Verification

Roy Carr-Hill and John Lintott
CONSUMPTION, JOBS AND THE ENVIRONMENT
A Fourth Way?

John N. Clarke and Geoffrey R. Edwards (*editors*)
GLOBAL GOVERNANCE IN THE TWENTY-FIRST CENTURY

Malcolm Dando
PREVENTING BIOLOGICAL WARFARE
The Failure of American Leadership

Toni Erskine (*editors*)
CAN INSTITUTIONS HAVE RESPONSIBILITIES?
Collective Moral Agency and International Relations

Brendan Gleeson and Nicholas Low (*editors*)
GOVERNING FOR THE ENVIRONMENT
Global Problems, Ethics and Democracy

Roger Jeffery and Bhaskar Vira (*editors*)
CONFLICT AND COOPERATION IN PARTICIPATORY NATURAL RESOURCE
MANAGEMENT

Ho-Won Jeong (*editor*)
GLOBAL ENVIRONMENTAL POLICIES
Institutions and Procedures

APPROACHES TO PEACEBUILDING

W. Andy Knight
A CHANGING UNITED NATIONS
Multilateral Evolution and the Quest for Global Governance

W. Andy Knight (*editor*)
ADAPTING THE UNITED NATIONS TO A POSTMODERN ERA
Lessons Learned

Kelley Lee
HEALTH IMPACTS OF GLOBALIZATION (*editor*)
Towards Global Governance

GLOBALIZATION AND HEALTH
An Introduction

Nicholas Low and Brendan Gleeson (*editors*)
MAKING URBAN TRANSPORT SUSTAINABLE

Graham S. Pearson
THE UNSCOM SAGA
Chemical and Biological Weapons Non-Proliferation

Andrew T. Price-Smith (*editor*)
PLAGUES AND POLITICS
Infectious Disease and International Policy

Michael Pugh (*editor*)
REGENERATION OF WAR-TORN SOCIETIES

Bhaskar Vira and Roger Jeffery (*editors*)
ANALYTICAL ISSUES IN PARTICIPATORY NATURAL RESOURCE MANAGEMENT

Simon M. Whitby
BIOLOGICAL WARFARE AGAINST CROPS

Global Issues Series
Series Standing Order ISBN 0–333–79483–4
(*outside North America only*)

You can receive future titles in this series as they are published by placing a standing order.
Please contact your bookseller or, in case of difficulty, write to us at the address below with
your name and address, the title of the series and the ISBN quoted above.

Customer Services Department, Macmillan Distribution Ltd, Houndmills, Basingstoke,
Hampshire RG21 6XS, England

Eliminating Weapons of Mass Destruction

Prospects for Effective International Verification

Berhanykun Andemicael
*Former Representative of the International Atomic
Energy Agency to the United Nations, USA*

and

John Mathiason
*Adjunct Professor of International Relations
Maxwell School of Citizenship and Public Affairs
Syracuse University, USA*

Foreword by

Hans Blix
*Former Executive Chairman of the United Nations Monitoring,
Verification and Inspection Commission*

First published in 2005 by
PALGRAVE MACMILLAN
Houndmills, Basingstoke, Hampshire RG21 6XS and
175 Fifth Avenue, New York, N.Y. 10010
Companies and representatives throughout the world.

PALGRAVE MACMILLAN is the global academic imprint of the Palgrave
Macmillan division of St. Martin's Press, LLC and of Palgrave Macmillan Ltd.
Macmillan® is a registered trademark in the United States, United Kingdom
and other countries. Palgrave is a registered trademark in the European
Union and other countries.

ISBN 13: 978–0–333–97034–8
ISBN 10: 0–333–97034–9

This book is printed on paper suitable for recycling and made from fully
managed and sustained forest sources.

A catalogue record for this book is available from the British Library.

Library of Congress Cataloging-in-Publication Data
Andemicael, Berhanykun.
    Eliminating weapons of mass destruction: prospects for effective
international verification / Berhanykun Andemicael and John Mathiason;
foreword by Hans Blix.
        p. cm.—(Global issues)
    Includes bibliographical references and index.
    ISBN 0–333–97034–9 (cloth)
        1. Nuclear nonproliferation. 2. Nuclear arms control. I. Mathiason,
John, 1942– II. Title. III. Global issues series (Palgrave Macmillan (Firm))
JZ5675.A53 2005
327.1′745—dc22   2004056899

10 9 8 7 6 5 4 3 2 1
14 13 12 11 10 09 08 07 06 05

Printed and bound in Great Britain by
Antony Rowe Ltd, Chippenham and Eastbourne

Contents

List of Tables and Figures

Tables

Figure

Foreword

This is a timely study and one that has emerged from the combination of an extensive examination of literature and a rich practical experience of how the issue of international verification of the elimination of weapons of mass destruction has been handled in the relevant international organizations and the Security Council. It contains a wealth of information and constructive ideas.

Inspectors – whether examining tax returns, imported articles, or elevators – are rarely loved by the public but as citizens we accept their activity because we know that it is in the public interest. Governments are traditionally rigidly averse to allowing any authorities not under their control to exercise any functions within their territories. They have not taken enthusiastically to international verification of arms control obligations, but as they are keen that neighbours and other states accept verification they have to do so themselves. It is in their interest.

Institutionalized and continuous on-site inspection and verification came only with the Non-Proliferation Treaty. A number of treaty provisions from the end of the nineteenth century and onward prohibited the *use* of specific weapons, which were deemed to cause 'unnecessary suffering' or to have indiscriminate effect, for example the dum-dum bullet. As such, uses would generally be visible and respect for the bans was expected to result from the risk of retaliation, they did not contain specific provisions for inspection or implementation. For the nuclear weapons, it was different. It was deemed that the safest way to prevent a use – by the non-nuclear-weapon States – was through a ban on acquisition and development: no weapon, no use! However, acquisition and development might not be visible but could be achieved in secret. To create confidence against cheating and unpleasant surprises, verification and inspection became necessary. The same pattern was followed later in the Chemical Weapons Convention and in the Comprehensive Test-Ban Treaty.

As this book demonstrates, the development of a professional independent verification system through the IAEA was not easy. It was the world's first modest – some would perhaps say shy – try of on-site inspection and it was geared to give confidence that there was no diversion of fissionable material from peaceful nuclear installations in advanced democratic and open societies. It did not create the means by which the

IAEA could satisfy itself that there were no *undeclared* installations for non-peaceful purposes. The first inspections by the IAEA in Iraq after the Gulf War in 1991 showed that this closed dictatorship had long violated the NPT without being found out. The safeguards inspectors had been limited to declared installations. In any case, in the absence of any intelligence information and satellite imagery, they would not have known where to look for non-declared secret installations in the closed police state.

The discovery in Iraq in 1991 persuaded the Member States of the IAEA that the system had to be drastically strengthened. They realized reluctantly that all had to accept a more intrusive system. Many new techniques, such as the use of automatic real time monitors, environmental sampling, commercial satellite imagery plus information about export and import and from national intelligence services, combined to make the new system more effective. It has yet to be accepted by the whole world community. It certainly is a leap forward from the traditional safeguards. At the same time, there should be no illusions that it could give guarantees about the discovery of small volumes of relevant activities, equipment or material. The laboratory production of gram quantities of enriched uranium or plutonium could easily be overlooked, if no one gives the inspectors information.

Some complain that the verification and inspection systems are without teeth, as they cannot stop illegal production of WMDs. However, on reflection it will be found that this is not really the function of inspectors. Rather, they are watchdogs with instruction to bark and alert governments to violations and even to non-cooperation by an inspected party. The power to intervene – by economic, diplomatic or other pressure – lies with the governments, which should also, as this book rightly stresses, back the inspectors in the performance of their tasks, and ensure that they have adequate resources of personnel and modern equipment.

Government support of international inspection systems should not develop into too close an embrace, however, lest the systems become suspected of being remote controlled instruments of specific States. To be acceptable to States subject to inspection and verification and to be credible, the verification systems must be independent, which, as this book rightly emphasizes, can only occur if they are run by intergovernmental organizations.

It is paradoxical that at a time when independent international inspection has developed into maturity and recently proved to come to rather accurate assessments of the weapons situation in Iraq, where national intelligence systems went very wrong, the United States, which has done so much to develop the systems, appears to be turning its back on them. During the Cold War the United States and many other States insisted that disarmament required verification. The Soviet Union agreed but took the view that only the destruction of arms should be verified – the 'bonfire'. What might remain in or later be added to the arsenals in the closed empire was no business of other States. No agreement was attainable. Gradually the Soviet Union became more open to inspection, not least in its bilateral arms control agreement with the United States.

Today it is the United States that is averse to verification and inspection! It declined to have a verification arrangement with Russia about the mutual reduction of nuclear warheads and barely accepted placing the measures in a formal agreement. It generally distrusts international verification and inspection mechanisms and prefers and trusts its own eyes and ears in the sky and spies on the ground. The US has rejected the Comprehensive Test-Ban Treaty, arguing, alone among States, that the verification would not be sufficiently reliable. It has rejected any verification mechanism for the Biological Weapons Convention and declared a negative attitude to verification of a convention prohibiting the production of fissile material for nuclear weapons (FMCT). The US has, however, continued to support the safeguards system of the IAEA and in the negotiations with the Democratic People's Republic of Korea it has insisted that an agreement must be verifiable.

It must be hoped that after the realization that the national intelligence, which the US and its allies relied upon before the armed action in Iraq in March 2003, was faulty and that the ignored inspection results of UNMOVIC and the IAEA were generally correct, there will be a reassessment in the US of the use of independent international verification. As the authors of this book stress, the reassessment should go even further. The negative attitude not only to international inspection but also to treaty commitments and to genuine cooperation with other States in the UN system has brought wide pessimism and malaise.

The Cold War is over. There is no risk of another war between great powers over territory or ideology, only of regional conflicts, civil war and of terrorist acts by the weak, disoriented and despairing. These acts do not signal a war of civilizations and we should not by our responses to them lead the world into such a war. It is difficult to understand that in this situation the United States should change to be a lone and angry wolf from being a respected lead wolf. It is not difficult to see how it could constructively lead again. The authors of this book rightly point to a programme of disarmament and to the use of mature international verification. A ratification of the Comprehensive Test-Ban Treaty would, in all likelihood, lead China, India, Pakistan and Iran and others to renounce all future testing. Not a small gain – also for the United States, which does not need any new types of nuclear weapons and which has no sympathy for other States developing their nuclear capabilities. The authors point further to a treaty to stop the production of more highly enriched uranium and plutonium for weapons. A reduction in the number of nuclear weapons needs to be coupled with an agreement not to make material for more weapons.

The list of possible and desirable measures for a cooperative reduction of the threats posed by weapons of mass destruction is long. This book shows that international verification has come a long way and can be put to good use as a tool to help in this process.

Stockholm

HANS BLIX
Former Executive Chairman of the United Nations Monitoring,
Verification and Inspection Commission
Director-General Emeritus of the
International Atomic Energy Agency
Chairman, Weapons of Mass Destruction Commission

Preface: Will Things Go Boom in the Night?

A belief in the real threat that someone will employ weapons of mass destruction (WMD) is one of the consequences of the events of September 11, 2001. The rhetoric of fear has become pervasive, with the United States declaring a policy of pre-emptive strikes whenever it feels that there is a potential that another State could acquire, develop or use a weapon of mass destruction.

In many respects, it recalls the medieval world that was full of unnamed, uncontrollable fears, towards which a traditional Scottish prayer was addressed:

> From ghoulies and ghosties
> And long-leggedy beasties
> And things that go bump in the night,
> Good Lord, deliver us!

At the beginning of the twenty-first century, the ghoulies, ghosties and long-leggedly beasties are chemical, biological and nuclear weapons, all of which could go *boom* in the night. Deliverance from them is a matter of disarmament, setting the conditions where these weapons can be eliminated from existing arsenals and from any future use.

Times do not seem propitious for optimism. The United States has clearly changed its course away from supporting and encouraging the development of an international regime to deal with WMD. While the real reason for this change is probably the renewed reverence for sovereignty and the desire to have unregulated use of the resources that the world's only remaining superpower could have, the formal argument against the international regime is that the institutions that are created to verify compliance will not work.

The central argument of the United States is that the international institutions that are now established, or could be established, cannot function well or plausibly enough to verify that existing weapons of mass destruction are destroyed or potential weapons are not created. On the other hand, for States like India, Pakistan, Iraq and North Korea, the argument is that disarmament should not only be effectively verified but should equally apply to the more powerful States that might threaten their own security. Both sides, however, seem to share the argument that international public organizations are not effective in safeguarding their national interests and that they can only rely on old-fashioned nation-state institutions for their security.

At the November 2001 meeting of States Parties to the Biological Weapons Convention, John Bolton, the United States Under-Secretary of State for Non-Proliferation, said:[1]

> The time for 'better than nothing' protocols is over. It is time for us to consider serious measures to address the BW threat. It is time to set aside years of diplomatic inertia. We will not be protected by a 'Maginot treaty' approach to the BW threat.

In rejecting a verification protocol to the Convention, he was asserting a new position: that international organizations were ineffective verifiers. This was the same position taken when the United States announced that it had no intention of ratifying the Comprehensive Nuclear Test-Ban Treaty, thus guaranteeing that it would not enter into force.

The present study tests this fundamental hypothesis: can international organizations realistically verify compliance with conventions to eliminate weapons of mass destruction? If so, can the objective be achieved more effectively by such multilateral means than by reliance predominantly on individual policies and national means for verification? From the answer to these two questions, a sense of what are the real disarmament issues of the day can be drawn. And finally an answer can be found to the question, can we keep things from going boom in the night?

The study presents an insider's view, based on our long experience as international officials and applying our combined research skills and knowledge of both disarmament and management issues within the United Nations system.

As authors, we wish to acknowledge with much appreciation the support and helpful comments we have received at different stages of this study. Hans Blix, and later Mohamed ElBaradei, as successive Directors General of the IAEA supported the idea of the project, and the former has now contributed a foreword to the book. We are most grateful to them. From the UN Department for Disarmament Affairs (DDA), we thank former Under-Secretary-General Jayantha Dhanapala and Randy Rydell for their critical advice on the original design of the project. We are also indebted to the late Professor Oscar Schachter for his inspiring ideas on the issue of compliance with norms, so central to the study. We also thank Joseph Cirincione of the Carnegie Endowment for International Peace, Patricia Lewis, Director of the UN Institute for Disarmament Research, Amy Smithson of the Henry L. Stimson Center and William C. Potter and Amy Sands from the Monterey Institute for International studies (MIIS), for making available helpful research material as well as for offering initial suggestions. On parts of the manuscript, valuable comments, suggestions and some corrections were received from Lawrence Scheinman and Jonathan B. Tucker of the MIIS Center for Nonproliferation Studies, Ralf Trapp of the Organization for the Prohibition of Chemical Weapons (OPCW), Gerardo Suarez, Daniela Rozgonova and Boris Kvok of the Comprehensive Test Ban Treaty Organization, from Mitchel Wallenstein, Dean of the Maxwell School of Syracuse University and Former Deputy Assistant Secretary of Defence for Counter-Proliferation Policy and also from Michael O. Wheeler of the Scientific Applications International Corporation; we are deeply indebted to them. We also thank Demetrius Perricos of the UN Monitoring, Verification and Inspection Commission (UNMOVIC) and Frank R. Cleminson of Rundle Virtual Research Group (Canada) for their comments on some specific proposals. Helpful corrections were also received from Julian Perry Robinson of the University of Sussex, Ewen Buchanan of UNMOVIC. We also gratefully acknowledge the liaison assistance provided by Gustavo Zlauvinen and Tarig Rauf of the IAEA, Tsutomu Kono of UN/DDA and Rafael M. Gross of the OPCW and the valuable news-clippings on proliferation issues we regularly received from Ewen, his colleague Geffrey Allan as well as Tracy Brown of the IAEA New York Office.

We thank Iobel and Stefan Andemicael for their helpful editing suggestions and Menkerios Andemicael for his design proposed for the book cover. We particularly appreciate Jan Clausen's effective work in preparing the final manuscript. Finally we are grateful to our families for their patience and moral support, especially Lisl Andemicael for her encouragement and passion for peace.

While greatly appreciative of all the help received, we are solely responsible for any remaining errors or inaccuracies in this book and are wholly responsible for the opinions expressed.

BERHANYKUN ANDEMICAEL
JOHN MATHIASON

Mt Tremper, New York

List of Abbreviations

ABACC	Argentine-Brazilian Agency for Accounting and Control of Nuclear Materials
ABM Treaty	Anti-Ballistic Missile Treaty
Agreed Framework	Agreed Framework between the United States of America and the Democratic People's Republic of Korea
Additional Protocol	Additional Protocol to the Agreements between States and the IAEA for the Application of Safeguards
Australia Group	Coalition of exporting States formed to restrict transfer of chemical weapon precursors and toxic chemicals
Baruch Plan	United States proposal to create an International Development Authority
BWC	Biological and Toxin Weapons Convention (Convention on the Prohibition of the Development, Production, and Stockpiling of Bacteriological (Biological) and Toxin Weapons and on Their Destruction)
CD	Conference on Disarmament
CFE Treaty	Conventional Arms Forces in Europe Treaty
CIA	Central Intelligence Agency
COCOM	Coordinating Committee for Multilateral Export Controls
CTBT	Comprehensive Nuclear Test-Ban Treaty
CTBTO	Comprehensive Nuclear Test-Ban Treaty Organization
CWC	Chemical Weapons Convention (Convention on the Prohibition of the Development, Production, Stockpiling and Use of Chemical Weapons and Their Destruction)
DDG	Deputy Director General
DG	Director General
EIF	Entry into force
ENDC	Eighteen-Nation Disarmament Committee
EU	European Union

EURATOM	European Atomic Energy Authority
FMCT	Fissile Material Cut-off Treaty
G-8	Group of Eight Heads of State and Government of the most economically significant States
GCD	General and Complete Disarmament
Geneva Protocol	Protocol for the Prohibition of the Use in War of Asphyxiating, Poisonous or Other Gases, and of Bacteriological Methods of Warfare
GCI	Global Communications Infrastructure
GPC	General Purpose Criterion
HEU	Highly-enriched uranium
IAEA	International Atomic Energy Agency
IDC	International Data Center
ILO	International Labour Organisation
IMS	International Monitoring System
INF Treaty	Intermediate-range Nuclear Forces Treaty
INFCIRC	IAEA's formal 'Information Circular' document
ISMA	International Satellite Monitoring Agency
KGB	Soviet central intelligence agency
US-USSR Principles	Agreed Principles for Disarmament Negotiations (McCloy-Zorin)
MAD	Mutual Assured Destruction
MCTR	Missile Technology Control Regime
MUF	Material unaccounted for
NAM	Non-Aligned Movement
NATO	North Atlantic Treaty Organization
NGO	Non-governmental organization
NNWS	Non-nuclear-weapon State
NPT	Nuclear Non-Proliferation Treaty (Treaty on the Non-Proliferation of Nuclear Weapons)
NSG	Nuclear Suppliers Group
NTM	National technical means
NWFZ	Nuclear-weapon-free zone
NWS	Nuclear-weapon State
OSI	On-site inspection
OPCW	Organization for the Prohibition of Chemical Weapons
P-5	Five permanent members of the UN Security Council
PMO	Policy-making organs
PTS	Provisional Technical Secretariat

PTBT	Partial Test-Ban Treaty (Treaty Banning Nuclear weapon Tests in the Atmosphere, in Outer Space and Under Water)
R & D	Research and development
SALT	Strategic Arms Limitation Treaty (SALT I, SALT II)
SIPRI	Stockholm International Peace Research Institute
SQ	Significant quantity of nuclear material (sufficient to make a nuclear explosive)
START	Strategic Arms Reduction Treaty (START I, START II)
SSOD	United Nations General Assembly's Special Session devoted to Disarmament
Treaty of Bangkock	Treaty on the South-East Asia Nuclear-Weapon-Free Zone
Treaty of Pelindaba	African Nuclear-Weapon-Free Zone Treaty
Treaty of Raratonga	South Pacific Nuclear-Weapon-Free Zone Treaty
Treaty of Tlateloco	Treaty for the Prohibition of Nuclear Weapons in Latin America and the Caribbean
UDOC	Unscheduled discrete organic chemicals
UN	United Nations
UNDC	United Nations Disarmament Commission
UNIDIR	United Nations Institute for Disarmament Research
UNMOVIC	United Nations Monitoring, Verification and Inspection Commission on Iraq
UNSCOM	United Nations Special Commission on Iraq
UK	United Kingdom of Great Britain and Northern Ireland
USSR	Union of Soviet Socialist Republics
US	United States of America
VERTIC	Verification Research, Training and Information Centre
VX	V chemical agent
WASSENAAR	Arrangement on Export Controls for Conventional Arms and Dual-use Goods and Technology
WIPO	World International Property Organization
WMD	Weapons of mass destruction
Zangger Committee	NPT Exporters Committee

Part I

Overview of the WMD Ban Regime

In order to fully understand the dynamics of today's debate on the process of arms control and disarmament and on the effectiveness of the existing verification mechanisms for the control of weapons of mass destruction (WMD), Part I presents an overview of the WMD control regime in both a conceptual and historical framework. The structure and logic of the regime to ban WMD is described in Chapter 1 while Chapter 2 traces the evolution of the emerging regime in the post-World War II era.

1
The Structure and Logic of the WMD Ban Regime

The issue of how to eliminate weapons of mass destruction was a major feature of international politics at the end of the twentieth century. It was also an essential part of the debate about international relations theory. The 'balance of terror', the possibilities loosed by technology of weapons that could destroy all human life on earth provided an incentive to find solutions. At the same time, it was the highest expression of the realist approach to international politics, dealing as it does with the ability of a State to defend itself.

The issue has gained much greater salience in the aftermath of the terrorist attacks on the World Trade Center and the Pentagon, for two reasons. First, it increased the fear that weapons of mass destruction could be used by a 'rogue' State or by a non-State actor. Second, the United States government took an increasingly unilateralist position and worked to reduce the scope of international agreements and institutions that were set up to eliminate the weapons of mass destruction (WMD). This position embodied a realist's cognitive set, with its assumption that only States could control the behaviour of other States and that the role of international organizations was minimal, if at all.

The WMD problem began with the one type of weapons that probably does not cause mass destruction: chemical weapons. The first disarmament efforts focused on banning these weapons, without, however, ignoring the potential of devastating germ warfare that had occasionally been crudely attempted in the past by spreading disease to the enemy without any technological refinements. Since the delivery of chemical weapons is localized, multiple bombs would be required to cause mass destruction. Chemical and biological weapons were considered abhorrent because they were indiscriminate. They could affect soldiers and civilians alike; they could not really be targeted in the same sense that

3

a conventional bomb or a mortar shell might be, for example as regards precision and control consistent with military objectives. Their prohibition in 1925 has largely been respected, notably during World War II, despite the precedents of chemical use set in the 1930s by Japan against China and Italy in Ethiopia and the use of chemical weapons half a century later by both sides in the Iran–Iraq War.

The real incentive for dealing with the unconventional weapons came with the nuclear age, since nuclear weapons are truly designed for mass destruction, on a major scale and with indiscriminate effects. While extensive and sustained conventional bombing can also wreak mass destruction, it cannot do as quite as effectively and efficiently as nuclear weapons. Indeed, the quantity of nuclear warheads assembled during the second half of the twentieth century could destroy human life several times over. The fear of these weapons is such that they have only been used twice during warfare, in Hiroshima and Nagasaki some sixty years ago.

The advances of biological science in the twentieth century led to the development of biological weapons, which are sometimes called 'the poor man's atom bomb'.[1] Deadly diseases like anthrax, botulism, the plague and even smallpox, rather than being eliminated, have been improved for weaponry. The reason that they are not a more public part of the arsenal is that the capacity to deliver or weaponize them effectively has lagged behind the technology to produce the agents. This partly explains why Iraq did not use them during the Gulf War (although the fear of their use meant that the military during Desert Storm were all vaccinated against anthrax).

An additional factor today is the concept of the 'rogue State', a government ruled by persons who are unwilling to abide by international norms and might even be so irrational as to use WMD against an enemy. Clearly, that is the position that was taken by the United States and some others on Iraq.

Add to this the idea that non-State actors, supported by various rogue States, might try to use these weapons for terrorism, as in the nerve-gas attack on the Tokyo subway by a quasi-religious group, the Aum Shinrikyo and, of course, potentially Al-Qaeda.

To deal with the threat of weapons of mass destruction, States have created an interlocking set of treaties providing for the elimination of WMD. At one level, the network of treaties is classic realism. The only way that the treaties can be enforced in the face of a State's defiance is through the use of force by other nation-States, as foreseen in Chapter VII of the United Nations Charter. The response of the

United States and others to Iraq's defiance of Security Council resolutions is a clear case.

At the same time, the treaties provide for mechanisms to verify that provisions are being met by the State Parties. Most provide for an international verification mechanism. This recognizes the inherent limitations of realism in a complex, interdependent world. Without a credible, authoritative and independent means of assuring all concerned States that a treaty is being broken, the prospects of obtaining an agreement to use coercive enforcement are limited. A case in point is the initial effort of the United States to obtain the consent of the Security Council in 2003 for such action in Iraq, the failure of which was used as a pretext to pursue a unilateral course.

The assurance that deviation from the provisions of the treaties will be effectively detected and lead to coercive action on a multilateral basis by stronger States is perhaps the greatest deterrence to States who might consider developing or proliferating weapons of mass destruction.

Behind this simple idea is a much more complex structure, based on certain assumptions about the nature of international politics, power and organizations. An overview of these assumptions is a necessary starting point to understanding and appraising the verification mechanisms.

The regime to ban WMD

When governments agreed on the various treaties that provided for the elimination of weapons of mass destruction, they were constructing an edifice of law and practice that transcended national borders and capacities. They were constructing what is usually called an international regime. We argue that the WMD ban is really a regime. In his study of UNSCOM (United Nations Special Commission), Graham Pearson refers to 'the web of deterrence' that, *inter alia*, includes 'comprehensive and effective arms control that clearly establishes the norm and has intrusive verification *regimes* to build confidence in compliance'.[2] Is it a single regime or several? The answer depends on how one defines a regime.

The term 'regime' in common usage refers to a mode or system of rule or government. Its application at the international level is derived from international relations theory, as a response to the inadequacy of the dominant realist model to explain international behaviour.

Realism posits that the international system is the consequence of the actions of individual States that weigh their national interest and use their power to promote that interest. For most of the twentieth century, it was in its various forms the dominant explanatory model for international politics.[3] It is a good theory to explain conflict, or justify the use of force in relations, but is not as good in explaining why States reach binding agreements and peaceful resolution of conflict.

The classic definition of a regime was given by Stephen Krasner in a seminal issue of the journal *International Organization* in 1983. He said:[4]

An international regime is a set of principles – explicit or implicit – norms, rules and decision-making procedures around which expectations of actors [States] converge in order to coordinate actors' behaviour with respect to a concern to them all.

The definition has four components:

- 'principles, norms, rules and decision-making procedures' represent elements of institutions, of regularity;
- 'expectations of actors' refers to cognitive and perceptual aspects rather than to actions;
- 'converge in order to coordinate' refers to the agreement to mutually affect possible behavior by indirect means rather than by authoritative means; and
- 'a concern to them all' refers to the fact that the collective pay-off is considered more important than the individual interest.

An international regime is an attempt to build an institutional structure of regulation without altering the basic institutional structure of the international system, based on State sovereignty. Within that context, international public institutions have a unique character.

The idea of regime theory was not originally related to the problem of regulating State behaviour in the WMD field, but was rather an attempt to explain what was happening in such areas as the Law of the Sea and the laws of outer space and the environment in general. The realist model did not have a place for such developments. The regime idea came at a point when neo-functionalist scholars saw an increasing amount of 'supranationalism' in trade and the economy (e.g. the European Community), even though the main building blocks were still sovereign States. Regime theory, in a Hegelian sense, was indeed a synthesis between the realist thesis and the functionalist antithesis. As a theory of international relations, regime theory had limited uses, and had more or less gone out of fashion by the end of the 1980s and was replaced by new approaches focused on international political economy and by concepts such as 'new institutionalism' and 'social construc-tivism'. Susan Strange's critique of regime theory in the 1983 volume of *International Organization*, 'Cave Hic Dragones!', was used by many as the definitive put-down.[5]

As scholars sought to use the concept, the real problem surfaced: it was difficult for theorists to apply it in practice. While treaty-based regimes, like the Law of the Sea, could fit, most international agreements were too amorphous to fit. There were some efforts to examine 'trade regimes' like the automobile industry, but they were particularly elusive. Regime theory fell from favour but still remains a useful source of concepts in regulating international organizations. As former international civil servants, regime theory resonates with us. We believe that it provides some useful explanatory tools for explaining the process of eliminating WMD, particularly the role of international secretariats.

Again, using Krasner's original definitions, the elements of a regime are the following:

- Principles are beliefs of fact, causation and rectitude;
- Norms are standards of behaviour defined in terms of rights and obligations;
- Rules are specific prescriptions and prohibitions with respect to actors' behaviour;
- Procedures are the prevailing practices for making and implementing collective choices.

To anyone who has participated, over a long period of time, in multilateral negotiations, this is exactly the order in which the negotiations proceed. There first has to be an agreement that a problem exists, a common understanding of its causal parameters and the need to resolve it through collective action ('rectitude'). States then have to define the normative parameters. Then States have to agree on rules, and finally they must set up institutions that will enable collective choices. A regime is not really complete until all four stages have been agreed, although things can begin to happen after stage two as soon as norms are established.

A complicating factor is that sometimes regimes overlap and often this overlapping makes the agreement process complex. In international negotiation this is called 'linkage', where an issue in one subject area is connected with an issue in another and both have to be resolved together if either is to be agreed.

At the international level, regimes are usually embodied in conventions, multilateral treaties that are binding on their parties. Moreover, there can be regimes that are formed somewhat less formally by less-binding kinds of agreements. However, fully articulated regimes inevitably have some form of treaty basis.

Applied to the issue of WMD, we can see that there was a consensus that the existence of WMD and the risk of proliferating them was destabilizing international relations and threatening to produce unacceptable outcomes. There was an agreement that the weapons could produce mass destruction. There was an agreement that eliminating these weapons would reduce the threat of conflict (causation) and was thus good.

There was also agreement that States that had WMD should not develop them further or give them, or their components, to States that did not have them, and that steps should be taken to eliminate and destroy the stocks of weapons. States had an obligation never to use them. States who lacked them had an obligation not to try to obtain them.

In significant recent publications, the Carnegie Endowment for International Peace has analyzed the problems and possibilities of 'repairing the regime' for preventing the spread of weapons of mass destruction and for tracking any signs of proliferation. The study is based on a useful definition: 'global non-proliferation regime is a network of interlocking treaties, organizations, unilateral and bilateral undertakings, and multi-lateral inspections aimed at halting the spread of nuclear, chemical and biological weapons'.[6] As the objective of these instruments goes beyond preventing proliferation, we prefer broadening the concept in this study to apply to the broader objective of WMD ban or elimination.

The WMD ban regime is centred on the following four WMD conventions, as buttressed by several regional and bilateral arrangements, norms and arrangements:

- The 1968 Treaty on the Non-Proliferation of Nuclear Weapons (NPT), which entered into force in 1970 and currently has over 190 parties, including the five nuclear-weapon States.
- The 1996 Comprehensive Nuclear Test-Ban Treaty (CTBT), which is not yet in force but has 172 signatories and 115 ratifications, including 33 of the 44 annex II countries.[7]
- The 1992 Convention on the Prohibition of the Development, Production, Stockpiling and Use of Chemical Weapons and on Their

Destruction (CWC), which entered into force in 1997 and has over 160 parties. And

- The 1972 Convention on the Prohibition of the Development, Production and Stockpiling of Bacteriological (Biological) and Toxin Weapons (BWC) and on their Destruction, which entered into force in 1975 and has over 150 parties.

All of these were negotiated within the context of the United Nations Conference on Disarmament as building blocks for a potential all-encompassing disarmament regime, initially conceived as a single system of General and Complete Disarmament (GCD), implemented by an international disarmament organization. The dichotomy between conventional and unconventional weapons had crystallized the concept of weapons of mass destruction as a useful category of the most lethal weapons for verified elimination. The WMD ban regime was to advance on the basis of separately negotiated 'partial measures', focused on each type of weapon, but forming a network of treaties interrelated by preambular cross references, common principles and norms, parallel mechanisms and procedures of recourse, ultimately to the UN Security Council.

Within each treaty system, the concept of regime is fully developed and we may clearly refer to the Nuclear Non-Proliferation Regime (including the NPT, the CTBT and regional arrangements), the CWC Regime and, to a lesser extent, the BWC Regime. However, the extent of progress towards an overarching WMD regime has been limited by political constraints undermining parallel development of all stages of a regime. While principles and norms for an obligatory ban of all WMD are fully agreed, rules and procedures as the third and fourth stages of regime-building are yet to be accepted across the board. That is particularly where the issue of verification comes into play.

In the early disarmament treaties of the twentieth century, following the realist model, it was assumed that the agreements would be self-policing. States, run by gentlemen, would simply honour their agreements. Unfortunately, many of the States, it seems, were not run by gentlemen.

In implementing disarmament treaties there are several dilemmas to be addressed, if compliance is to take place:

- States involved in the elimination of WMD confront almost a classic version of the Prisoner's Dilemma game. While the best outcome is that both parties disarm, what happens if one does, in good faith, and the other does not? In that case the one that does not will dominate the one that did, thus increasing the cost of compliance.

- States may be run by leaders who are unscrupulous and irrational and who might not comply. If one of these 'rogue States' acquires WMD, they could wreak their irrational national interests on all States that had complied. Thus, there is a reason for non-rogue States not to eliminate their WMD.
- Non-State actors who, by definition, are not bound by international conventions, might obtain WMD from States that have them, or even develop some themselves to pose a threat.

The dilemmas have to be resolved by having clear and credible information about whether States are in compliance. The issue here is how to obtain that clear and credible information. If the information is flawed, as was the case with WMD and the invasion of Iraq, action to enforce compliance can be considered illegitimate. If the information is not credible – that is, not from a trusted source – it may not be believed.

In this, the importance of legitimacy, both of the actions and of the information on which it is based, is high. To understand why this is the case, we have to reflect on the nature of power in international politics today.

We can take power to be the ability to make someone else do something that they might not otherwise do. In the classic thinking of the Realist model of international relations, this is done by the threat of use of force or other sanctions. In an earlier time this would be done by alliances, would be reflected in a balance of power. Even in the contentious debates between the realists (or neo-realists) and the constructivists, there is a recognition that power is an essential factor in international politics.[8]

Max Weber reflected on the nature of power. In effect, he distinguished three types of power: coercive, utilitarian and legitimate. This has been well examined by Hurd:[9]

Consider three generic reasons why an actor might obey a rule: (1) because the actor fears the punishment of rule enforcers, (2) because the actor sees the rule as in its own self-interest, and (3) because the actor feels the rule is legitimate and ought to be obeyed. The trait distinguishing the superior from the subordinate is different in each case. In the first, it is asymmetry of physical capacity; in the second, a particular distribution of incentives; and in the third, a normative structure of status and legitimacy.

Hurd's analysis, like those of others, notes that focus has always been on legitimate power. There are good reasons for this.

Coercive power, the ability to make someone do something by inflicting pain – or threatening to – of a physical or financial nature is the ultimate form, but also the costliest. What Hurd calls self-interest, but what we prefer to term utilitarian power, is making someone do something by providing them with material rewards (tax incentives, trade agreements, bribes) is a second type. This is also costly.

Legitimate power, or making someone do something simply because it is the right thing to do, is the least costly. It is also largely self-enforcing. There is an element of self-interest in this, in the sense that order in society, the economy and politics is in most persons' (or nations') interest, by removing uncertainty in transactions and expectations of behaviour.

Translated to the international level, as Franck says,[10] 'A partial definition of legitimacy adapted to the international system could be formulated thus: *a property of a rule or rulemaking institution which itself exerts a pull towards compliance on those addressed normatively.*' [Emphasis in the original.]

In terms of WMD, States could use coercion to enforce compliance, but this would be very costly, particularly if it was based on an erroneous diagnosis of the situation, as was clearly the case for the United States and its coalition in Iraq. Using utilitarian incentives would also be costly, if the nature of the situation were to be incorrectly interpreted, as seems to have been the case between the United States and North Korea.

To look at sources of power in a multilateral system, it is obvious that we have to look to the third type of power, legitimate power.

There are several elements to legitimate power. The first is that the rule on which legitimacy is based has to have been agreed by all. Without this consensus, the rule will not be legitimate. This aspect was clearly set out in early regime theory, where a critical stage in regime formation was agreement on rules and procedures to implement agreed norms and principles. In this sense, legitimacy is affected by the nature of the principles (beliefs of fact and causality) and norms (beliefs about what is right behaviour). It is also affected by the operation of the rules and procedures. As Franck has put it:[11]

The perception of those addressed by a rule or a rule-making institution that the rule or institution has come into being and operates in accordance with generally accepted principles of right process.

Legitimacy thus is affected by the institutions who either operate or oversee the rules. Since one of the characteristics of most international regimes is that the operation of the regime is usually – if not always – entrusted to an international organization, any inquiry about the use of the legitimation power must focus, at least in part, on these organizations. For the unilateralists in the United States government, there is a rejection of this premise. The position was clearly stated by John Bolton, the United States' Under-Secretary of State for Arms Control and International Security:[12]

The question of legitimacy is frequently raised as a veiled attempt to restrain American discretion in undertaking unilateral action, or multilateral action taken outside the confines of an international organization, even when our actions are legitimated by the operation of that Constitutional system. The fact, however, is that this criticism would delegitimize the operation of our own Constitutional system, while doing nothing to confront the threats we are facing. Our actions, taken consistently with Constitutional principles, require no separate, external validation to make them legitimate. Whether it is removing a rogue Iraqi regime and replacing it, preventing WMD proliferation, or protecting Americans against an unaccountable Court, the United States will utilize its institutions of representative government, adhere to its Constitutional strictures, and follow its values when measuring the legitimacy of its actions. This is as it should be, in the continuing international struggle to protect our national interests and preserve our liberties.

Put succinctly, the United States will decide what is legitimate and what is not and can do so because of its coercive power. It is a philosophy based, at least in part, on 'might makes right'.

In exploring the role of legitimate power, several elements have to be examined. Clearly, the first is whether States will accept rules as legitimate and therefore as binding. Hurd (1999, p. 398; see note 9) notes that for some States, the reputation for 'rule-following' is an essential element in national identity. Certainly the Scandinavian States would be included in that. Other States, however, consciously refuse to comply with international norms. Often they are branded as 'rogue States' by other States.

Which rules are legitimate and therefore binding is clearly not a simple matter. At one level, there are clearly universal norms that all States are expected to observe. This would include the Charter of the United

Nations, where commitment to the provisions is a condition for membership in the community of nations. At another level, are the norms embodied in international treaties. Most international regimes are constructed around such international conventions. Adherence to the obligations of being a State party is a critical element in international order. Because adherence to a convention becomes a legal matter, the act of ratifying or acceding to a convention is a sober one for most States.

There are two types of conventions, in effect. Some conventions set out obligations for contracting States but have no enforcement or monitoring mechanism. An example is the Biological and Toxin Weapons Convention. These conventions are easier for States to become party to because there are no reporting requirements, but make it less easy to determine non-compliance.

Other conventions, particularly those in the area of human rights, have verification and monitoring mechanisms. The Nuclear Non-Proliferation Treaty and the Chemical Weapons Convention are examples of these, as is the set of conventions in the World Trade Organization.

Whether any of these international rules can be used for the purpose of legitimate power is a matter of degree. Franck in his work on the role of legitimacy in international law, states that:[13]

> Specifically, four indicators of a rule's and a rule-making process's legitimacy will be hypothesized ... These indicators of rule-legitimacy in the community of states are: *determinacy, symbolic validation, coherence,* and *adherence* ... The hypothesis asserts that, to the extent a rule, or rule process, exhibits these four properties it will exert a strong pull on states to comply. To the extent these properties are not present, the institution will be easier to ignore and the rule easier to avoid by a state tempted to pursue its short-term self-interest.

Franck's analysis points in the direction of factors that will determine whether a State will accept the rule. Clearly, the State has to have accepted the rule in the first place, either by becoming a Party to the Convention or by having voted in favour of a resolution. That is one reason why so much time is taken in crafting resolutions and why, in many cases, ambiguous language is adopted. The more ambiguous the language, the less incentive there is to comply. In practice, a State that did not vote for a resolution, like a State that has not become a party to a convention, is not bound by the content of that text.

That States take these obligations seriously is shown by the fact that very few States have withdrawn from conventions to which they had previously subscribed, even though most provide procedures for withdrawing. The action by North Korea is withdrawing from the Non-Proliferation Treaty was one example. The unusual action by the United States in trying to withdraw its signature from the convention establishing the International Criminal Court (even though by merely signing, the United States had not taken on a legal obligation) is another.

Once a negotiation is under way to address an issue with an international norm or rule, there is a clear incentive for States to participate. Unless the State has been involved in the agreement and is willing to accept the rule, it really has no standing in that area. Since in the United Nations no rule can really be adopted unless all States agree, there is little possibility of a rule being adopted without a State's implicit consent. However, once a norm moves from a moral to a legal plane, there is a further incentive to become a party. Most conventions insist that if a State is not a party to the convention, it cannot be a decision-maker about it.

One reason for accepting conventions is that, in practice, there are clear linkages among rules at the international level. For example, rules in one area, such as copyrights, have implications for rules in others, such as trade in services. Issues of linkage are often key facilitators or obstacles in multilateral negotiation. In many ways the agreed international rule structure is held together by overlapping and intermingled rules, so that there is an inherent incentive to maintain the coherence of the whole by avoiding non-compliance on parts. The degree to which this is important to a State is in direct proportion to the number and importance of issues in the whole. For the United States, there are few areas of international rule-making in which the country does not have an interest. As Franck puts it:[14]

> A government's failure to comply with a legitimate rule usually arouses the concern of other states, even those not directly affected by the breach. A state's failure to discharge its normative obligation frequently is seen by such other states as threatening their interests indirectly: by undermining the legitimacy of a rule of which they approve and on which they rely, and by weakening the fabric of the community's rule system as a whole.

Given an agreed structure of norms, the next element of legitimacy is the process by which compliance or non-compliance is determined. One option is for individual States to decide whether other States are in compliance. The danger in this, of course, is that no State in a system of sovereign States can be considered neutral and therefore able to credibly argue that another State is in violation of its obligations. For example, the United States claimed that North Korea was in breach of its obligations under the 1994 Framework Agreement, whereas North Korea claimed that it was the United States that was in breach.

One function of the Security Council is to avoid this problem by reaching, among a Membership that is diverse in interests, a consensus on whether States whose actions are referred to the Council are in breach or not, and this is not easy to obtain. Without this consensus, as the United States learned in Iraq, the legitimacy of State action is not assured.

While in a Westphalian system, legitimacy might be expected to be conveyed by States acting in concert, as the international system has evolved through the second half of the twentieth century the role of certifying the legitimacy of State actions and the detection of non-compliance has been assumed increasingly by international organizations and international civil society, sometimes separately, often working together.

It is a multifaceted role. It involves helping to set the basis for agreeing on a rule and trying to ensure that the rule's content is clear – what Franck calls *determinacy*.[15] Once the rule is agreed, the role has to do with maintaining the process of verifying compliance. As Franck puts it:[16]

> Whether the clarifying process is successful in transforming rule indeterminacy into determinacy depends on the legitimacy that the members of the international system ascribe to the specific process. This implicates such factors of legitimacy as *who* is doing the interpreting, their *pedigree* or authority to interpret, and the *coherence* of the principles the interpreters apply.

This element of verification has become a central role of international organizations, who must perform the role with authority and due regard to the political environment in which they operate.

Put another way, the regimes that States have created can only function effectively if the international mechanisms that were formed to facilitate their operation are competent and effective.

Returning to the dilemmas inherent in implementing the rules for the elimination of WMD and State compliance with them, the answer is to have rules and procedures that can credibly verify that everyone is complying with their obligations. How this is done is of critical importance.

On the one hand, since the international system is based on sovereign States, an intrusive verification system would threaten the wider issue of sovereignty. (For example, a verification system that required disclosure of trade secrets in the biochemical industry was considered unacceptable by the US in the case of the BWC.)

On the other hand, a system that relied on verification by one or the other of the States parties would not be trustworthy. (For example, Iraq argued that US inspectors in UNSCOM were actually spies, and it seems that some were.)

The three treaties that provide for verification all try to cope with the issues of access and intrusiveness which are central to the entire WMD ban regime. Major political obstacles would have to be removed before the BWC may also have a verification mechanism based on the precedents of the other three.

Verification in a broader context

According to the United Nations, 'verification is a process which establishes whether the States Parties are complying with their obligations under an agreement'.[17] It is a process of gathering and analyzing information to make a judgment about parties' compliance or non-compliance. The multiple aim of verification is: to generate confidence among the parties; to deter non-compliance by threatening timely detection; and to provide early warning about non-compliance.[18]

Basically there are three categories of disarmament verification, based on combinations of two dimensions: the bilateral–multilateral dimension and the adversarial–cooperative dimension. They can be represented by three models:

Model 1. Bilateral adversarial verification between rival States, for example the US and the USSR during the Cold War. The guiding principle is reciprocity of obligations, which may permit consensual, cooperative measures for intrusive verification. The process is simply inter-State, with parallel or joint mechanisms for implementation. The main examples are the INF and the START bilateral treaties on nuclear disarmament.

Model 2. This involves multilateral adversarial verification, as in the case of the disarmament of Iraq under the Gulf War Cease Fire resolution of the UN Security Council (Resolution 687 (1991)). The guiding principle is verification as part of imposed enforcement action by the international community against a non-compliant State. The process has three stages and sets of interaction: (a) interaction between the suspected State and the inspectors or other investigators; (b) consultations between that State and the community of States seeking to uphold the norm, with or without inspection reports; and (c) between the Security Council as an enforcement mechanism and the non-compliant State, if it continues, in its defiance, to pose a threat to international peace and security. The full process is available to the International Atomic Energy Agency (IAEA), the Comprehensive Test-Ban Treaty Organization (CTBTO) and the Organization for the Prohibition of Chemical Weapons (OPCW). However, only the third phase is available to the State parties of the Biological Weapons Convention, who have to rely on their own information to report non-compliance directly to the Council, The BWC has no mechanism to verify non-compliance.

Model 3. Multilateral cooperative verification which is based on an international agreement. The guiding principle is consensual arrangement among State parties for an international verification mechanism and compliance procedures linked to the UN Security Council. This process is the most comprehensive as it subsumes model 2 in extreme cases of non-compliance, such as Iraq and North Korea in the case of the IAEA and Iraq. It relies on an institutionalized system of implementation comprising four tiers: (a) consultative process among State Parties (general conferences and review conferences); (a) governance by elected boards and executive heads; (c) secretariat management and inspectorate; and (d) compliance process involving interaction between the organization's decision-making bodies and the security Council. Member States are both targets and beneficiaries of a consent-based verification system. The main examples of this model are verification organizations serving the NPT, the CTBT and the CWC but includes also the various verification arrangements for other multilateral disarmament treaties.

Elements of the regime

The WMD ban regime consists of a series of rules about what States are expected to do and a series of procedures to show that they are complying with these expectations. Each treaty is a bit different, but they have common elements in the procedures to be followed. In most cases, the procedures have not been tested. However, the experience of both the IAEA and the United Nations Special Commission in Iraq has given very valuable lessons on the efficacy of the different elements.[19]

The main elements of the regime are: (a) legal undertakings to progressively ban weapons of mass destruction; (b) State declarations and periodic reports on all relevant items; (c) procurement accounting;

(d) ongoing technical monitoring; (e) inspections; (f) compliance procedures; and (g) specific institutions to consolidate all these elements. Together these elements are designed to allow for independent verification without, however, intruding too greatly on State sovereignty.

Legal undertakings

By becoming party to the international conventions, States take on a legal obligation to implement the agreed terms. Often this involves making subsidiary agreements that specify State responsibilities in more detail. The Safeguards agreements that are part of the NPT are an example of these. The extent of obligation is defined by the undertakings that States make and, in practice, not all States have made the same undertakings. For example, until 2004, Iran (along with a number of other countries) did not accept enhanced safeguards agreements.

Declarations and reports

The basic element is the declaration. Each State agrees to declare whether it has WMD, their components or any items relevant to their production, in what quantities and where they are located. The initial declarations set the baseline for determining the pace at which weapon destruction, relevant peaceful activities or other agreed action is taking place. There are international procedures to determine the criteria and format of reporting, and international organizations analyze the declarations according to common standards. The declarations are updated by periodic reports as part of an ongoing process of State accounting and control.

The difficulty, of course, is that States might lie on their declarations. Iraq, for example, provided the IAEA with correct information about its declared programme, but had a parallel, undeclared programme. Had a bit more time passed, the undeclared programme would have been able to produce fissile material that would have allowed Iraq to develop a usable nuclear weapon, even without using the declared material. As UNSCOM found out in the 1990s, Iraq simply told lies about biological weapons and half-lies about chemical.

Procurement accounting

The issue of verifying that there is no WMD proliferation is addressed by monitoring trade in certain commodities. For nuclear weapons, there is a system of reporting on all movement of nuclear material and related sensitive items from one country to another. Exporters are required to obtain licences and the quantities exported under these licences are reported to the IAEA by voluntary arrangements. In the case of chemical weapons, so-called precursor chemicals are required to be licensed for export and these trades are to be reported to the OPCW. And there is an agreement among many States (the so-called Australia group) to report on precursors for both biological and chemical weapons.

The dilemma here is that there can be a time-lag in reporting and the material may have been shipped and received before this is noticed (as happened in the case of chemical and biological weapons in Iraq). Also, there is a problem if some states do not report or if material is sold clandestinely and smuggled across borders.

Technical monitoring

In order to verify compliance in ways that do not depend on either declarations or accounting, procedures of different kinds have been agreed that allow indirect monitoring (in the sense of remote systems that are automatic). The CTBT is almost entirely about indirect monitoring. The International Monitoring System is a complex of seismic, radionuclide and maritime remote sensors that can detect automatically whether a nuclear explosion has taken place by sending data via satellite to the International Data Centre in Vienna, where analysts can determine whether the pattern of the sound or the radionuclide signal came from a nuclear source. Technical monitoring is also extensively used in the nuclear non-proliferation area and in the chemical weapons field in support of human inspections. In the wake of the Iraq problem, the IAEA's new verification protocol for enhanced safeguards provides for remote environmental sensing and for more intrusive methods at nuclear sites as a supplement to declarations and inspections.

Inspections

The ultimate means of verification is inspections. The three treaties with verification components all provide for on-site inspections. In the case of the IAEA, there are both regular (routine) inspections at declared sites and special inspections at newly designated sites. This model is also foreseen in the CWC. In the case of the CTBT, the on-site inspection is triggered whenever one of the States alleges that another State has detonated a nuclear device. A similar challenge procedure exists in the CWC.

The problems with inspections have to do with the extent to which State sovereignty precludes surprises and the extent to which inspectors will have full access. The Iraqis were masters at trying to hide things from inspectors and a major change in the new IAEA protocol has to do with giving inspectors multiple entry visas so that they can appear unannounced.

Compliance procedures

Finally, the results of the various prior stages have to lead to procedures that will encourage compliance, it that is not found. This can be procedures for adjudicating disagreements, for raising the stakes of non-compliance and for providing incentives for compliance.

The specific institutions of the regime

For each of the conventions that have verification elements, a public international organization has been given the responsibility for managing verification. As with any institutional development, the newer institutions have learned from the older ones. It should be emphasized, however, that each institution is independent of the others and, to some observers, this is a disadvantage. There are many reasons why this took place: different patterns of States parties, different professional and bureaucratic bases within States, and the desire to have organizations located in different countries.

For example, when the CTBT was adopted, one idea was for the organization to be located in the IAEA, which, after all, dealt with the NPT and things nuclear. The counter-argument was that the IAEA lacked a capacity in the seismic field. It was also said that until the treaty entered into force, the provisional secretariat was a temporary organization and should not be part of a permanent one.

IAEA

The IAEA was established in order to facilitate (and, to an extent, regulate) the use of nuclear energy. In terms of WMD, its charge was to ensure that nuclear material for peaceful purposes was not diverted for other purposes. It did not, at the time, have a mandate to deal with existing nuclear weapons (that were, then, in the hands of the US, the then USSR and the UK, followed later by France and China, the other Permanent Members of the Security Council). Under the NPT, it was charged with monitoring nuclear facilities to verify that no diversion was taking place. The programme to do this was called, appropriately, Safeguards. Each party to the IAEA Statute was expected to reach a safeguards agreement that would specify how the Agency would monitor and inspect nuclear facilities. In the wake of the Gulf War and the discovery of the clandestine Iraqi nuclear programme, the safeguards procedures were thoroughly reviewed and strengthened.

As nuclear energy has, for the time being, become reduced in importance, the IAEA has increasingly become the focus for intellectual and scientific work on things nuclear. It is the classical technical agency and one of its activities consists of research on new methods of monitoring, including the development of equipment and software.

CTBTO

The CTBTO in Vienna is the most technologically dependent verification organization. Its Provisional Technical Secretariat (of the Preparatory Commission for the CTBTO) is in the process of putting into place what one of their staff called 'the world's first international burglar alarm'. The premise is that if States cannot test nuclear weapons, they will not be able to convince anyone that (a) they have weapons and (b) that if they claim to have them, that they work. This in itself will help prevent the proliferation of these weapons. The International Monitoring System, designed by seismologists, will be able to detect when a small earthquake occurs in Siberia or when a building is dynamited in downtown Syracuse and, from the patterns, be sure that the explosion was not nuclear.

The treaty will only come into force, however, when all of the States who were deemed to have the potential to develop nuclear weapons have ratified. Some of them are waiting on the United States, which, of course, has the most weapons and did the most testing, although it had a moratorium throughout the Clinton presidency and still does today. There are fears, however, that the Bush administration actually wants to be able to test nuclear weapons and that is why they are not ratifying the treaty.

OPCW

The Organization for the Prohibition of Chemical Weapons at The Hague has the task of monitoring the CWC. There are two types of chemicals that were subject to the CWC's prohibitions: those used for chemical warfare (toxic chemicals and their precursors) and those used by the police and others for law enforcement, including RIOT control (tear gas, for example). But the production of the same toxic and precursor chemicals either for weapons or for a variety of peaceful uses is problematic. The focus of verification is thus on dual-use chemicals, the chemical factories and other chemical facilities in the country. The task of the OPCW is to look at the data, and inspect the facilities, to be sure that the purpose is legitimate and that the activities at the facility are consistent with the obligations assumed under the CWC. They also have to oversee the destruction of existing weapons, not an easy process in the best of times. The organization has had major problems (including having its executive head fired).

Biological weapons

In contrast to the other conventions, the BWC has no verification institution. The original treaty essentially gave the verification responsibility to the UN Security Council. Article VI of the Convention authorizes any State Party to lodge a complaint with the UN Security Council accompanied by possible evidence that another party is violating the provisions of the Convention. Each State Party has undertaken to cooperate in carrying out any investigation that the Council may initiate in response to the complaint.

Given the problems of the Security Council, it is not clear what this would mean. Part of the problem with verification of this treaty is a belief on the part of the United States that verification is, in fact, impossible. An article in the 26 July 2001 issue of the *Financial Times* enumerates a number of seemingly insurmountable problems and suggests as an observance of a voluntary code of conduct as a preferable alternative to a permanent verification mechanism.[20]

What does management have to do with all of this?

So now we finally come to the question, to what extent does the viability of the WMD ban regime depend on public management?

The first point is that management of international public organizations is qualitatively different from the management of national public sector institutions or the private sector. What is learned from that experience is only partially applicable to international management. Management of non-sovereign international public organizations means that the direct enforcement of decisions is impossible, revenue cannot be collected, national political processes cannot be tapped and, most significantly, managers cannot appear to be basically in charge of managing the system. If one applies the open systems approach to international public administration, one will learn that internal management is far, far less important than dealing with the external environment. In fact, the external environment is virtually the only space for management.

A second point is that who the managers are is not completely clear. On the one hand, they would seem to be the civil servants who staff the secretariats of the international organizations. Yet, constitutionally, it is the boards of governors and executive boards who are formally responsible for decision-making. In practice, as we will see, it is usually the civil servants, visibly the executive head, working with the elected government representatives (in the form of the chairperson of the executive board) who are the real decision-makers.

A third factor is that the organizations have to ensure geographic balance, in order to ensure credibility. The senior positions are distributed among different countries. For example, the IAEA recently had a Director General from Egypt (Africa) – the DG is always from a country with nuclear knowledge, but not a nuclear-weapon State – the Deputy Director General (DDG) for technical cooperation was from China, the DDG for nuclear power is from the Russian Federation, the DDG for safety was from Canada, the DDG for safeguards was from Belgium and the DDG for management was from the United States. Keeping these different nationalities working on a common basis is not easy.

The success of any organization, and especially of the verification organizations, depends on the ability of those managers to run their institutions in such a way that the tasks are carried out successfully.

We now turn to the main management issues that will be dealt with in detail later.

Leadership

Leadership in an international organization is very different from that in a national government, a private sector corporation or an nongovernmental organization (NGO). Leaders of international organizations have to lead without appearing to. If they take too many positions, they risk becoming part of the problem rather than be catalysts for a solution.

An example of effective leadership is taking an initiative to reform an organization. The success of the effort may depend not only on good ideas but also on how leadership is exercised by the executive head of an organization.

A case in point is former UN Secretary-General Boutros Boutros Ghali, who tried to exercise his powers overtly and ended up alienating some of the major powers to such an extent that they prevented his re-election. Another is Mary Robinson, who, reflecting a moralist's view of human rights, also managed to offend some influential quarters. In leadership, style matters as well as substance.

In the case of verification, we have two quite different approaches: Mohamed ElBaradei of the IAEA (like his predecessor, who now heads the UN's Iraq verification organization) is low-key and correct. The first head of the OPCW, Bustani, who was direct, became controversial and was fired, the first elected head of an international organization to be so.

Strategic planning in the face of uncertainty

The WMD ban regime is one that is in many ways incomplete and evolving. Moreover, the funding of the system is not assured at all. And yet, the evolution of the system is one that is expected to take a long time (indeed, unlike national administration, where the time horizon is constrained by the electoral process, international administration can and must use a longer time horizon).

Each of the managers of the three verification institutions has to find a way to do real strategic planning in the face of uncertainty. The uncertainty has to do with issues of political support finance and technological developments. Strategic planning means looking at a future desirable state and working back to the present by setting out things that need to happen.

A good example is the CTBT. The uncertainty lies in the date when the convention will come into force. As things now stand, this cannot happen before 2005, assuming that George W. Bush, who seems to have little faith in WMD multilateral treaties, were not to be re-elected. One of the strange elements of the CTBT is that the monitoring system is expected to be in place on the date that the convention enters into force, so the estimated date for this is very important. A dilemma is that, as part of the compromise on staffing, governments stated that no staff could work longer than seven years. If correct, the day the convention comes into force, all of the experienced staff will have left. So, the Executive Director has been working on a plan to phase in the system on the basis of an expected date.

Finance and budget

Much of the intellectual work is actually constrained by mundane details of finance and budget. Unlike a national administration that can levy taxes and receive revenue, or a private sector entity that can raise capital by selling shares, an international organization is dependent on the funds that the national legislatures of its members are willing to appropriate. Only one UN organization, the World Intellectual Property Organization (WIPO), has to date been allowed to charge user fees, and do so well financially, and only the Bretton Woods institutions are able to raise funds from bonds in the financial markets – and to finance administrative costs out of interest income from their loans to Member States. These are somewhat of an anomaly. In effect the Member States determine how much they are willing to give to the organization and, within that envelope, a budget can be drawn. Usually it is expressed as a kind of zero growth (real or nominal).

Convincing the Member States that the budget needs are real, that adequate financial probity exists and that the money is well spent is a major management imperative. So too is coping with the problems of late payment. All UN organizations use a calendar year budget, but few Member States do. (The US fiscal year begins in October, whereas the UN systems begin in January, which means that the US payment is always late.) The Financial Crisis of the United Nations has been an agenda item since the 1950s, which probably makes it the longest-running crisis in history. It is essentially a cash-flow crisis.

IAEA's Director General ElBaradei is considered fortunate in that for the last couple of years he has been given a zero real growth budget (others got zero nominal, which means a reduction in real terms). As even this was deemed insufficient, he had to institute results-based budgeting, which the major contributors wanted against the preferences of the developing countries (Group of 77), before asking for additional funds.

Personnel

A main reason for having an international organization responsible for verification is that it is more credible than a national organization. Credibility is dependent on a combination of political neutrality and technical competence. This means hiring and socializing technically competent persons who will acquire some of the characteristics of neutral diplomats. Finding a way to achieve both is a major problem of personnel administration. It is a particularly acute problem in the verification organizations. Two stories illustrate this.

The IAEA has a strong policy of rotation. The assumption is that a staff member is only there temporarily. However, for many jobs, you do need career people. Apparently the original reason for the rotation policy was a desire to ensure that the safeguards department remained neutral and that rotation was expected to ensure it. At the beginning of the Agency only the US and the USSR had technicians who could be inspectors, and many of these were in the intelligence services. Rotation was expected to prevent the Safeguards Department from becoming mini-CIAs or mini-KGBs. The irony is that the Agency is the only place in the world where inspectors can be hired; the Agency trains the inspectors and as a result the Safeguards Department has a very high percentage of staff on long-term (i.e. greater than seven years) contracts.

When the CTBTO was started on a provisional basis, almost all of the staff was new to international service. They tried to bring their national approaches to bear, and the result was not pretty. One solution was to have an outside consultant facilitate management retreats where they could learn how international management was different. Over time, we have noticed that the senior managers are becoming more adept at navigating the international external environment. The irony is that the rotation policy, if not changed, will force many of these to leave, just as they are becoming adept.

The rotation problem has also been reported regarding the OPCW. This regime, with its structure, institutions and management issues, is the result of an evolution over time – a long process during which the international political system itself evolved. This historical context has shaped the regime as it is today and will constrain the directions in which it can evolve further. We must therefore turn to the historical context of the regime in Chapter 2.

2
Evolution of the WMD Control Regime

A historical perspective is necessary for understanding the importance of verification as an indispensable element of any disarmament process, especially with respect to weapons of mass destruction. Verification is the process of gathering, analyzing and evaluating information to determine whether a State is complying with its obligations under a treaty or another type of agreement.[1] The concept of verified disarmament is an integral part of the broader concept of arms control, which includes the regulation of armaments, the limitation of armed forces and the various measures to ensure transparency and build mutual confidence. Arms control was first defined in the 1960s as including 'all the forms of military cooperation between potential enemies in the interest of reducing the likelihood of war, its scope and violence if it occurs, and the political and economic costs of being prepared for it'.[2] A more concise recent definition broadens the concept to apply it to the century-old process by stressing security enhancement as a goal of all States: it presents arms control as 'measures directly related to military forces, adopted by governments to contain the costs and harmful consequences of the continued existence of arms, within the overall objective of sustaining or enhancing their security'.[3]

Today's drive for a ban of weapons of mass destruction – nuclear, chemical and biological – has its origins in a concept of arms control first articulated in 1899 at the First Hague International Peace Conference. Governments then were driven mainly by a humanitarian desire to restrict the means and methods of warfare by banning the use of chemical and bacteriological agents as terror weapons; they were also concerned about the burden of armaments. While the concepts of alleviating human suffering and reducing the economic and social burdens were more explicit, there was also an implicit recognition of the need to reduce military insecurity in an international system of sovereign States which lacked moral, cultural and behavioural restraint on the use of force. Hague was an effort to mitigate the inhumanity of war and to limit armaments by generating consensus for possible international law in the area. No attempt was made however to create any institutions.[4]

During World War I, The Hague consensus was largely disregarded, resulting in extensive use of poison gas. The horrible experience necessitated an elaboration of provisions in the Covenant of the League of Nations for the reduction of armaments and later for codification of the ban on the use of chemical and biological weapons. Apart from the imposed disarmament of the vanquished States, the most significant arms control achievements of the inter-war years were the 1922 Washington Treaty on limitation of naval armaments and the 1925 Geneva Protocol for the Prohibition of the Use in War of Asphyxiating, Poisonous or Other Gases and of Bacteriological Methods of Warfare. Although the issues of verification and enforcement were seriously discussed then, no mechanism was considered feasible. Provision was made only for the investigation of any allegation of illicit use of biological and chemical agents. States were not prepared then to extend the ban to the development and possession of chemical and biological weapons. Ambitious inter-war negotiations for arms reduction had already failed when Hitler's government defiantly embarked on a massive rearmament of Nazi Germany. Furthermore, despite the restrictions of the Geneva Protocol, Japan and Italy were not deterred from using chemical weapons in the 1930s, in their wars of invasion against weaker States – China and Ethiopia.

However, it was significant that the ban was observed by all combatants during World War II, more likely for fear of retaliation than in observance of international norms. Indeed the devastating use of conventional weapons was not limited to the battlefield but was deliberately extended to civilian non-combatants, thus setting the stage for the horrors of the atomic destruction of Hiroshima and Nagasaki.

The UN Charter and disarmament

It is unfortunate that, from the perspective of arms control, the United Nations Charter was signed just before the atomic explosions, thus rendering the disarmament provisions of the Charter suddenly inadequate for the emerging nuclear age. It is remarkable, however, that, even before these calamities, the shock of massive and indiscriminate devastation by conventional weapons was sufficient to compel the drafters of the UN Charter to prescribe a sweeping ban on war itself.

This profound ideal was embodied in the preamble to the Charter, which opens with the words: *'We the peoples of the United Nations determined to save succeeding generations from the scourge of war.'* Peace and security became the organization's paramount objective. The Charter proclaimed the maintenance of international peace and security as the first purpose of the United Nations (Article 1.1). Accordingly, the Charter prohibited the threat or use of force in international relations (Article 2.4), provided for the peaceful settlement of disputes (Chapter VI) and created a new mechanism – the Security Council – for international action regarding threats to peace, breaches of the peace and acts of aggression (Chapter VII).

Those provisions established the general legal and political framework for pursuing the goal of arms regulation and disarmament and for a special role of the United Nations. No doubt was left that disarmament would serve as one of the pillars to achieve the overarching goal of peace and security. The General Assembly and the Security Council were assigned joint responsibility in this area. The Assembly was to consider 'principles governing disarmament and the regulation of armaments' and make 'recommendations to the Members or to the Security Council or to both' (Article 11). The Council, in performing its function of promoting the establishment and maintenance of international peace and security, was to formulate, with the assistance of its Military Staff Committee, 'plans to be submitted to the Members of the United nations for the establishment of a system for the reduction of armaments' (Article 26). The Charter speaks of principles and plans for arms regulation and disarmament but makes no mention of verification to sustain the process.[5]

In order to understand fully the nature and prospects of effective disarmament verification in the twenty-first century, we need to trace its evolution, both as a concept and as a process in constant adaptation to changing political and security circumstances. Such an understanding may help in defining the challenges and possibilities for strengthening the regime for controlling the threat from weapons of mass destruction. We will begin with a brief overview.

A radical beginning

With the use of the atom bomb as a weapon of mass destruction, the scope and significance of the disarmament provisions of the Charter were instantly transformed. In 1946, the very first UN General Assembly resolution was devoted to nuclear disarmament. It established an Atomic Energy Commission as the first subsidiary body of the General Assembly. In what became known as the Baruch Plan, the United States offered to end its monopoly of nuclear weapons if its far-reaching proposal would be accepted. The plan was to create an international atomic development authority to assume ownership of all fissionable material as well as its production and distribution, and to provide oversight and control over the peaceful uses of all the material.

A sweeping remedy was thus proposed to end the vague reference in the UN Charter about the importance of disarmament and the silence about weapons of mass destruction. However, this radical proposal that involved an unprecedented delegation of authority to an international organization, was vehemently opposed by the Soviet Union, which preferred to pursue its own nuclear ambitions. Both the notion of international ownership and the emphasis on international inspection were rejected as a significant infringement on national sovereignty. The Soviet Union's insistence on a *disarmament-first* approach was diametrically opposed to the *control-first* approach of the United States. This removed any possibility for meaningful negotiation. A deep gulf was created in the nuclear arms control debate between the Soviet approach of sweeping nuclear disarmament and the American focus on arms control with strict verification. This Soviet–American difference marked a deep and constant fault line in East–West disarmament negotiations during most of the Cold War.

Concept of WMD

Although the new emphasis was on nuclear disarmament, other major armaments were not ignored. Indeed the often-cited first resolution of the General Assembly envisaged in 1946 also the elimination of 'all other major weapons adaptable to mass destruction'. By 1948, the Security Council also recognized the urgency of reducing conventional armaments by establishing a separate commission on those weapons. Curiously, the first definition of weapons of mass destruction was formulated by the Commission on Conventional Armaments in an effort to confine the scope of its work. Thus, it proposed: 'weapons of mass destruction should be defined to include atomic explosive weapons, radioactive material weapons, lethal chemical and biological weapons and any weapons developed in the future which have characteristics comparable in destructive effect'.[6]

Verification as a central issue

In the post-World War II era, the evolution of the verification issue has been at the centre of the debate on security and disarmament. It has been shaped by an interplay among various factors affecting national and international security, especially perceptions about future military threats, notions about arms control and the need to preserve national sovereignty. The significance of the verification issue was enhanced by the dynamics of the East–West nuclear arms race, which was fuelled by technological innovations, always adding complexity to arms control as an issue in the tortuous negotiations. Verification indeed became a buzzword with a misleadingly simple meaning but with multiple implications depending on who used the term and in what context. In addition to its core meaning of verification of compliance, the term was used occasionally as a political tool. The US would accuse the Soviet Union of empty propaganda or would use the term to impress a domestic disarmament lobby about its own serious approach. The Soviet Union would use it to charge that the United States was promoting it for espionage and sabotage without even the benefit of real disarmament.

Nuclear focus of the Cold War

From 1945 until the end of the 1980s arms control was a key feature of Cold War diplomacy that had created an elaborate network of treaties and processes to regulate the nuclear balance, reduce the risk of East–West military confrontations and prevent the spread of nuclear weapons to additional States or to uninhabited environments. The quest was for comprehensive balance in nuclear and conventional forces, but the debate was dominated by the nuclear equation. Chemical and biological weapons, already banned from use, hardly figured as an issue in the balance. The proposals and the debate on verification were shaped by the changes in the Cold War itself. East–West detente meant gradual relaxation of ideological rigidities and pragmatism in strategic calculations. It permitted progress in the diplomacy of arms control within the context of a constant condition of geopolitical bipolarity and 'balance of terror', represented by the doctrines of 'mutual assured destruction' (MAD) and 'nuclear deterrence'. Over the years, verification was transformed from a major issue of contention to an agreed process for monitoring compliance with treaty obligations.

Historically, a remarkable evolution took place, from the absence of any verification of treaty commitments and reliance only on national technical means (NTM), to a network of cooperative verification measures supported by NTMs and from bilateral mechanisms to regional and international institutions dedicated to verification.

Refocusing on WMD

After the end of the Cold War, during the 1990s the transformation of the geopolitical map generated a more diffuse and more complex set of security problems. Today's rapidly changing world poses new threats, which are inherent in uncertainties and instabilities in different regions. The collapse of communism in Eastern Europe accompanied by the break-up of the Soviet Union and the end of the ideological division in Europe have removed old Cold War issues and the constraints of balanced bipolarity. The loosening of the existing tight controls has unleashed traditional issues of nationalism, ethnicity, religious fanaticism and territorial claims and has also highlighted dormant global issues. In arms control terms, a serious issue today is the threat of proliferation not only of nuclear weapons but also of other weapons of mass destruction, particularly in regions of frequent armed conflict. An equally disturbing new risk is the illicit trafficking in material for such weapons, with access possibly acquired by terrorist groups. The end of the Cold War thus poses new challenges stemming from the problems of instability and uncertainty. It also opens new opportunities for arms control based on a web of interrelated multilateral treaties with complementary mechanisms for international verification.[7]

Evolution of the verification issue in disarmament

In order to assess today's challenges and opportunities facing the international community in trying to preserve and build upon the WMD control regime, we need to trace the evolution of the concept and practice of verification during six distinct phases after World War II.[8] Four of these phases correspond with the evolution of the Cold War from tense confrontation to peaceful coexistence, and to detente and reciprocity leading to selective close cooperation. The remaining two phases cover the post-Cold War era, beginning with immediate and extensive international cooperation, which gave way to the current phase dominated by unilateralist tendencies in the policies of the sole remaining superpower, the United States of America. The last phase has been energized by the outrage and sudden perception of insecurity resulting from the terrorist attacks of 11 September 2001 in both New York City and Washington DC.

The evolution results from the interplay among three interrelated factors: the geopolitical strategic environment; the arms control preoccupations; and the modalities of verification proposed or adopted. The various modalities of arms control verification today share common roots and were originally conceived as parts of a comprehensive verification system. However, the case-by-case negotiation of partial measures, although practical and productive, has perpetuated centrifugal tendencies and fragmentation in the approach to international verification. A historical examination will demonstrate that few of today's ideas on disarmaments and proliferation control are indeed new. Many of the proposals were shelved on the grounds that they were ahead of their time, but they may still serve as a source of inspiration for progress towards the regime envisaged soon after World War II. A retrospective analysis can point the way to possibilities for a coherent and complementary management of the crucial verification function to sustain the WMD treaties.

Verification during the Cold War

The nuclear arms race and the Baruch Plan, 1945–1953

The first phase in the evolution of verification covers the period from the Hiroshima atomic bomb to the Soviet achievement of thermonuclear parity. This phase coincides with the period from the establishment of the United Nations to the death of Stalin and the end of the Korean War.

Early in the nuclear age, two conflicting tendencies emerged in the early years of the United Nations: an unfettered nuclear arms race and an initiative to harness the atom exclusively for peaceful purposes. In 1946, the first tendency was reflected in the Baruch Plan to create an international atomic development authority, a far-reaching US proposal that was seriously considered by the newly established Atomic Energy Commission of the United Nations. Under the Plan, once a system of controls and sanctions was effectively in place, further production of atomic weapons would cease, all existing stocks would be destroyed under appropriate verification, and all technological information would be communicated to that authority.

It was a plan for a nuclear-weapon-free world under the control of an international authority that could approve sanctions against violators, without being blocked by a veto. The US would initially hold on to its monopoly of the technology but would share it with the authority when the authority's control and sanctions mechanism was effectively operating. The idea of this unprecedented delegation of authority to a supranational institution controlled by the US was, however, opposed by the Soviet Union. The latter's Gromyko Plan reversed the priorities in order to avoid control before disarmament and insisted on negotiating a treaty that would prohibit the production and use of atomic weapons and provide for the destruction of all such weapons within three months. This fundamental disagreement set the stage for a full-scale nuclear arms race lasting almost half a century. The approach of both sides to keep talking while arming themselves became a feature of the Cold War dynamics.[9]

Nuclear balance and bipolarity was on the way. When the Soviet Union tested its first atomic bomb in 1949, the strategic landscape was raised to a dangerous level. The situation was aggravated by the victory of Mao Zedong's communist regime in China, which deepened the ideological division in the world. When the new regime was excluded from the United Nations, the Soviet Union responded by boycotting Security Council sessions at a crucial time when it was debating the Korean War. The Council's launching of a US-led international operation free of the Soviet veto so deepened the diplomatic crisis that all dialogue ceased, ushering in a breathless nuclear arms race between the two powers. When the US achieved a thermonuclear breakthrough in its 1952 test, the Soviet Union was able to match that achievement just a year later. By then, the nuclear status was not confined to the two leading powers since the United Kingdom also was able to test an atomic bomb in 1952. The tension continued to build until bipolarity became virtually global. The establishment of the US-led North Atlantic Treaty Organization (NATO) in 1949 was matched five years later by the consolidation of the Soviet control in Eastern Europe in the form of the Soviet-led Warsaw Treaty Organization. By this time, the risk of nuclear war had increased to such an extent that the two sides found it prudent to seek some relief by reviving the arms control debate at the United Nations.

Despite the deep ideological division, the risk of war and strategic calculations compelled the two sides to explore once again a new approach to disarmament. A comprehensive approach became attractive when the Korean War demonstrated that atomic weapons could not be used advantageously and that, in such cases, only superiority in conventional armaments would confer a real advantage.[10] Institutionally, the existing parallel commissions on atomic energy and on conventional weapons were integrated to form the UN Disarmament Commission in order to address issues comprehensively.

The elimination of nuclear and other weapons of mass destruction was to be negotiated in the same context as the regulation, limitation and balanced reduction of armed forces and conventional armaments, 'under effective international control'. Different perceptions of military balance and suspicions about the adversary's sincerity in negotiations dictated different arms control strategies. The Soviet Union, which initially trailed in the nuclear arms race, persisted in its approach of 'nuclear disarmament first', starting with early discontinuance of nuclear testing and a pledge not to use nuclear weapons. On the other hand, the US and its allies placed particular emphasis on the necessity of effective verification and, as initial measures, a balanced reduction of conventional armaments and armed forces, areas in which the Soviet Union was believed to retain superiority.

The upshot of the first phase was the crystallization of the concept of nuclear deterrence while exploring the whole spectrum of arms control, including the reduction of conventional weapons. Although the concept of weapons of mass destruction was introduced as a category separate from conventional weapons, its nuclear, chemical and biological components were not presented as interrelated elements. Nor was much attention given to chemical and biological weapons since the debate was dominated by concerns about nuclear weapons and also by the preoccupation with the imbalances in conventional armaments, especially in Europe. Time was not ripe for the concept of verification since the Soviet Union was not ready to open up its closed society and was still deeply preoccupied about the political risk of espionage and control by the West.

Peaceful coexistence: disarmament principles
and atoms for peace, 1953–1963

The second phase was a seminal stage in arms control negotiations. In geopolitical terms, this phase was governed by a concept of East–West 'peaceful co-existence' under conditions of nuclear deterrence. With the involvement of the former colonies as newly independent States, it was possible to explore all aspects of arms control and to gain wide recognition for verification as an integral part of disarmament. Strategically, the new thermonuclear parity and the Korean armistice set the stage for less confrontational policies by the Eisenhower and Kennedy Administrations in Washington and by Chairman Nikita Krushchev in Moscow. However, there were many bumps along the way. These included the Soviet concern about the 1955 admission of West Germany to full membership in NATO with its implications for arms control in Europe, the 1960 atomic tests by France and the 1962 Cuban missile crisis between the US and the USSR.

During this phase, the focus shifted gradually from broadly addressing the issue of disarmament to concentrating on selected partial or collateral measures that could pave the way for general disarmament.[11] A whole range of measures was identified for future negotiations: a nuclear test-ban, the cut-off of production of fissionable materials for weapons; the transfer of fissionable material from military to peaceful uses; various transparency measures to reduce the risk of surprise attack; and proposals for peaceful use of outer space. An important benefit of this pragmatic à-la-carte approach was to make the contentious issue of verification more acceptable in the context of certain partial measures.

IAEA precedent and non-proliferation. The most significant achievement of the period was the establishment of the International Atomic Energy Agency (IAEA) in 1957 to promote the peaceful uses of atomic energy. For the first time, an international body was equipped with a mechanism for international verification of arms control commitments. When President Eisenhower made his 'Atoms for Peace' speech at the 1953 session of the UN General Assembly, the idea was partly to slow down the nuclear arms race by transferring fissionable material away from military weapons to a new agency devoted to peaceful application. The second part was to discourage nuclear-weapons proliferation by facilitating the acquisition of nuclear materials and technology under strict control. Although the first part did not materialize as envisaged, the principle of transfer still remains part of the IAEA's Statute.

Of great significance was the acceptance by the vast majority of UN Member States of the non-proliferation objective and the installation of an international mechanism for peaceful nuclear cooperation among States, especially between the nuclear 'haves' and 'have-nots'. Non-proliferation would be pursued under international safeguards against diversion, including the right to on-site inspection (OSI). Although the idea of inspection in the territory of a nuclear-weapon State was still unacceptable, IAEA's safeguards established an important precedent: on the basis of negotiated instruments, non-nuclear-weapon States agreed to accept certain limits on their sovereignty in this sensitive area of arms control. Another notable though less significant precedent, was the verification procedure embodied in the Antarctic Treaty of 1959 whereby the uninhabited environment of Antarctica was subjected to multilateral inspection as regards all stations, installations, equipment, ships and aircraft of any State, including the nuclear-weapon States.

The test-ban issue. The quest for arms control involved not only efforts to prevent proliferation but also to halt nuclear testing and thereby control the pace of the nuclear arms race. The goal was to conclude a comprehensive test-ban treaty, with effective international verification. The Cuban missile crisis of October 1962 was a stark reminder of the immediate risk of nuclear confrontation in an atmosphere of unfettered arms race. A major initial impact of the crisis was to intensify efforts towards a comprehensive test-ban treaty.

By mid-1963, negotiations by the US, the UK and the Soviet Union were close to success. As scientific discussions showed that national technical means could reliably detect all tests except the small underground explosions, the three powers agreed in principle that on-site inspection could be limited only to those explosions. However, a stalemate developed over the modalities and number of required annual inspections and became so intractable that the issue of inspection was put aside, while a provisional solution was sought to reduce the nuclear risk.

In a sudden shift, the two sides settled for a more modest but immediately achievable goal: a limited test-ban treaty, without the requirement of on-site inspection. The Treaty Banning Nuclear-Weapon Tests in the Atmosphere, in Outer Space and under Water (or Partial Test-Ban Treaty – PTBT), concluded by the US, the USSR and the UK in October 1963, relied exclusively on national technical means for its verification. As the first international nuclear agreement of worldwide scope, the PTBT was the second major achievement at this phase.

Multilateral disarmament agenda. The end of the second phase was also marked by a significant consolidation of issues for rational agenda-setting in a multilateral context. The revived comprehensive approach introduced the concept of 'General and Complete Disarmament' (GCD), which negotiators exploited for a desperately needed momentum going beyond its propaganda dimensions. This was made possible by two major developments: the enlargement of the United Nations towards global membership and the breakthrough in US–Soviet talks on the principles for general disarmament.

As regards the first point, the admission of newly independent States from Africa and Asia into the United Nations had an impact not only on general multilateral diplomacy but also on the disarmament debate. The new members chose to keep away from Cold War alliances but not to remain passive; they were keen to express their independent voice in world affairs. In the transformed political environment, the enlarged UN membership came to serve a dual function for the Cold War rivals: as a forum to exercise political and ideological influence, and as a source of ideas and initiatives by new Third World actors.

In 1959, at the suggestion of Soviet Chairman Khrushchev, the General Assembly had proclaimed that the ultimate goal of disarmament efforts was to achieve *General and Complete Disarmament under effective international control.* The Assembly requested the existing disarmament bodies to elaborate proposals towards this goal. With the vigorous endorsement of the concept by the newly established Non-Aligned Movement (NAM) and by the General Assembly itself, the momentum was carried on in Geneva.

Globalization of the disarmament issue was thus under way. The East–West dialogue itself was transformed into a global debate, with the non-aligned States as full participants. The contrasting East–West positions served as the points of reference for a debate on how to consolidate familiar elements from past proposals into a single architecture for general disarmament.

US–USSR agreed principles. The East–West breakthrough on principles of disarmament was in part a product of the interplay between bilateral and global diplomacy. It was made possible by a new understanding reached in September 1961 between Moscow and the new Kennedy Administration in Washington. The result was the Agreed Principles for Disarmament Negotiations – the 'McCloy–Zorin Principles'. The following eight principles were agreed as a foundation for all future negotiations:

1. The goal of negotiations is to achieve General and Complete Disarmament accompanied by procedures for the peaceful settlement of disputes;
2. Disarmament should allow the retention of only non-nuclear armaments, forces and facilities necessary for internal order and security and contingencies for a UN peace force;
3. Disarmament should consist of: (a) the reduction of conventional armaments, military establishments and budgets; (b) the elimination of weapons of mass destruction – nuclear, chemical, biological and any other WMDs – along with the means of delivery; (c) the abolition of military organizations and academies;
4. Disarmament should be conducted on a stage-by-stage basis, within a specified time limit for each stage, and transition upon a verified and satisfactory completion of each phase;
5. Balanced reductions should be ensured at each stage, with no military advantage for any party but equal security for all;
6. Disarmament should be implemented under strict and effective international control carried out by an International Disarmament Organization established within the framework of the UN;
7. Disarmament should be accompanied by measures to strengthen institutions of peace and security and supported by an international peace force; and
8. Negotiations should be conducted without interruption to aim at the widest possible agreement at the earliest possible date.

Geneva negotiations. In 1962, with the blessing of the General Assembly, the Agreed Principles were used to guide negotiations in Geneva. The ten-nation negotiating body, which represented the Eastern and Western powers equally, was expanded to include eight 'Non-Aligned States'. For two years, they formed the basis for negotiations at the Eighteen Nation Committee on Disarmament (ENDC), where the US and the USSR presented different proposals and elaborated them with some concessions to accommodate suggestions made by the non-aligned States.[12] However, the effort was notable more for the innovation on process than for the progress on substance. Significantly, it demonstrated the futility of an ambitious approach to negotiate a single, comprehensive treaty on disarmament, with a single international organization to verify implementation. Equally, it underscored the potential of negotiating partial measures in accordance with certain logical priorities, with each success generating the confidence needed to negotiate other measures and leading to the ultimate goal of general and complete disarmament.

Negotiators were aware not only of the interrelatedness of the partial disarmament measures but also of the appropriate verification mechanisms to be provided for them. The partial test-ban treaty was seen as a modest step towards an internationally verified comprehensive ban of all tests, including those carried out underground. Such progress would in turn serve as a litmus test about the determination to halt and reverse the nuclear arms race. The implications were significant for future negotiations as the subject of disarmament was to be organized into logical segments and sequences. The verification issue would be negotiated on a pragmatic basis to ensure incremental progress.

The stage was thus set for a tenuous balance between the quest for coherent progress and that for practical results in selected areas that were negotiable at the moment. Thus, as regards non-proliferation, it was possible to set a precedent on verification by agreeing on the international safeguards of the IAEA to discourage proliferation outside the nuclear club, the same type of safeguards being applicable to denuclearization arrangements negotiated for particular regions. For the Antarctica Treaty, which covered an uninhabited environment, it was sufficient to rely on monitoring by the State parties themselves.

A more significant precedent on self-reliance in monitoring was established by the Partial Test-Ban Treaty: only national technical means were to be used to verify compliance. An oft-mentioned saying in Geneva then was 'don't make the perfect the enemy of the good'. The lessons for future arms control talks were contradictory: one of fear – that the two sides would fend off international pressure by settling for token agreements; the other of hope – that agreement on even portions of important partial measures without inspection requirements may help progress on bigger issues in the long run.[13]

Détente: verified non-proliferation and disarmament plan, 1964–1979

The third phase was a period of growing stability in the strategic relations between the US and the Soviet Union, but it was also one of tension in Asia, especially involving China. China's emergence as a major power had shown early signs when it prevailed over India in their 1962 border war, but it was its emergence as a nuclear power that complicated the global equation and intensified American security concerns in the context of the long Vietnam War.

While a period of détente set in between the US and the Soviet Union, the People's Republic of China was already having security problems with both those powers. The renewed interest in the non-proliferation issue was in large measure due to concern about China's nuclear breakthrough which had taken place despite the Soviet Union's attempts to constrain it. Top priority was thus given to the negotiations for a nuclear non-proliferation treaty as effort continued to identify other collateral measures of worldwide scope that might be amenable to international verification. For strictly East–West arms control issues, negotiations were to rely on the prospect of advances in national scientific techniques to obviate the need for on-site inspections. This was notably the case with the 1972 Anti-Ballistic Missile Treaty, which became a cornerstone for future strategic arms control agreements between the US and the Soviet Union.

Control of weapons of mass destruction

When the Geneva negotiations gave priority to proliferation-related partial measures, the approach to verification was pragmatic. The parties would agree on adequate methods that would balance two factors – effectiveness versus minimum intrusiveness. The methods used were thus tailored to the various non-proliferation measures that were agreed.

The most significant global agreement was the Treaty on the Non-Proliferation of Nuclear Weapons (NPT) of 1968, preceded the year before by the first regional treaty – the Treaty for the Prohibition of Nuclear Weapons in Latin America (Treaty of Tlatelolco). The nuclear preoccupation led also to treaties on Outer Space (1967) and the Sea-Bed (1971).[14] Upon the failure of all efforts to conclude a single convention on biological and chemical weapons, the negotiators singled out the first part and agreed in 1972 on a Biological Weapons Convention (BWC) with the longest name (Convention on the Prohibition of the Development, Production and Stockpiling of Bacteriological (Biological) and Toxin Weapons and on their Destruction) but without any verification mechanism. The verification measures adopted were of three types: (a) international safeguards against nuclear proliferation, administered by the IAEA under the NPT and also applicable to zonal denuclearization agreements such as the Tlatelolco Treaty for Latin America; (b) verification by the State parties themselves to ensure the exclusion of WMD from Outer Space and the Sea-Bed by the observation of relevant activities of any State party, with the right to inspect any facilities in those uninhabited environments; and (c) reliance on national technical means to detect any violation of the Biological Weapons Convention, since international verification was deemed unachievable at the time.

NPT and IAEA safeguards. Although the founding of the IAEA was motivated by a concern about nuclear proliferation, it did not deter France and China from joining the nuclear club. It was only after the Chinese bomb that non-proliferation became a dominant issue. In 1965, the US and the USSR were able to negotiate and present identical texts of a draft treaty to the Eighteen Nation Disarmament Committee (ENDC). By mid-1968, amendments by other States ensured additions reflecting their particular concerns. These included, most notably:

(a) The availability to all parties of the benefits of nuclear technology for peaceful purposes (Article IV), including the potential benefits of peaceful nuclear explosives (Article V).
(b) The undertaking to pursue negotiations in good faith on effective measures to end the nuclear arms race at an early date and to achieve nuclear and other disarmament (Article VI).
(c) Affirmation of the right of groups of States to establish nuclear-weapon-free zones (Article VII). Significantly, international verification was a key element in designing the nuclear non-proliferation regime.

Article III of the Treaty required non-nuclear-weapon States to negotiate with the IAEA for the application of its safeguards system to all their nuclear facilities. Interestingly, a linkage with other mechanisms was added in the preamble of the NPT, in the form of a reiteration of the commitment made previously by the parties to the PTBT as a goal to pursue after achieving a Comprehensive Nuclear Test-Ban Treaty (CTBT).

A breakthrough was made possible by a precedent-setting compromise reached on the key issue of unbalanced obligations or 'discrimination' and that of 'confidentiality'. To at least partially address the discrimination between nuclear and non-nuclear-weapon States, whereby the peaceful nuclear industry of the nuclear-weapons States were exempted from the IAEA's full-scope safeguards, those States extended a voluntary offer to accept IAEA inspections in their civilian nuclear facilities. To cope with the confidentiality of commercial secrets raised by members of the European Community, those countries were allowed to continue to rely basically on their own collective EURATOM safeguards system, with arrangements negotiated with the IAEA to ensure international monitoring of that system in accordance with the Agency's safeguards requirements. Equally significant was the provision made in the Treaty for the Prohibition of Nuclear Weapons in Latin America: to have its parties utilize IAEA safeguards or comparable international verification for that treaty regime.

Biological Weapons Convention.   The inadequacy of the 1925 Geneva Protocol prohibiting the use of biological and chemical weapons had long been recognized. However, all efforts to expand the scope of the prohibition in both fields to include possession and also to add a verification mechanism had failed. In the context of the growing détente of the early 1970s, biological weapons were singled out for a total ban because of a special concern about the impact of the genetics revolution on the biological arms race. Accordingly, the US and the Soviet Union proposed a draft for negotiating a Biological Weapons Convention to the ENDC. The BWC instrument was adopted with the understanding that it would represent a first step in the search for a comprehensive ban in the interrelated biological and chemical areas, with appropriate international verification machinery.

Outer space and sea-bed treaties.   In a parallel process, prohibitions with respect to all weapons of mass destruction in the uninhabited environments of the sea-bed and outer space were achieved also. These were areas that were outside national jurisdiction under international law. Joint US–USSR draft treaties were used without much difficulty to negotiate instruments with vague verification procedures that relied mainly on national bilateral initiatives. The Outer Space Treaty, negotiated in 1967 in a special Committee of the UN General Assembly for the exploration and use of that environment, declares that State parties shall not place any WMD around the Earth's orbit, in any celestial bodies or anywhere in outer space but shall use those areas exclusively for peaceful purposes.

The verification provisions of the Treaty require the parties to inform the UN Secretary-General about all relevant activities. They include observation of flights of space objects by any interested parties and general on-site inspection with respect to the moon and other celestial bodies, on the basis of reciprocity (Articles X, XI and XII). Similarly, the Sea-Bed Treaty, which was negotiated at the ENDC in 1972, prohibited placement of WMD on or under the sea-bed, beyond the 12-mile coastal zone. The verification provisions include observation of activities on the sea-bed by any party or through appropriate bilateral or international inspection arrangements, with the possibility of referring unresolved issues to the UN Security Council (Article III).

Bilateral issues and NTM. The arms race between the US and the Soviet Union had to be regulated to reduce the risk of war. Even as methods of international verification were refined to fit specific multilateral treaties, technological progress on national technical means (NTM) opened up new opportunities for East–West arms control. During most of the 1970s, the US–Soviet negotiations focused on the Strategic Arms Limitation Talks (SALT I and II) and achieved a limitation of strategic delivery vehicles without requiring on-site inspection.

In sidestepping this difficult issue, the two sides were satisfied with the adequacy of the existing national technical means for this area of bilateral arms control. Since China and France were still boycotting any test-ban talks, the issue remained essentially a bilateral one for the US/UK alliance and for the Soviet Union. A comprehensive ban remained elusive because of the continued stalemate over on-site inspection. Once again, the three signatories of the PTBT settled on another small measure – the 1974 Threshold Test-Ban Treaty, which banned only large underground tests (above 150 kiloton) that could be monitored effectively by national technical means. Thus, international verification was still excluded from this East–West agreement, although it remained the preferred method for multilateral treaties of global scope.

New plan for coherent disarmament

Phase three ended with a major initiative by the whole international community to take stock of what had been achieved thus far and to chart the future course. By 1978, 33 years of disarmament negotiations had explored approaches ranging from comprehensive to partial measures and achieved agreement only on certain partial measures where consensus was possible. The progress was unsystematic and lacked an integrated, step-by-step approach. Worse still, no real progress had been made in halting the arms race, which had become more complex and increasingly global in scope. Against this background, the UN General Assembly convened its First Special Session Devoted to Disarmament (SSOD I) to take stock and organize future efforts. For the first time in the history of disarmament negotiations, the international community achieved consensus on a comprehensive disarmament strategy. The Final Document of the session was a landmark document universally accepted as a design for all future disarmament efforts within and outside the United Nations. It elevated the 1961 US–Soviet Agreed Principles to a higher level as regards scope, structure and reach.

The Document stated: 'genuine and lasting peace can only be created through the effective implementation of the security system ... and the speedy and substantial reduction of arms and armed forces, by international agreement and mutual example, leading ultimately to general and complete disarmament under effective international control.' Negotiations on general and complete disarmament were to be conducted concurrently with negotiations on partial measures of disarmament. It stated: 'Priorities in disarmament negotiations shall be: nuclear disarmament, other weapons of mass destruction ... conventional weapons ... and reduction of armed forces.' However, it made it clear that the control and elimination of weapons of mass destruction should remain at the top of the agenda.

As refined and elaborated further by the UN Disarmament Commission in the following year, the order of priorities for the WMD disarmament was to be: nuclear test-ban; cessation of nuclear arms race by halting weapons development and production and cutting off fissile material for weapons; reduction of nuclear weapons; nuclear non-proliferation and creation of nuclear-free zones; and prohibition of chemical and radiological weapons. Verification methods and procedures would be negotiated for the specific disarmament measures to facilitate effective implementation of the agreements and to create confidence among States.[15]

International satellite monitoring.   The Special Session was significant not only as a global conference for review and planning but also as a source of new verification methods. A far-reaching proposal was made by France to establish an International Satellite Monitoring Agency (ISMA) in order to strengthen the existing verification system. The idea was so well received that the General Assembly launched a feasibility study on it. In 1982, the Assembly endorsed the conclusion of the expert group that satellite monitoring would make a valuable contribution to the verification of disarmament agreements and requested the Secretary-General to examine the practical modalities with respect to the institutional aspects of an ISMA. However, the proposal failed to command unanimous support from the nuclear-weapons States: while France, China and the UK were joined by the vast majority of States in favour of implementing it, the Soviet Union opposed the idea and the US abstained on it.[16] The proposal was left aside for possible review at a more propitious time. It remains among the proposals whose time is yet to come.

Towards entente: verified bilateral
disarmament, 1980–1991

Despite the guidelines set by the Special Session, the 1980s were initially years of recrimination and tension between the superpowers that hindered progress in multilateral talks. In phase four, the decade began with a sense of American weakness represented by humiliation during the Iran hostage crisis and the Soviet invasion of Afghanistan, resulting in acceleration of the arms race. However, towards the mid-1980s, a sudden awareness of the real dangers of pre-emptive nuclear strike by either side induced a transformation of perspectives that allowed the emergence of a genuine dialogue.[17]

The radical reforms introduced by General Secretary Mikhail Gorbachev in the Soviet Union, and particularly his Glasnost policy of transparency, were accompanied by a rethinking of Soviet military doctrine, moving away from the total reliance on the doctrine of 'mutual assured destruction (MAD)' towards Andrei Sakharov's notion of 'mutual security'. This shift ensured a positive Soviet response to President Ronald Reagan's call for reciprocal verification, including on-site inspection, as an essential foundation for far-reaching disarmament measures. In addition to national technical means, mutual on-site inspection and ongoing monitoring became integral elements of verification for the US and the USSR.

The whole verification package was embodied in the two landmark bilateral agreements between the two superpowers: the 1987 Intermediate-Range Nuclear Forces Treaty (INF Treaty) for the elimination of delivery vehicles, and the 1991 Strategic Arms Reduction Treaty (START I Treaty) for the substantial reduction of both warheads and their delivery vehicles. A similar verification approach was used for the 1990 Treaty on Conventional Armed Forces in Europe (CFE) to balance forces between the NATO and the Warsaw Pact groupings and build mutual confidence and security.[18]

Thus, with the rapid improvement in US–Soviet relations, US proposals for on-site inspection became an instrument to achieve effective verification rather than as a tool of domestic politics and external propaganda. In the past, excessive US demands for verification methods had served to induce Soviet rejection, which would in turn be used to justify the shelving by the US of any undesirable disarmament proposals. The acceptance of such intrusive verification measures thus opened a new future for the concept in all contexts. Verification became a permanent feature of future disarmament negotiations, with appropriate adjustments on access and transparency requirements. The result was the emergence of a multitude of verification mechanisms, varying in intrusiveness as one moved from the bilateral to the multilateral spheres.[19]

Verification after the Cold War

The early 1990s represented the most radical transformation of the post-World War II geopolitical landscape. The changes in the strategic environment have created both opportunities and challenges for multilateral arms control, especially for the concept of disarmament verification. A perceptive essay by Michel Moodie[20] outlines the following factors as accounting for the main changes in the international environment, which had an impact on the direction taken by arms control today. First, the concept of security has evolved from a primary focus on military aspects to a more complex notion having significant political, economic and even environmental dimensions. The combination of regional stability, economic strength and political cooperation has become important in enhancing the security of States. This underlines the need for international cooperation and for multilateral arms control.

The second, and more dramatic change, has to do with the ending of the Cold War which characterized the nature of East–West relations for 45 years. As a consequence, East–West issues have given ground to more pressing problems of instability and conflict in different parts of the world.

Third, the breakup of the Soviet Union and the emergence of successor States as new players has affected the implementation of existing treaties and introduced new proliferation concerns and arms control dynamics.

The fourth major transforming factor was Iraq's war of aggression and the revelation about its clandestine WMD programme in flagrant violation of existing treaties. The Iraq experience prompted very close cooperation within the international community and also unity in establishing an unprecedented regime of intrusive verification for disarming Iraq.

International terrorism is the fifth factor affecting the international environment that emerged in the 1990s. It became a major transforming factor especially since the catastrophic events of September 11, 2001 in New York and Washington DC and the anxiety created by the mysterious subsequent attacks with mailed anthrax.

Verified WMD conventions, 1990–2000

In phase five, the changes in the strategic environment have had a significant impact on the organization of priorities in the arms control field. While continuing successful bilateral efforts between the US and the Soviet Union for deeper nuclear disarmament under a START II Treaty, there was a major effort to revitalize the United Nations, to intensify multilateral diplomacy and to strengthen international norms for both global and regional disarmament.

Lessons from Iraq. Significant benefits were gained from the Iraq experience. The first lesson was to strengthen the authority of the Security Council in the field of disarmament. Two major developments combined to enhance the role of the Council in this regard.

First, the Security Council put in place an enforcement mechanism compelling Iraq to disarm its weapons of mass destruction and its offensive missiles (range exceeding 150 km). This had positive implications for arms control as an issue of international security. The Council's Resolution 687 (1991) on the cease-fire after the Persian Gulf War established an integrated verification regime for dismantling Iraq's nuclear, chemical, biological and missile programmes. The regime would be executed cooperatively by two agencies: the IAEA, which would focus on the nuclear part; and a Special Commission (UNSCOM), which would concentrate on the chemical, biological and missiles components. As a subsidiary body of the Council, UNSCOM would receive intelligence information from Member States, designate inspection sites and provide assistance and cooperation to the IAEA teams. The effective dismantlement of Iraq's WMD programme was to serve as a step towards the creation of a zone free of weapons of mass destruction in the Middle East.

The second development was the unanimous adoption by members of the Security Council at the level of Heads of State and Government of a 'Presidential Statement'. The statement, which was announced on

31 January 1992 by the President of the Council, declared as follows: 'The proliferation of weapons of mass destruction constitutes a threat to international peace and security. The members commit themselves to working to prevent the spread of technology related to the research for or production of such weapons and to take appropriate action to that end.' On nuclear proliferation, the members of the Council pledged that they 'will take appropriate measures in the case of any violations notified to them by the IAEA'.[21] Significantly, the international community may infer from this declaration that weapons of mass destruction are not neutral in relation to international peace and security but that their very existence may pose an international threat.[22]

Strengthening IAEA safeguards. For the IAEA, the Iraq lesson enabled Director General Hans Blix to persuade Member States to overhaul the safeguards system in a manner that would enable detection of undeclared activities and any diversion of declared items by NPT parties. After six years of intensive study and deliberations, the Board of Governors of IAEA accepted his proposal in the form of a Model Additional Protocol to be annexed to existing Safeguards Agreements upon acceptance by the parties concerned (IAEA document INFCIRC/ 540, corr.). The main elements of the strengthened system aim to uncover relevant undeclared activities, particularly: (a) by improving IAEA's knowledge of the nature and location of all *nuclear activities* and also of any relevant *nuclear-related activities* of a non-nuclear-weapon State; and (b) by expanding the inspectors' physical access to locations beyond the strategic points in a nuclear facility. This would include not only nuclear sites but also other locations such as research facilities and relevant open spaces for monitoring.[23] The indefinite extension of the NPT in 1995 provided a stable framework for full implementation of the strengthened safeguards system.

Chemical and biological weapons conventions. The third lesson was related to Iraq's extensive use of chemical weapons against Iran and against Iraqi Kurds. At the Conference on Disarmament in Geneva, Member States were motivated to redouble efforts towards a Chemical Weapons Convention (CWC). The new consensus-oriented diplomacy made it possible to fulfil the pledge to follow up the Biological Weapons Convention (BWC) with a separate and more effective convention on chemical weapons. For the new convention, it was deemed necessary to devise an effective verification mechanism, which was absent from both the 1925 Geneva Protocol and the BWC.

In 1992, it was finally possible after two decades of on-and-off negotiations, to agree on a text which would constitute the first comprehensively verifiable multilateral treaty that would totally eliminate an
entire class of weapons and would bring potential production facilities
under strict monitoring. With the entry into force of the Convention in
1997, the Provisional Technical Secretariat at The Hague, the OPCW,
became a permanent mechanism for verification. The inspection procedures go far beyond routine monitoring and inspection of declared
industrial and military facilities of State parties, and are not 'discriminatory'. They also provide for 'challenge inspection' initiated by any
concerned State party.[24]

Although the proposals for a verification protocol for the BWC go
back to the mid-1980s, the idea has moved to centre stage only in the
second half of the 1990s. Difficult negotiations within an Ad Hoc Group
of State parties were able to produce a draft protocol acceptable to
almost all the State parties, except the most influential one, the United
States. More recently, the United States went even beyond rejecting the
proposal to question the verifiability of the Convention.[25]

Comprehensive Test-Ban Treaty. The momentum gathered from the
indefinite extension of the NPT and the agreement on the CWC was
helpful in sustaining the effort to resolve differences over the nuclear-
test-ban issue. All the positive post-Cold War factors were brought to
bear on the negotiations at the Conference on Disarmament to achieve
a treaty banning testing in all environments and relying on an elaborate
mechanism for verification. The 1996 Comprehensive Test-Ban Treaty
(CTBT) was the culmination of over four decades of bilateral and multilateral negotiations. Unlike the 1963 Limited Test-Ban Treaty and the
1974 Threshold Test-Ban Treaty, which relied on verification by national
technical means, the CTBT established an international verification
machinery combining a complex of global monitoring systems
involving seismological, infrasound, hydro-acoustic and radionuclide
networks, with on-site inspection.[26]

Unlike the NPT which was mainly directed at non-nuclear-weapon
States, the CTBT's main impact is on the nuclear-weapon States and
other nuclear-capable States, notably the so-called 'threshold' States –
India, Israel and Pakistan. Remarkably, all the nuclear powers came
on board and India's veto of a consensus at the Conference on
Disarmament was not allowed to block adoption of the text by the
United Nations General Assembly to launch the process of signing and
ratification by States. However, entry into force has been blocked by a

few significant hold-out States. It still awaits ratification by China and the United States and signing and ratification by India, Israel and Pakistan.

Present trends

The sixth and final phase began with the shift in American foreign policy under the new Bush Administration from a vigorous multilateral approach to scepticism and a shift towards unilateralism. The transformation became complete after the catastrophic terrorist events of 11 September.

The threat from international terrorists was not new. It had already been recognized in the mid-1990s as one of the new threats but did not dominate the foreign policy agenda. Truck bombing of crowded buildings by terrorists had already become more frequent. Even the spectre of terrorism with chemical and biological agents could no longer be dismissed as unrealistic, following the 1995 terrorist release of sarin nerve gas in the Tokyo subway system. Aum Shinrikyo, the wealthy apocalyptic Japanese cult, was responsible for the fatal incident that tried earlier and failed to cause harm by releasing biological agents. However, it was after the massive Al Qaeda attacks of 2001 in New York and Washington DC and the limited but frightening anthrax attacks in the eastern part of the United States that the possibility of major terrorist attacks with WMD became of highest concern. Al Qaedas's international threat has embodied a frightening combination of factors: an extreme Islamist ideology, an unrestrained motivation to inflict mass civilian casualties against the US and its allies, an interest to acquire materials for WMD, a talent for organizational efficiency and a reputation in fund-raising. Its capacity to operate covertly from safe havens within the chaos of a client failed State makes these factors even more dangerous for States and for people anywhere.

In this light, the war against Al Qaeda and other international terrorist groups has transformed the international security environment to such an extent that the US, as the only remaining superpower, has tended to rely more on short-term unilateral responses than on the well-trodden path of multilateralism.

To recapitulate, we have traced the evolution of disarmament verification in six phases, ranging from a comprehensive and centralized approach to one based on partial arms control measures selected according to their negotiability. The advent of the nuclear age under US atomic monopoly had initially focused attention on the radical idea of pooling nuclear weapons under a supranational authority but gave way first to a more traditional approach to achieve general and complete disarmament under effective verification. The latter was a more comprehensive approach designed to balance security concerns in the areas of weapons of mass destruction with preoccupation about a growing conventional arms race.

In the context of extreme Cold War rivalry and the emergence of the Non-Aligned Movement, proposals were so driven by calculations of strategic and propaganda advantage that the issue of effective verification by a single disarmament organization became the linchpin for the entire process. A significant consequence of the confrontation during the Cuban missile crisis was to seek realistic measures to avoid a nuclear war.

As the ultimate goal of GCD receded into the background, a new pragmatic approach was adopted, embodying a step-by-step course of partial measures. The result was a set of interrelated treaties adopted with separate verification mechanisms. Breakthroughs in verification technology also made it possible for the main nuclear powers to push forward on bilateral measures without insisting on intrusive inspections and to institute a two-track approach to arms control: a bilateral approach between the superpowers, relying on detection by national technical means; and a multilateral approach to prohibit proliferation of weapons of mass destruction, based on international verification.

As the Cold War gave way to deténte and cooperation between the superpowers, another breakthrough in arms control diplomacy brought about mutual acceptance of reciprocal monitoring and extensive on-site inspections. Such verification arrangements in bilateral treaties are more intrusive than the corresponding mechanisms negotiated for multilateral treaties. Such intrusiveness can be instructive in refining the process of international verification but cannot be expected under multilateral agreements. It has been possible in a bilateral setting because sovereignty concerns are alleviated by the symmetry of security concerns, by the balance of obligations and the opportunities for reciprocal action, and ultimately by the expectation of retaliation or easy withdrawal from the treaty if non-compliance threatens national security.

Various combinations of verification mechanisms – NTM and bilateral or multilateral methods – have long been routinely used to sustain the overall arms control system. However, they are facing today a number of challenges beyond the old ones, especially from the new unilateral tendencies in American foreign policy.

Challenges for effective WMD verification

Before outlining the challenges to WMD verification, it is helpful to reiterate the points from Chapter 1 regarding the nature of the verification mechanisms based on the NPT, CTBT and the CWC. The organizations concerned share the common purpose of verifying compliance by States with their treaty obligations. The multiple aims of verification are:

- To assess continuously treaty implementation;
- To remove uncertainties about honest implementation;
- To generate confidence among the parties;
- To discourage non-compliance by threatening timely detection; and
- To provide early warning of any non-compliance.

The IAEA, the CTBTO and the OPCW use similar or functionally comparable methods to carry out their verification responsibilities, which include:

(a) *Establishing baseline information*: For the IAEA and the OPCW, the declaration of relevant items by a State is the starting point in order to verify the 'correctness and completeness' of the declarations. National technical means and intelligence information from States can assist in the initial inspections to establish a baseline for future on-site inspections. Each member maintains a *State accounting and control system*, a form of bookkeeping to help each organization audit and monitor the technical operation of relevant facilities and review any changes in material balance that have taken place since the last declaration. For the CTBT, the functional equivalent is the record of scientific data accumulated from past nuclear tests, seismological events and other relevant information.

(b) *Installing monitoring equipment*: Equipment for surveillance (cameras), containment (seals) and other means for monitoring are installed by the IAEA and OPCW to ensure preservation of data on any development, for analysis by their own laboratories. For the CTBT, the system includes global monitoring networks for registering seismological, hydro-acoustic, infrasound and radionuclide information for analysis.

(c) *Procurement monitoring*: As part of the verification agreements and supplementary agreed procedures, the IAEA and the OPCW have arrangements to receive information from Member States of any transfers in designated materials and technologies of particular relevance to their non-proliferation objectives.

(d) *On-site inspection*: All three organizations include on-site inspection as a major part of their verification method. The IAEA and OPCW conduct routine periodic inspections at pre-selected sites to observe as well as retrieve recorded information and gather samples for analysis. But they differ considerably on how to follow up when further investigation is required to resolve inconsistencies or suspicious activities. They both have special measures available to handle suspicious cases. The IAEA Secretariat may request *special inspection* when the information provided by a State party is not adequate and its explanations are not satisfactory. The Secretariat is given considerable power in determining when investigation is necessary. The CWC's functional equivalent is the *challenge inspection*, which is initiated by a State party rather than by the technical secretariat in order to clarify any questions concerning possible non-compliance. Under the CTBT, the *on-site inspection* is only of one kind: challenge inspection similar to that of CWC. It is the State parties that request such inspection if the technical data suggests suspicious events on the basis of information assembled by the secretariats as well as by their own means.

These subjects will be taken up individually for a detailed comparative analysis of the verification systems of the IAEA, the CTBTO and the OPCW.

Effective verification is crucial for the fulfilment of the objectives of any disarmament treaty, not least in the WMD fields. The effectiveness of the verification package depends on a number of factors, some inherent in the agreed structure and others related to the type of responses demanded by emerging challenges. The Iraq experience about dismantling its WMD programme is instructive for any effort to strengthen existing systems of multilateral verification. However, it should not be regarded as a direct model for any treaty-based verification. The mandates of the Special Commission on Iraq (UNSCOM/UNMOVIC) and of the IAEA were based not on the consent of a host State but on binding enforcement resolutions of the Security Council under Chapter VII of the UN Charter.

The resolutions impose disarmament measures on a vanquished aggressor and treaty violator, and provide inspectors the right of intrusive access to territory, of unrestricted use of intelligence information and technology and of prompt access to the Security Council for enforcement action. The main value of the Iraq experience is to help in understanding the interaction of the various components of a verification regime in coping with clandestine violations of WMD treaties. It also serves as a source of ideas on ways to strengthen existing systems in order to respond effectively to current security challenges. As State parties seek to balance their individual sovereignty rights with the common security concerns reflected in WMD treaties, the following issues are identified as posing special challenges: (a) *Structural*: lack of membership universality, regime stagnation and fragmentation, and erosion of multilateralism; (b) *Substantive*: territorial intrusiveness, technology transfer, confidentiality of information and compliance issues.

Structural challenges

Universality issue

The WMD treaty regimes are global in concept, as norms against the acquisition or proliferation of the proscribed weapons. They are open to all States and are in this sense designed for universality in membership. It has to be recognized, however, that the NPT, unlike other WMD treaties, prescribes differing obligations for nuclear and non-nuclear-weapon States. The greatest challenge for all these treaties is their failure to achieve universality of membership, especially as regards the non-accession by certain militarily significant States.

The absence from the NPT of three nuclear-capable States – India, Pakistan and Israel – is a source of weakness for the nuclear non-proliferation regime. The non-acceptance of the CTBT by India and Pakistan and some other States and the non-ratification of the Treaty by the US are a serious setback in the effort to consolidate the provisional CTBT verification system. The 1998 nuclear tests by India and Pakistan were a major setback to the nuclear non-proliferation objective embodied in both the NPT and the CTBT. Many Middle East countries that are parties to the NPT have not accepted the CWC because of security concerns over the nuclear capability of Israel and the failure to advance towards a nuclear-weapon-free zone in the Middle East. The problem for the BWC is not so much lack of universality as it is a lack of consensus on how to ensure verification of compliance. In all cases, a major challenge is to enhance universality, especially by securing commitments from all militarily significant States to join in.

Regime-building issues

As each treaty was negotiated separately, the overall WMD verification function is fragmented, lacks coherence and leaves major gaps, especially in the areas of biological weapons and missile delivery systems and also in the sphere of export/import control. Effective synergy among existing systems cannot be expected unless State parties are persuaded of the value of building a common WMD regime. This will require an effort going beyond the independent strengthening of each verification system. The Iraq experience demonstrates the inter-relatedness of the weapons of mass destruction and the importance of a coordinated approach as a means of ensuring both security and disarmament, particularly in unstable regions such as the Middle East. What could be done to build linkages between the verification organizations to maximize synergy? In this regard, would the approach of joint protocols to existing treaties be feasible? What can be done to build practical cooperation among the IAEA, the CTBTO and the OPCW? How could they build on the statutory links with the Security Council provided in their respective treaties? These are some of the questions to consider.

Erosion of multilateralism

The challenge to multilateralism in the United States goes back at least a decade when conservative elements in the US Congress began blocking the President's plans to replenish regular budgets of international organizations. It became worse towards the end of President Clinton's term when ratification was denied to a number of signed conventions, including the CTBT. Under the Bush Administration, especially after 11 September, the dominance of conservative ideology in both Congress and the Executive branch has tended to accelerate the erosion of the traditional multilateral perspective of the United States. The recent unilateral withdrawal by the United States from the Anti-Ballistic Missiles (ABM) Treaty and its unprecedented announcement to nullify the US signature in selected treaties awaiting ratification including presumably the CTBT, are widely seen as an attempt to redefine the concept of international cooperation. If this unilateralist tendency is sustained, it might pose the greatest challenge to the established treaties and verification systems, as well as hinder their further development. The mechanisms for international verification will need to demonstrate their effectiveness as an essential tool to promote international security, in addition to the technical and other means at the disposal of individual States. To do so, the substantive issues of verification need to be addressed.

Substantive challenges

Intrusiveness issue

The effectiveness of a verification mechanism is determined not in absolute and objective terms but by how the parties judge its adequacy for the job in terms of cost–benefit. Intrusiveness of the system is one of the issues to consider. Unlike the Iraq disarmament operation, treaty-based verification operates within a consensual framework and is constrained by the security and other concerns of national sovereignty. An excessively intrusive system may provide dividends in detection of non-compliance but it would be costly in terms of sovereignty concessions and in budgetary terms. Territorial intrusiveness in the form of on-site inspection can be kept to a necessary minimum by resort to advanced technical means for monitoring events by remote sensing or on-site. The challenge is not selecting one or the other but how to combine them for effective results and in a manner acceptable to all parties. It is a dynamic balance depending both on changes in attitudes towards the issue of intrusiveness as confidence is built and in the innovations in monitoring technology.

Transfer of technology issue

All the WMD treaties seek to preserve the right of States to acquire dual use technology for peaceful development and not to hinder legitimate transfer of technology. At the same time, they provide rules to prevent diversion of such technology to proscribed military activities. The challenge is how best to control trade in such technology without detriment to the advancement of countries, especially the less developed ones. At issue is the effectiveness of the existing export/import mechanisms governing sensitive items relating to weapons of mass destruction.

Confidentiality issue

The confidentiality issue, which relates to the sovereignty issue, cuts both ways. A verification system relies mainly on information declared by States and officially gathered by the verification body. However, its effectiveness is enhanced in suspicious cases by relevant intelligence information made available by States that have it. Prudent use of intelligence information by international organizations is not unknown, but it remains controversial unless it is officially authorized, as it was in the case of the Iraq operation, or used internally with utmost discretion in planning official information gathering. Seeking broader understanding on the issue is part of the challenge. The other aspect of confidentiality relates to the protection of commercial or security secrets of the host country as it opens its treaty-related facilities for international monitoring. Balancing the host's need for confidentiality and the inspectors' demands for transparency is the other side of the challenge. This is again a dynamic relationship that can be developed in a manner to enhance effectiveness of the verification system.

Compliance issue

If non-compliance is demonstrated, does the present system provide adequate recourse? The answer at present is negative and that is a major challenge to all the WMD treaties. The compliance mechanism is weak and rudimentary; it relies basically on consultative procedures within the treaty organization, with the possibility of referring non-compliance cases to the UN Security Council, the only body that can impose international sanctions and other collective measures. The Council has sufficient guidelines to be more responsive, on the basis of the 1992 Presidential Statement of its 1992 Summit Session. However, at present it lacks consensus on whether and when it may take up disarmament-related issues other than that on Iraq.

Part II

Verification Mechanisms

The regime for elimination of weapons of mass destruction, as it has evolved, depends on the operation of a number of verification mechanisms. The focus is on the verification systems established under the Nuclear Non-Proliferation Treaty (NPT), the Comprehensive Test-Ban Treaty (CTBT) and the Chemical Weapons Convention (CWC). Each system comprises a diverse set of technical mechanisms, ranging from satellite imagery and sophisticated seismic measurement to visual inspection by human experts, and each has its own history, limitations and political context. However, there are also similarities in overall objectives, patterns of operation and problems encountered in ensuring compliance by States with their treaty obligations. Part II analyzes the mechanisms from their starting point in setting baseline information through technical monitoring and procurement control to proactive methods like on-site inspections. It provides a comparative analysis of the three verification systems in order to identify their strengths and weaknesses as components of an emerging broader WMD control regime.

Part II

Verification Mechanisms

3
Baseline Information: Declarations and Data Collection

The foundation of disarmament inspections is the declaration of weapons capabilities and of activities with dual-use purposes. The information submitted is crucial for effective verification, but it does not exist in a vacuum. Its accuracy and completeness cannot be guaranteed irrespective of the goodwill of submitting States, but needs to be checked against the totality of available information assembled from other sources, including existing data banks, media sources and future inspections.

Completeness and correctness are the two concepts underlying the value of the information base as a means to verify compliance with disarmament and non-proliferation commitments. At the first level, the correctness of declared information is checked by inspections in order to provide factual assurances about the peaceful use of declared material and facilities and about the dismantlement of any weapons programmes. The analysis of information is focused on discovering inconsistencies or ambiguities that require clarification or remedial action to ensure continued compliance. However, this is not sufficient to reveal clandestine activities. Verifying the completeness of information forms the second level. Completeness often depends on additional information that States are asked to provide, supplemented by information assembled by the inspectorate from other sources. The combination is expected to provide a reasonable assurance regarding the absence of undeclared material, facilities and illicit activities.

Declarations are used to plan inspections to validate the information and build a coherent picture of all relevant activities whose peaceful status will be routinely checked in the future. The necessity of declarations is stressed in agreements between States, concluded bilaterally or multilaterally, and in some decisions of the United Nations, notably by the

Security Council as regards the disarmament of Iraq. Disarmament and non-proliferation treaties invariably include commitments by contracting parties to submit at the outset a full catalogue of information about the state of armaments within a country or the potential to develop or acquire the weapons in question. State parties that have peaceful nuclear or chemical programmes as well as States that possess chemical weapons or the agents for such weapons are required to declare all relevant items. Specifically, they have to report not only the relevant materials but also the production, storage, conversion and destruction facilities in order to provide an information framework for subsequent inspections. There is no comparable requirement in the biological area, as the Biological Weapons Convention has no provision for a verification mechanism.

Initial declarations are used for establishing a baseline for checking the completeness and reliability of the submitted data. Without reference to baseline information inspectors are not able to identify missing elements or detect cheating. The declarations are updated by the submission of annual and other periodic reports that form the basis for ongoing evaluation of compliance with the disarmament and non-proliferation obligations undertaken in each treaty. The declarations and periodic reports include information on domestic production, the transfer of designated items within a country and any acquisition of such material and equipment from abroad.

The importance of declarations under the NPT and the CWC is underscored by the fact that most of the inspectors' time is spent on correlating activities at declared sites with the data submitted about them. It is usually when anomalies are found between the declared data and the activities at a site that more intrusive methods are employed. In the case of the CTBT, the already existing databanks on earthquakes and on past nuclear weapons tests form the functional equivalent of State declarations as a baseline for identifying suspicious events. In comparing the effectiveness of the baseline-setting processes prescribed by the treaties, the central issue is whether the information base is complete, coherent and accurate and whether it provides a systematic framework for verification work. The main elements in the declarations are:

1. *Transparency objective* designed to build confidence and ensure deterrence;
2. *Inventory accountancy* involving items of relevance to a weapons programme: nuclear material or chemical agents and any relevant equipment;

3. *Activities list* regarding the process of production and use of the dual-use material – the nuclear fuel cycle from uranium mining to electricity and fissile material and the chemical process from various precursors to industrial chemicals and warfare agents;
4. *Locations*, including the sites and the facilities for production, use and storage or disposal of the nuclear or chemical material; and
5. *Timelines* for the declarations, including the periods covered, the deadlines for submission and the frequency of updates.

The scope of the required information ranges from comprehensive and overarching, as in the case of chemical disarmament, to a narrower focus, as in the case of nuclear non-proliferation and the nuclear test ban. In all cases the contents are organized in such a way as to enable the inspectorate to identify 'high-risk' sites, facilities and activities for more focused attention. The process of assembling and analyzing the information ranges from the OPCW's extensive and highly structured approach that spans the entire chemical field, to the IAEA's uranium-based approach that focuses on the nuclear fuel cycle, with some flexibility to broaden the information base. However complete, declarations by themselves may not provide the total picture of a State's weapons capabilities and its aspirations.

Both the OPCW and the IAEA are therefore keen to establish effective data banks, with declared information at their core but supplemented by other information from official or open sources, ranging from science to the media. The setting of an information base indeed represents the core of the CTBT's monitoring system, which integrates and builds upon existing networks of scientific data on seismology and past nuclear tests, to form a baseline for detecting any possible future tests.

OPCW's comprehensive declarations

State declarations under the CWC encompass the civilian as well as the military sector to form a basis for the OPCW to *monitor* the destruction of chemical weapons and any associated facilities, to *oversee* the legitimate activities and to *deter* against the diversion of dual-use chemicals to weapons production. They are intended to ensure maximum transparency among State parties by providing comprehensive data as a basis for verifying both the completeness and correctness of the information on weapons programmes and on the chemical industry. The Convention does not limit the definition of chemical weapons to 'munitions and devices, specifically designed to cause death or other harm' but extends it to 'toxic chemicals and their precursors, except when intended for purposes not prohibited under the Convention, as long as the types and quantities are consistent with such purposes'. In principle, therefore, this general-purpose criterion (GPC), based on type, quantity and end-use of the chemicals, extends the declaration requirements to the entire chemical field, far beyond the agreed categories and lists of dual-use items.

However, in order to keep the verification burden and the intrusiveness to a minimum, the focus has to be mainly on certain agreed categories and lists. These form the basis for determining the nature and scope of information to be declared and the degree of intrusiveness required for each type of inspection. Obviously, chemical weapons and warfare agents are given priority for detailed reporting and intensive monitoring.

The declaration requirements for chemical-weapon States include the submission of full information: on chemical-weapons stockpiles and on facilities for their production, storage and destruction, or conversion, as appropriate; on commercial sites and facilities that were previously involved in weapons production; and on chemical weapons abandoned by a State within its territory or elsewhere. In the civilian sector, all State parties are required to submit declarations on their production and, as applicable, processing and consumption of 43 chemicals or groups of chemicals, organized under three itemized categories, and a declaration of production facilities for most other organic chemicals. The list of each schedule of controlled chemicals is given in Table 3.1. The categories of chemicals are ranked on the basis of two criteria: their military potential and the extent of their legitimate civilian use:

- *Schedule 1* comprises 12 chemical warfare agents (e.g. sarin, mustard gas, VX), as well as some key precursors for them, which have little or no commercial use but are permitted in limited quantities for various peaceful purposes – scientific research, medical applications, pharmaceutical production or protective purposes.
- *Schedule 2* comprises 14 high-risk chemicals and precursors that are moderately used in commerce and industry, such as herbicides and ceramics.
- *Schedule 3* lists 17 less-risky chemicals and precursors that are used by industry in large quantities.
- *Other unscheduled chemicals*, labelled 'unscheduled discrete organic chemicals' (UDOC), which are not listed but whose production facilities are not exempt from declaration and some inspection.

Table 3.1   CWC schedules of controlled chemicals

Schedule 1: Military agents with no or low commercial use

Toxic chemicals
1. O-Alkyl phosphonofluoridates (e.g. the nerve agents Sarin and Soman). [Chemical Abstracts Registry Numbers (CAS #), 107-44-8; 96-64-0]
2. O-Alkyl phosphoramidocyanidates (e.g. the nerve agent Tabun). [CAS # 77-81-6]
3. O-Alkyl aminoethyl alkyl, phosphonothiolates and corresponding alkylated or protonated salts (e.g. the nerve gas VX). [CAS # 50782-69-9]
4. Sulfur mustards (9 types, e.g. mustard gas). [CAS # 2625-76-5; 505-60-2; 63869-13-6; 3563-36-8; 63905-10-2; 142868-93-7; 142868-93-7; 142868-94-8; 63918-90-1; 63918-89-8]
5. Lewisites (3 types). [CAS # 541-25-3; 40334-69-8; 40334-70-1]
6. Nitrogen mustards (3 types). [CAS # 538-07-8; 51-75-2; 555-77-1]
7. Saxitoxin. [CAS #35523-89-8]
8. Ricin. [CAS # 9009-86-3]

Precursors
9. Alkyl phosphonyldifluorides (e.g. DF). [CAS # 676-99-3]
10. O-Alkyl O-2-dialkyl aminoethyl alkyl phosphonite and corresponding alkylated or protonated salts (e.g. QL, a key precursor for VX). [CAS # 57856-11-8]
11. Chlorosarin. [CAS # 1445-76-7]
12. Chlorosoman. [CAS # 7040-57-5]

Schedule 2: High risk precursors and toxic chemicals with moderate commercial use

Toxic chemicals
1. Amiton: O, O-Diethyl S-[2-(diethylamino)ethyl] phosphorothiolate and corresponding alkylated or protonated salts. [CAS # 78-53-5]
2. PFIB 1,1,3,3,3-Pentafluoro-2-(trifluoromethyl)-1-propene. [CAS # 382-21-8]
3. BZ: 3-Quinuclidinyl benzilate. [CAS # 6581-06-2]

Precursors
4. Chemicals, except those listed in Schedule 1, containing a phosphorus atom to which is bonded one methyl, ethyl or propyl (normal or iso) group but not further carbon atoms (e.g. methylphosphonyl dichloride, dimethyl methylphosphonate). [CAS # 676-97-1; 756-79-6]
   Exemption: Fonofos: O-ethyl S-phenyl ethylphosphonothiolothionate. [CAS # 944-22-9]
5. N-N-Dialkyl phosphoramidic dihalides.
6. Diakyl N,N-dialkyl phosphoramidates.
7. Arsenic trichloride. [CAS # 7784-34-1]
8. 2,2-Diphenyl-2-hydroxyacetic acid. [76-93-7]
9. Quinuclidin-3-ol. [CAS # 1619-34-7]
10. N,N-Dialkyl aminoethyl-2-chlorides and corresponding protonated salts.
11. N,N-Dialkyl aminoethane-2-ols and corresponding protonated salts
    Exemptions: N,N-Dimethylaminoethnol and corresponding protonated salts [CAS # 108-01-0]; and N,N-Diethylaminoethanol and corresponding protonated salts. [CAS # 100-37-8]

Continued

Table 3.1   Continued

12. N,N-Dialkyl aminoethane-2-thiols and corresponding salts.
13. Thiodiglycol: Bis(2-hydroxyethyl)sulfide. [CAS # 111-48-8]
14. Pinacolyl alcohol: 3,3-Dimethylbutan-2-ol. [CAS # 464-07-3]

Schedule 3: High commercial volume dual-use chemicals

Toxic chemicals
1. Phosgene: carbonyl dichloride. [CAS # 75-44-5]
2. Cyanogen chloride. [CAS # 506-77-4]
3. Hydrogen Cyanide. [CAS # 74-90-8]
4. Chloropicrin: Trichloronitromethane. [76-06-2]

Precursors
5. Phosphorus oxychloride. [CAS # 10025-87-3]
6. Phosphorus trichloride. [CAS # 7719-12-2]
7. Phosphorus pentachloride. [CAS # 10026-13-8]
8. Trimethyl phosphite. [CAS # 121-45-9]
9. Triethyl phosphite. [CAS # 122-52-1]
10. Dimethyl phosphite. [CAS # 868-85-9]
11. Diethyl phosphite. [CAS # 762-04-9]
12. Sulfur monochloride. [CAS # 10025-67-9]
13. Sulfur dichloride. [CAS # 10545-99-0]
14. Thionyl chloride. [CAS # 7719-09-7]
15. Ethyldiethanolamine. [CAS # 139-87-7]
16. Methyldiethanolamine. [CAS # 105-59-9]
17. Triethanolamine. [CAS # 102-71-6]

Source: Chemical Weapons convention's Annex on Chemicals; see http://www.opcw.org/html

Whether a particular chemical industry facility should or should not be declared is determined by two criteria: whether it produces, processes, or utilizes one or more of the scheduled chemicals; and whether the annual amount of chemicals processed exceeds specified quantity thresholds.[1] Table 3.2 provides the lowest thresholds for reporting on annual production levels for chemicals under each schedule. It also gives the corresponding thresholds for inspections, which are much higher, except for the warfare agents under Schedule 1.

Chemical weapons

States that possess chemical weapons are required to declare, within thirty days after ratifying the Convention, key aspects of their weapons programmes, including stockholding of chemical weapons. This must

Table 3.2 Thresholds for annual data declarations and routine inspections

Type of facility	Type of activity to be reported for previous calendar year and anticipated for next calendar year	Annual production threshold for reporting	Threshold for inspectioins
Schedule 1	Production, processing, consumption, acquisition import/ export data	– 100 g	– 100 g
Schedule 2	Production, processing, consumption, import/export data	– 1 kg benzilate – 100 kg (Amiton, PFIB) – 1 metric ton for other Schedule 2 chemicals	– 10 kg benzilate – 1 metric ton (Amiton, PFIB) – 10 metric ton for other Schedule 2 chemicals
Schedule 3	Production, import/ export data	– 30 metric tons	– 200 metric tons
Other chemicals production facilities	Production data for previous calendar year only	– 30 metric tons for discrete organic chemicals containing phosphorus, sulphur, or fluorine	– 200 metric tons

Source: Chemical Weapons Convention, Verification Annex, Part VI, paras 10,1, 28; Part VII, paras 3, 12; Part VIII, paras 3, 12; Part IX, paras 1, 9; cited from Amy E. Smithson, *Rudderless: The Chemical Weapons Convention at 11/2* (Washington, DC, 1998), p. 7.

include data on the aggregate quantity and toxicity of each declared chemical agent, the associated equipment, munitions and other components, and the location and inventory of each storage facility. It must also include data on chemical weapon production and development facilities. States are required to halt promptly all production of chemical weapons and identify each facility with precise information on location, ownership and operating history going back to the end of World War II. Such historical information and timeline is also required of former chemical-weapon States as regards any abandoned, decommissioned, or converted weapons production facilities. January 1946 is also used as the earliest date for retroactive reporting on the commercial sites of any State that had previously produced scheduled chemicals for weapons, with an account of the production history of each facility, going all the way back. This history should also include information on past transfers of chemical weapons between States. A complete, accurate and timely declaration of chemical weapons and related facilities was considered essential for meeting the ambitious 10-year deadline for dismantling them. Unfortunately, the whole process of destruction has been slowed down by undue delays caused by a number of factors beyond the slowness of initial declarations: mainly, lack of leadership in assigning priority and funding for the task, legal complications and technical difficulties associated with CW destruction operations.

Permitted warfare agents

Declarations are also required of any of the warfare agents listed in Schedule 1 that are produced for scientific research or for medical, pharmaceutical, protective or other peaceful purposes. States are permitted to produce a yearly aggregate of no more than one metric ton of such chemicals for these purposes. Examples of defensive applications include the development of vaccines and treatments for CW poisoning and the testing of detectors, protective masks and clothing. Production for such protective purposes is allowed at only two facilities defined by capacity: one single small-scale production facility where, *inter alia*, the reactor vessels cannot exceed 100 litres and the annual production must not exceed one metric ton, and a second designated facility capable of an annual production of up to 10 kilograms of the toxic chemicals. In addition to a detailed description of those facilities, the initial declaration must also include information on any other facilities producing such chemicals in lesser amounts for other peaceful purposes, the lowest reporting threshold being 100 grams per year.

It is important to have timely and precise initial and annual data declarations on the permitted warfare agents. Evidently, it is facilitated by the ability to focus verification efforts on the facilities dedicated to the production of Schedule 1 chemicals for peaceful application. Furthermore, declarations are required in each transfer of a Schedule 1 chemical between States Parties (both in advance of the transfer and again in the annual declaration). What is not so obvious is the usefulness of the aggregated information on annual production, which is a key reference point for detecting discrepancies between gross figures and the findings from inspecting all declared plants, including those producing dual-use chemicals.

Dual-use chemicals

Initial and annual data declarations on sites and facilities in the chemical industry focus on the dual-use chemicals. These involve the chemicals listed in Schedules 2 and 3, with more demanding reporting requirements on the former because of the higher risk factor. Each State must declare the nature of the activities at all its industrial sites that produce or consume the dual-use chemicals and report the aggregate national amounts of Schedule 2 and 3 chemicals. The aggregates represent the balance of what is produced, processed, consumed, imported and exported in one year. In addition, detailed data must be submitted for each commercial facility where production, processing or consumption of those scheduled chemicals exceeded the threshold quantities outlined in Table 3.2. The reporting thresholds vary in accordance with the risk factor. For example, for Schedule 2 chemicals there are three levels: one kilogram for highly toxic chemicals that had previously been used for weapons, 100 kilograms for chemicals that could also be easily weaponized, and one metric ton for other chemicals and their precursors. For Schedule 3 chemicals, the threshold rises to 30 metric tons per year. The data on individual facilities must include precise information on the declared site, the location and activities of each plant.

Other industrial chemicals

The reporting requirement on other chemical production facilities is not structured, but an initial list of facilities that have the potential to produce any of the scheduled activities must be submitted and updated annually. In the case of facilities that produce discrete organic chemicals containing some basic building blocks for making weapons – phosphorus, sulphur or fluorine (PSF) – the threshold for annual reporting by a facility is 30 metric tons, similar to that of Schedule 3 chemicals. For other chemicals, a plant need not report unless its annual production exceeds 200 metric tons.

Problems encountered

Four types of problems were encountered by the OPCW during its first seven years that hindered smooth functioning of the verification system: delays in reporting, incompleteness of declarations, ambiguities in the submissions, and inconsistencies in applying the agreed criteria, or lack of some criteria in some cases.

First, although States were required to submit initial declarations not later than 30 days after becoming parties, this deadline was rarely met. Most States took months, and some, including the United States, several years to do so.[2] This problem has seriously disrupted plans for timely and systematic initial inspections, especially in the civilian sectors. Consequently, there have been complaints about pace, balance and equity of the verification missions.

Second, as a number of countries had submitted partial or otherwise incomplete declarations much effort was required to obtain the missing information. As of March 2002, the Secretariat was able to identify potentially declarable industrial activities in 44 States – half of the States that had not previously declared those industrial activities.[3] Open-source information was helpful in this regard.

Third, as many declarations had contained significant ambiguities, or inconsistencies the secretariat had to engage in protracted exchanges to obtain clarifications. The inconsistencies were reflected also in the data sets declared by pairs of States regarding their trade in scheduled chemicals in the same calendar year. For example, in 2000 requests for clarification were made to over eighty States parties but the answers were slow in coming.[4]

A fourth problem is the OPCW's inconsistency in the thresholds criteria that has occurred in some areas. The broad concept used in the Convention is to keep the amount of data gathered to the minimum required to verify compliance with the CWC. However this concept has encountered conflicting interpretations. The United States has posed a major problem in this regard. It has excluded from its declaration inventories with low concentration of scheduled chemicals and facilities that produce a mixture of reportable unscheduled discrete chemicals with other unreportable chemicals.[5] Another problem is the difficulty faced by the OPCW in harmonizing the inter-State trade aggregates concerning scheduled chemicals in order to ensure correct overall material balance. The main reason is that some States have applied differing reporting thresholds for domestic production and export controls. Other reasons include the difficulty of identifying mixtures containing scheduled chemicals (which in transfer regulations are often classified differently from the original chemicals), the impact of free ports and zones, and the effect of material in transit at the end of the year.[6]

IAEA declarations: towards an integrated system

The IAEA's baseline information is currently based on a dual system of safeguards, involving the collection and evaluation of information from NPT parties. The first is based on the State's declaration covering its peaceful nuclear activities, which focus primarily on the nuclear-fuel cycle.

The declaration requirements are outlined in the Comprehensive Safeguards Agreements, based on a model document known as INFCIRC/153. The second emerging system is based on expanded declarations designed to cover all aspects of a State's nuclear programme and all related material, equipment and activities, as embodied in the Additional Protocols to the Safeguards Agreements. It is based on a more recent model document known as INFCIRC/540. The next step is to develop an integrated safeguards system for each State that accepts the Additional Protocol to supplement its existing Comprehensive Safeguards. The purpose is to implement the two agreements as a single instrument resulting in a unified safeguards system.

Declarations under traditional safeguards

Comprehensive Safeguards Agreements are based on the concept of 'material accountancy', which represents the submission by a State to the IAEA of its inventory of nuclear material and any associated facilities to be verified for *correctness*. This is done by auditing the operator records and by checking the physical inventory at each facility. The IAEA flags any inconsistencies first by comparing the declarations with the records. Then it identifies by inspection any discrepancies between the records and the physical inventories in order to determine whether there is 'material unaccounted for' (MUF). Beyond that, the findings cannot give a credible assurance that the declarations were complete in the first place. The capacity of the traditional safeguards system is too limited to verify the completeness of the declarations. Although both the IAEA Statute and the NPT are broad enough to cover verification of undeclared material and facilities, Member States had decided early in the 1970s on a less intrusive system incapable of assuring completeness of information.

In the traditional safeguards system, the main items reported in a State's initial and periodic declarations are:

- *Nuclear material*: Information on a State's stocks of material subject to safeguards, with details on each facility's material balance. Reportable nuclear material refers to uranium oxide or metal as the source, uranium fuel assemblies, low-enriched uranium, radioisotopes, special fissionable material, and spent reactor fuel in storage or under reprocessing. Special fissionable material, comprising highly enriched uranium and plutonium, is the most sensitive since it is usable for weapons. Only small quantities of nuclear material at the lower end of the fuel cycle are exempted from safeguards.[7]

- *Fuel cycle*: Information on a State's fuel cycle activities – uranium ore conversion, uranium enrichment, fuel fabrication, reactor operation, spent fuel reprocessing and waste management.
- *Reactor design*: Detailed information on the design, features and location of each nuclear facility 'as early as possible' before nuclear material is introduced into it. This includes power and research reactors, conversion and fuel-fabrication plants, reprocessing plants, isotope separation plants and relevant storage facilities.

The central feature of the traditional safeguards system is the pragmatic approach of facility-by-facility evaluation of the State's declaration and its focus on verifying the inventory of nuclear material as it flows in the nuclear fuel cycle. The emphasis is on checking for discrepancies between the declared information and the facts on the ground. At the plant sites the focus is on strategic inspection points where measurements and samples are taken and also where containment and surveillance equipment is installed. It is a selective and strategic approach and thus deliberately less than comprehensive despite the designation. Its inadequacy was clearly revealed after the discovery in Iraq of a clandestine nuclear weapons programme in the early 1990s. It then became imperative to enhance the detection capabilities by expanding the information gathering and evaluation capabilities of the IAEA.

Expanded declarations to detect concealment

The problem of providing assurances regarding the completeness of a State's declarations has three aspects: (a) information on the continuing peaceful status of the current nuclear energy programmes of NPT State parties; (b) information on the history of dismantled, transferred or otherwise converted nuclear-weapons programmes; and (c) information on whether any State parties exempted from safeguards now possess sufficient quantities of nuclear material requiring termination of the waiver. The third aspect involves approximately 120 small States with limited industrial capabilities and is considered not to pose any serious problem.[8]

Significantly, the four existing cases of voluntary nuclear disarmament also did not pose a problem of cooperation with the IAEA. These were: the South African case involving verification by the IAEA of the history of a recently dismantled nuclear-weapons programme, and the cases of three former Soviet Republics – Belarus, Kazakhstan and Ukraine – involving monitoring and verification by the IAEA of the dismantlement or transfer of nuclear weapons to Russia. All these required extensive initial declarations and clarifications. Cooperation with the IAEA was exemplary, as all those States had firmly decided to dispose of their nuclear weapons and accede to the NPT with a clean slate as non-nuclear-weapon States.

The main focus of the strengthened safeguards system is therefore on the first aspect, which covers about 60 States that are required to submit the fullest possible declarations on their peaceful nuclear programmes. In order to strengthen the capabilities for detecting undeclared nuclear activities, the new Additional Protocol system combines four major factors: first, increased nuclear transparency in the form of extended declarations by States; second, an expanded physical access for IAEA inspectors; third, new technical measures for environmental sampling (e.g. air, water, soil, vegetation), with the right to apply them beyond declared locations; fourth, an evaluation system based on the totality of available information and on State-wide rather than on a facility-by-facility assessment. The first and fourth factors are of particular relevance in setting a comprehensive information system to address a problem of undeclared nuclear activities. Accordingly, the extended declarations include the following categories of information:

- Information on all aspects of a State's nuclear fuel cycle, extending coverage to uranium mines, and also going beyond the usual nuclear facilities to cover any other location where nuclear material is available for non-nuclear applications;
- Information on all buildings at a nuclear site, going beyond previously designated premises;
- Information about research and development related to the fuel cycle, which was not required before; and
- Information going beyond nuclear material and activities to include the manufacturing and export of sensitive nuclear-related technologies.

In the new system, the State Declarations are continuously compared with the totality of the information available to the IAEA. This includes information from open sources (technical journals, trade publications and the news media), information from various States and data from previous inspections. It is by such comparison that inconsistencies are identified and resolved by credible explanations or by the submission of any missing information. An integrated system combines the material accountancy approach of the traditional comprehensive safeguards and the broader approach of the Additional Protocol covering all relevant activities. The regular declaration for each facility provides the basis for verifying whether the declared items are correct or, technically speaking, 'accounted for'. On the other hand, an extended declaration, with supplementary information from the data bank of the Agency, provides a broader basis for evaluating the information for completeness. In order to enhance the credibility of the findings, the evaluation is done not merely on a facility-by-facility basis but on a Statewide basis.

Problems encountered

Two major problems are encountered by the IAEA as regards the expansion of its information base: the slow pace of legal acceptance by Member States of the strengthened safeguards system and, consequently, the delay in establishing for each State an integrated system that supplements the existing comprehensive safeguards agreement with the provisions of the Additional Protocol. By mid-2004, seven years after the Board of Governors approved the Model Additional Protocol, only 84 States had the Additional Protocol, of which only 59 had brought it into force. This means only about two-fifths of the 148 NPT parties with a comprehensive safeguards agreement in force have concluded an Additional Protocol. The next step of integrating safeguards for each State is complex, costly and time-consuming. The methodology has been refined and modest progress is being made to implement it in a number of States. More encouraging is the significant progress made recently within the IAEA to establish a whole new infrastructure for broad information collection and management, with evaluation by multidisciplinary teams.

Iran as an illustration

The importance of baseline information for an effective verification system can be illustrated by the case of Iran with respect to both the chemical and nuclear aspects of weapons of mass destruction. It demonstrates the importance of full transparency by a State that claims to comply with the technical requirements of reporting while withholding essential information on its present or past weapons programme.

In the chemical field, when Iran ratified the CWC in November 1997, it denied that it had a chemical weapons programme. It was not until a year later that it acknowledged the truth. It confirmed the unambiguous information collected from other sources that it had developed a chemical weapons capability during the Iran–Iraq war but that the process was reversed and 'terminated' after the 1988 ceasefire. Today, Iran is a CWC member in good standing, having declared three former chemical weapons production facilities and several industrial sites. However, despite successful corroboration by OPCW inspections, the US has continued to doubt the completeness of Iran's declaration, unfortunately without submitting any information to justify its suspicions.[9]

In the nuclear field, the transparency problem in Iran is even worse. As a party to the NPT with a safeguards agreement in force since 1974, Iran had routinely updated its initial declaration about its peaceful nuclear programme, but without revealing the full extent of its activities since the onset of its war with Iraq. It was not until credible information was received in 2002 from members of an opposition group that the IAEA was able to confirm that Iran's declarations since 1985 were incomplete and misleading. By June 2003, the IAEA Director General was able to confirm to the Board of Governors that Iran had failed (a) to declare its 1991 import of natural uranium, its subsequent enrichment efforts, and its processing and storage facilities, and (b) to provide any information on the existence, let alone the design, of its covert uranium enrichment facilities.[10] In the aftermath of the 2003 US-led invasion of Iraq, it required diplomatic pressure to persuade Iran to open up its entire programme in accordance with the reporting requirements of the Additional Protocol.

CTBTO's global monitoring data centre

Under the terms of the CTBT, the verification regime being established will rely not on State declarations but on an ongoing International Monitoring System (IMS), based on a global network of sensors of different types, a Global Communication Infrastructure (GCI) to transmit the data in real-time, and an International Data Centre (IDC) to manage the information process. It is the IDC, located at the CTBTO headquarters in Vienna, which analyzes the technologically gathered information for detecting and locating events that might be nuclear tests. The Centre processes the raw data into a standard product to be used as an objective basis for further analysis, both by the OPCW and by the individual Member States with whom it is shared. It is on the basis of such analysis, backed by any other information at their disposal, that a State may request a challenge inspection against another State.

The work of the IDC will be discussed in more detail as part of the subject of ongoing monitoring in the following chapter on technical monitoring.

4
Technical Monitoring

The advances in information technologies, coupled with the development of more sensitive measuring instruments have meant that verification increasingly depends on ongoing, indirect monitoring. Called technical monitoring, it addresses the problem of intrusiveness into sovereign territory by making the detection mechanism mechanical and automatic. 'Look, Ma, no hands', so to speak.

This type of monitoring is particularly effective with nuclear weapons, where production or testing is physically notable. Testing can be heard or felt, production can be observed by monitoring instruments.

The management issues in this type of verification centre on the establishment and maintenance of the systems, and the financing required for this.

While the IAEA has always placed some reliance on recording devices, the new expanded verification protocol means that increasingly the Agency is planning to use indirect techniques to verify compliance under expanded safeguards. Still, the clearest example of this approach to verification is found in the CTBTO.

The CTBTO model

The most elaborate of the ongoing technical monitoring is included in the Comprehensive Test-Ban Treaty. In that treaty, the main verification mechanism is the International Monitoring System that, until the Treaty enters into force, is managed by the Provisional Technical Secretariat of the CTBTO. The CTBTO describes the system in this way:

The International Monitoring System (IMS) comprises a network of 321 monitoring stations and 16 radionuclide laboratories that monitor the earth for evidence of nuclear explosions in all environments. The system uses four verification methods, utilizing the most modern technology available.

When completed, the IMS will have stations throughout the world and should be able to detect any nuclear tests.

The premise behind the system is that for a nuclear weapon to be credible a country has to be able to prove that it works. This is necessary for two different reasons. A State would not want to threaten to use a weapon that it had not tested. And other States would not be deterred if the weapons were not tested. Thus, testing is an essential element of any strategy to use nuclear weapons.

Now, testing involving a large explosion, particularly in the atmosphere, would not require a verification system; the explosion would be very noticeable. However, for most of the last forty years tests have taken place below ground or under the ocean, and the sizes of the explosions have become smaller. Monitored from a distance, nuclear tests could be confused with normal seismic movements or non-nuclear man-made explosions.

Two types of problems have to be addressed by the verification system: (i) undetected testing that would allow a State to complete development of a nuclear weapon before steps could be taken to prevent this, or (ii) State use of a normal seismic event or a non-nuclear explosion to pretend to have developed and tested a weapon.

For a State to be able to prove that it has nuclear weapons, at least one weapon has to be tested, or appear to have been tested. However, if testing can be instantly detected and responded to, there are strong disincentives to attempt a clandestine test. Similarly, if the difference between a nuclear test, a non-nuclear explosion, and a normal seismic event can be detected, the possibility of 'false positives' is reduced.

Under this logic, the potential for detecting nuclear tests serves as a disincentive for their development and for the threat of their use.

For a verification organization, as well, there has to be credible evidence that the testing can be detected. Developing a system that will provide that credible evidence has been the main work of the CTBTO in its first years.

The most recent nuclear tests were those carried out by India and Pakistan in May 1998. The monitoring system was not yet in place, and the Provisional Technical Secretariat of the CTBTO was just beginning to become organized. Even with this, the few existing IMS facilities clearly detected the explosions.

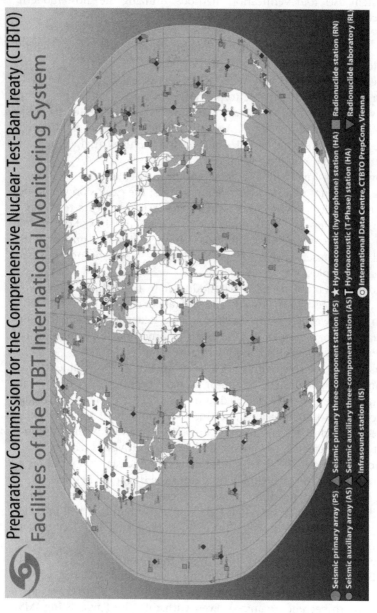

Figure 4.1 Preparatory Commission for the Comprehensive Nuclear Test-Ban Treaty Organization (CTBTO) facilities of the CTBT International Monitoring System

Source: Comprehensive Test-Ban Treaty Organization, 2004.

The key to the system is the International Data Centre. This centre is computer-based and located in Vienna, but receives its data automatically through satellite transmission from the monitoring stations. In describing the IDC, the CTBTO states that:

- Over 100 stations are already transmitting data to the IDC, many of them continuously.
- Global coverage is being ensured through the Global Communications Infrastructure (GCI), which receives and distributes data and reporting products relevant to Treaty verification. Data are received and distributed through a network of three satellites.
- The GCI became functional in mid-1999.
- Five GCI hubs have been installed and GCI terminals have so far been set up at 46 IMS stations, national data centres and development sites.
- The GCI hubs are connected via terrestrial links to the IDC in Vienna.

Will it work?

The real issue behind the IMS is whether it will work. In the debates in the United States on ratifying the CTBT, it was argued that the system was incapable of detecting an underground explosion of less than 1 kiloton. Similarly questions were raised about whether the system would be able to distinguish between a low-level nuclear explosion and a natural seismic event. If the system were unable to detect low-level explosions, or determine whether they were nuclear, non-nuclear man-made or natural seismic events, the purpose of the Treaty would not be served.

The issue turns on two factors: the coverage of the system, and the sensitivity of the measuring instruments.

The coverage issue is central to the need for an international verification mechanism. In the period before the CTBT, once above-ground testing was abandoned in favour of underground tests, an explosion would have to be detected through what are termed 'national means', seismic, radionuclide or infrasound stations that were under national control. Thus, for the United States to detect an explosion in the former Soviet Union, the means would be a seismic station under US control. Similarly, the Soviet Union would detect explosions in the United States through its own seismic stations. This would not be a problem for large explosions, but for smaller explosions the distance from the site could make detection at best ambiguous.

In defining the system for the CTBT, the concept was to have a network that literally covered the globe, with enough stations that no explosion, anywhere, could go undetected. The network would consist of existing stations as well as new stations. Each would be under the control of the respective government, but would follow an agreed standard and would be linked by a common telecommunications system. The Protocol to the Treaty stated:

4. In accordance with appropriate agreements or arrangements and procedures, a State Party or other State hosting or otherwise taking responsibility for International Monitoring System facilities and the Technical Secretariat shall agree and cooperate in establishing, operating, upgrading, financing, and maintaining monitoring facilities, related certified laboratories and respective means of communication within areas under its jurisdiction or control or elsewhere in conformity with international law. Such cooperation shall be in accordance with the security and authentication requirements and technical specifications contained in the relevant operational manuals. Such a State shall give the Technical Secretariat authority to access a monitoring facility for checking equipment and communication links, and shall agree to make the necessary changes in the equipment and the operational procedures to meet agreed requirements.

The Protocol also specified exactly where these stations should be located.

There were to be 50 primary seismological stations from which data would be transmitted automatically and uninterrupted to the International Data Centre. In addition, there were to be 120 auxiliary stations from which the CTBTO could request data that should be 'immediately available through on-line computer connections'. These stations would be able to detect movements of the earth, and because the patterns of underground explosions are different from natural seismic events this would detect underground tests.

To detect above-ground tests (as well as any radioactivity that would escape from an underground, or underwater test), a network of 80 stations to measure radionuclides in the atmosphere is to be set up. Each station uses air samplers to detect radioactive particles released from atmospheric explosions and vented from underground or underwater explosions. The relative abundance of different radionuclides in these samples can distinguish between materials produced by a nuclear reactor and a nuclear explosion. Each of these would have a corresponding laboratory that was certified by the Technical Secretariat and paid by the CTBTO to analyze samples. The results of this analysis would be sent directly to the International Data Centre.

For underwater explosions, the treaty provided that a network of hydroacoustic stations comprised of six hydrophone and five T-phase stations would be set up. The six hydrophone stations use underwater microphones (hydrophones) that capture signals underwater and then transmit them via cable to the shore station. Hydrophone stations are extremely sensitive and pick up acoustic waves from underwater events, including explosions, occurring very far away. Such stations are expensive to install and costly to maintain, so the network also consists of five T-phase (seismic) stations. These stations are located on oceanic islands and use seismometers to detect the acoustic waves that are converted to seismic waves when they hit the island. The data from the hydroacoustic stations are used in the verification system to distinguish between underwater explosions and other phenomena, such as sub-sea volcanoes and earthquakes, which also propagate acoustic energy into the oceans.

Finally, a network of 60 infrasound stations was provided that use microbarographs (acoustic pressure sensors) to detect very low-frequency sound waves in the atmosphere produced by natural and man-made events. These stations are arrays of 4–8 sensors, which are located 1 to 3 km apart. This network is designed to provide data that will locate and distinguish between atmospheric explosions and natural phenomena such as meteorites, explosive volcanoes and meteorological events, and man-made phenomena such as re-entering space debris, rocket launches and supersonic aircraft.

Taken together, the four types of measuring instruments, once established and connected to the International Data Centre, will make sure that any explosion anywhere cannot avoid detection. The added value of the international system, in comparison to the national means that were heretofore used, is that stations will be located in places where, due to political conflicts, no single power would have complete access. For example, it would not be expected that the United States would be able to place stations in Iran.

Process of constructing the system

Under the Convention, the verification system is expected to be operational at the moment the treaty enters into force. While some of the elements of the system existed prior to the convention, especially in those States where seismological research was common, a large number of stations have to be built in countries where no previous stations have existed. In addition, for the system to operate successfully, many of the pre-existing facilities need to be upgraded.

The system is currently scheduled to be finished in 2007. Assuming that funding levels are maintained, the process of completing the system will continue. With the existing stations, the system is already operational. The greatest problems are in establishing stations in countries that do not have them, and which lack the technical expertise and infrastructure. For these the stations have to be designed to be almost automatic.

Additionally, the construction process involves developing procedures and software to analyse the different kinds of wave forms that will distinguish a nuclear explosion from a natural event like an earthquake. This is also well under way.

Maintenance of the system

Once constructed, the system needs to be maintained. Here the issue is how to keep a very technically complex system working in countries where technological expertise in certain areas is scarce. The issue is made more difficult by having to do maintenance on a system that is not yet formally operational. The longer the time between construction and entry-into-force, the more likely that the system will deteriorate unless funding levels are maintained.

The delay in entry-into-force, however, may influence the ability to maintain the system. Unlike most international organizations, but like the IAEA in some areas, the Provisional Technical Secretariat (PTS) was set up to provide rotation of staff. This meant that staff was expected to have relatively short, three- to five-year, assignments. The maximum permitted was to be seven years. Five years have now elapsed and there is already beginning to be a turnover. So far, the turnover has not affected key senior management positions, but without a new policy, by the time the system is completely operational, the staff that had planned and constructed it will be gone.

Operation of the system

The system has yet to be tested by a nuclear explosion, but in this case there is a side benefit: in addition to detecting nuclear-weapons testing, the IMS can provide invaluable data on natural events.

The issue of credibility is key here: can the conclusions drawn from the data in the system be trusted? This depends on the staff and the procedures being followed. The first head of the IMS is a Mexican seismologist, and the first head of the International Data Centre is from Egypt. This kind of mix is what gives international agencies the sense of political objectivity.

The IAEA experience

The IAEA has always maintained remote devices like cameras and various types of counters. However, the data acquired from these had to be obtained during inspections. Under the expanded safeguards protocol, the Agency is permitted to install monitors that can provide data to Vienna in real time.

The use of these systems has been increasing and the 2003 Safeguards Report issued by the Agency stated:[1]

55. To improve the efficiency of its safeguards implementation, the Agency continues to increase the number of installed unattended monitoring systems. At the end of 2003, there were 88 systems installed in 40 facilities in 22 States: 10 new systems and five replacement systems were installed during the year. Remote monitoring of surveillance data as an effectiveness and efficiency measure continues to expand. At the end of 2003, the Agency had 44 such systems with 109 cameras operating in nine States.

During the period that the IAEA conducted inspections together with UNMOVIC, it installed remote monitoring systems in Iraq that were said to have functioned well.

5
Controlling Supply: Procurement and Import/Export Monitoring

While remote monitoring, such as is envisaged by the Comprehensive Test-Ban Treaty and the Expanded Safeguards Agreements, can determine with reasonable certainty whether a State is testing nuclear weapons or has moved material around internally, it cannot actually prevent or control the development and production of weapons, especially chemical and biological weapons.

Development of weapons of mass destruction requires research and production facilities as well as raw material. If the supply of the necessary equipment and material can be controlled, the spread of weapons can be prevented. Similarly, if the flow of this type of equipment and material can be monitored, the elimination of weapons can also be verified.

A major verification method that has evolved over time is the monitoring of imports and exports of material that could be used to develop or produce weapons of mass destruction. In some ways, this was an easy choice as a method. International trade involves considerable record-keeping, originally because of the need to collect taxes and tariffs on imports and exports, but also to prevent the flow of prohibited products in global commerce. Shipments often require export licences and bills of lading, that are checked when the cargo leaves one country and when it enters another. Goods in international trade are classified according to commonly agreed systems, making identification of content both easy and consistent.

For much of the equipment and materials being tracked, the only possible suppliers are in developed countries, and to the extent that these can place controls on exports, the likelihood of diversion is lessened. However, three new factors have entered into play here. First, supplies can be diverted to third countries and therefore escape scrutiny. The supplies and equipment can be shipped legally to a country, but then can be re-sold and shipped to another country, Second, and more important, there are now countries that are not part of the non-proliferation regimes, like North Korea, Israel, India and Pakistan, that have the industrial capacity to produce at least some of the necessary equipment. And, finally, materials that have 'gone missing' as a result of political chaos, as happened in the former Soviet Union, can enter into a clandestine market for equipment and material. The issue is complicated by the fact that most of the material are by nature dual-use.

The international transfer of nuclear material is formally regulated under the Nuclear Non-Proliferation Treaty and related Safeguards Agreements. As a result, any transit of such materials is expected to be reported routinely to the IAEA. The same is true of other materials, such as centrifuges and their parts that could be used for enrichment of uranium. There is considerable evidence that reporting by States parties to the NPT is reasonably effective.

The issue is more complex for chemical and biological weapons. Here, in addition to agreeing to destroy declared weapons facilities, State parties to the Chemical Weapons Convention also agree to monitor the transfer of a series of chemicals listed in annexes to the Convention. Some of these are single-use chemicals, whose only known use is in the production of a weapon, except in small amounts for Research, Protection or medical/pharmaceutical purposes. Most, however, are dual-use, in the sense that they could either be used for peaceful purposes or as weapons. The Biological and Toxin Weapons Convention also includes a prohibition on acquisition or supply of those weapons, including their precursors, if to be used for non-peaceful purposes. Most material that would be covered by this part of this Convention would also be for dual use, and the Convention itself, unlike the Chemical Weapons Convention, lacks a definition of which materials should be included.

None of the international verification organizations have programmes that directly monitor trade flows in the equipment and material that could be used. Instead, they depend on a series of informal agreements among suppliers that could provide the required information. The question to be discussed in this chapter is whether these arrangements can work in the current situation and, if not, whether there are reasonable prospects where international verification organizations could provide an effective replacement.

The nuclear material gentlemen's agreement

With regard to nuclear material, the Director General of the IAEA, Mohamed ElBaradei, has already made his judgment, writing in an op-ed essay published in the *New York Times* on February 12, 2004, referring to steps needed to strengthen the existing non-proliferation regime:[1]

> The first step is to tighten controls over the export of nuclear material. The current system relies on a gentlemen's agreement that is not only non-binding, but also limited in its membership: it does not include many countries with growing industrial capacity. And even some members fail to control the exports of companies unaffiliated with government enterprise.
>
> We must universalize the export control system, remove these loopholes, and enact binding, treaty-based controls – while preserving the rights of all States to peaceful nuclear technology. We should also criminalize the acts of people who seek to assist others in proliferation.

The gentleman's agreement to which the Director General referred consists of three groups of suppliers: the Zangger Committee which periodically updates a list of material whose export should be controlled, the Nuclear Suppliers Group that agrees on guidelines for licensing export of these materials, and the Wassenaar Arrangement that agrees on common procedures for controlling exports. The most comprehensive is the NSG, with 44 members. Table 5.1 shows the members of the three groups. The functions, however, are slightly different.

Some of the exceptions are significant. China, a major industrial power, is a member of the Zangger Committee and the NSG. Brazil, another industrialized State, is only a member of the NSG.

The Zangger Committee

The Zangger Committee was the first of the arrangements. Named after its first chairperson, Claude Zangger of Switzerland who continued to serve for some twenty years, the Committee was formed in 1971 'to reach common understandings on how to implement Article III.2 of the NPT with a view to facilitating consistent interpretation of the obligations arising from that Article'.[2] Article III.2 states:

> Each State Party to the Treaty undertakes not to provide: (a) source or special fissionable material, or (b) equipment or material especially

Table 5.1 Members of the three groups dealing with export controls in the nuclear field

Zangger Committee	Nuclear Suppliers Group	Wassenaar Arrangement
Argentina	Argentina	Argentina
Australia	Australia	Australia
Austria	Austria	Austria
–	Belarus	
Belgium	Belgium	Belgium
	Brazil	
Bulgaria	Bulgaria	Bulgaria
Canada	Canada	Canada
China	China	
	Cyprus	
Czech Republic	Czech Republic	Czech Republic
Denmark	Denmark	Denmark
Finland	Finland	Finland
France	France	France
Germany	Germany	Germany
Greece	Greece	Greece
Hungary	Hungary	Hungary
Ireland	Ireland	Ireland
Italy	Italy	Italy
Japan	Japan	Japan
	Kazakhstan	
	Latvia	
	Lithuania	
Luxembourg	Luxembourg	Luxembourg
	Malta	
Netherlands	Netherlands	Netherlands
	New Zealand	New Zealand
Norway	Norway	Norway
Poland	Poland	Poland
Portugal	Portugal	Portugal
Republic of Korea	Republic of Korea	Republic of Korea
Romania	Romania	Romania
Russian Federation	Russian Federation	Russian Federation
Slovakia	Slovakia	Slovakia
Slovenia	Slovenia	
South Africa	South Africa	
Spain	Spain	Spain
Sweden	Sweden	Sweden
Switzerland	Switzerland	Switzerland
Turkey	Turkey	Turkey
Ukraine	Ukraine	Ukraine
United Kingdom	United Kingdom	United Kingdom
United States	United States	United States

designed or prepared for the processing, use or production of special fissionable material, to any non-nuclear-weapon State for peaceful purposes, unless the source or special fissionable material shall be subject to the safeguards required by this Article.

However, the definition of what specifically was meant by 'source or special fissionable material' or what 'equipment or material' was covered had been left open. The Zangger Committee met between 1971 and 1974 and produced what was termed the 'trigger list', consisting of 'items which would "trigger" a requirement for Safeguards and guidelines ("common understandings") governing the export, direct or indirect, of those items to non-nuclear-weapon States (NNWS) that are not party to the NPT'.[3]

Over the next quarter century, the Committee updated the list to take into account technological changes. These were periodically reported to the IAEA and issued as INFCIRC documents.

The Committee's informal structure was reflected in its procedures. As described by its current chairman, Fritz W. Schmidt,[4] the Committee would meet twice a year for a half day, usually at the Austrian Ministry of Foreign Affairs in Vienna, and reach agreements. These would be written up by the Committee secretary, who was always provided by the United Kingdom permanent mission to the IAEA, in the form of a draft note verbale that, once approved, would be exchanged among the members. As Schmidt states: 'These notes, known as "Internal Notes," take the form of identically-worded unilateral declarations to the effect that the export of the items in question will be controlled through domestic legislation.' The implementation of the agreements would be undertaken by each member, but they would also inform the IAEA of their agreements and these would be issued as a revision to the INFCIRC documents.

There were efforts during the 1995 Review Conference on the Nuclear Non-Proliferation Treaty to give official status to the Zangger Committee, whose work was recognized in one of the reports of the Conference. However, this was not agreed. At the 2000 Review Conference, the issue of coordination of export controls in terms of the 'trigger list' was also taken up, but no agreement was reached.[5]

The Nuclear Suppliers Group (NSG)

The Nuclear Supplier's Group was formed in 1974 as a response to the testing of a nuclear weapon by India. As the Group's website says,[6] this 'demonstrated that nuclear technology transferred for peaceful purposes could be misused'. Over the next four years, the Group elaborated its own trigger list and guidelines to cover 'nuclear transfers to any non-nuclear-weapon State for peaceful purposes'. Unlike the Zangger Committee, whose trigger list referred to any export of material mentioned specifically in the Non-Proliferation Treaty, the NSG focused on precursors of these also, and on the non-nuclear weapons states, as well as on ensuring that the materials transferred would not be diverted to other uses.

The NSG was dormant between 1978 and 1992, but was revived following the discovery that Iraq, a party to the NPT, had been able to develop a clandestine weapons programme. As the Group stated in its report in 2000:[7]

> it became apparent that export control provisions then in force had not prevented Iraq, a party to the NPT, from pursuing a clandestine nuclear weapons programme, which later prompted UN Security Council action. A large part of Iraq's effort had been the acquisition of dual-use items not covered by the NSG Guidelines and then building its own Trigger List items. This gave major impetus to the NSG's development of its Dual-Use Guidelines. In doing so, the NSG demonstrated its commitment to nuclear non-proliferation by ensuring that items like those used by Iraq would from now on be controlled to ensure their non-explosive use. These items would, however, continue to be available for peaceful nuclear activities subject to IAEA Safeguards, as well as for other industrial activities where they would not contribute to nuclear proliferation.

The NSG revised its guidelines in 1992 to include dual-use products. It decided:[8]

- To establish guidelines for transfers of nuclear-related dual-use equipment, material and technology (items which have both nuclear and non-nuclear applications) that could make a significant contribution to an unsafeguarded nuclear fuel cycle or nuclear explosive activity. These Dual-Use Guidelines were published as Part 2 of INFCIRC/254, and the original Guidelines published in 1978 became Part 1 of INFCIRC/254;
- To establish a framework for consultation on the Dual-Use Guidelines, for the exchange of information on their implementation and on procurement activities of potential proliferation concern;
- To establish procedures for exchanging notifications that have been issued as a result of national decisions not to authorize transfers of dual-use equipment or technology and to ensure that NSG participants

do not approve transfers of such items without first consulting with the State that issued the notification;

- To make a full-scope safeguards agreement with the IAEA a condition for the future supply of Trigger List items to any non-nuclear-weapon State. This decision ensured that only NPT parties and other States with full-scope safeguards agreements could benefit from nuclear transfers.

The NSG seeks to prevent the proliferation of weapons by ensuring that 'a supplier, notwithstanding other provisions in the NSG Guidelines, authorizes a transfer only when satisfied that the transfer would not contribute to the proliferation of nuclear weapons'.[9]

While the agreement is fairly clear and detailed, the implementation arrangements are generally less formal. The NSG Plenary, with a rotating chair, meets twice a year. There are working groups that meet intersessionally, whose results form the bulk of the plenary agenda. There are two standing subsidiary bodies, the Consultative Group (CG) and the Information Exchange Meeting (IEM) with Chairs that also rotate annually. The CG meets at least twice a year and is tasked to hold consultations on issues associated with the Guidelines on nuclear supply and the technical annexes. The IEM precedes the NSG Plenary and provides another opportunity for NSG participants to share information and developments of relevance to the objectives and content of the NSG Guidelines.

The Group in practice meets less frequently. Its last meeting was held in May 2004 in Sweden. The NSG emphasizes that implementation of its guidelines be determined by national laws and practices, and although states are encouraged to exchange information, and some procedures are in place for notification of shipment of goods on the trigger lists, these are neither mandatory nor universal.

The NSG exchanges information on denials of export permits and is one of two agreements to use electronic means to do so.

The Wassenaar Arrangement

The third gentlemen's agreement is now called the Wassenaar Arrangement that was established in March 1994. It replaced a previous arrangement, called COCOM, which was concerned with controlling arms exports to the former Soviet Union, the other states that were party to the Warsaw Pact and China. The purpose of the arrangement was to 'contribute to regional and international security and stability, by promoting transparency and greater responsibility in transfers of conventional arms and dual-use goods and technologies, thus preventing destabilizing accumulations'.[10] While its main focus is on trade in conventional arms, its concern with dual-use material is relevant to nuclear non-proliferation in that dual use-material is a major risk factor in trade. In addition to agreeing on the list of items to be covered by the Arrangement, a central principle is that 'Participating States agree to exchange general information on risks associated with transfers of conventional arms and dual-use goods and technologies in order to consider, where necessary, the scope for co-ordinating national control policies to combat these risks.'[11]

In practice, with regard to dual-use material, this includes exchanging information on licences. The Arrangement has made three lists – the dual-use list, the sensitive list and the very sensitive list. For the dual-use list, which is the most comprehensive, information on licences denied is to be exchanged twice a year. For items on the sensitive or very sensitive list, denials are to be reported within 60 days of the date of denial. Finally, for items on the sensitive or very sensitive list, the complete list of licences issued is to be exchanged on a twice-yearly basis. A weakness of the arrangement that has been noted by many critics is that members do not have an obligation *not* to export items that have been denied by other parties.[12]

Unlike the other two agreements where secretariat services are provided, to the extent necessary, by staff of the members, the Wassenaar Arrangement provides for a secretariat that is located in Vienna. This means that information can be channelled through a single office. Moreover, the WA uses electronic means to exchange information.

Flaws in the ointment

Besides the obvious problem that the existing arrangements are not universal, there are serious problems in establishing effective national export controls. Orlov's analysis of Russian export control policy noted weak political leadership, poor inter-agency coordination, government corruption and penetration by export interests, financial and technical problems, lack of an export control culture, weak punishment of violations, and loopholes created by regional factors as elements undercutting the procedures in that country.[13] On the other hand, Zaborsky's analysis of the Brazilian export control system found that it was very effective.[14] Clearly the effectiveness of the system depends on the individual country.

The real difficulty with the system is that there is no clear procedure to cumulate the information that is produced. Some information, like licences given for items on the dual-use list of the Wassenaar Agreement, is not collected or disseminated. The information is not necessarily in the same form, although in some cases the information requirement is set out in the agreements.

More importantly, none of the arrangements involves a systematic collection or publication of information. The information is exchanged, but not analyzed centrally, and it is up to the individual Members to use the information as they see fit. Moreover, not all States report even the limited amount of information on denials of export permits that they are supposed to report.[15] Without this information there is no credible method for verifying that, even for the States members of the gentlemen's agreements on nuclear materials, exports or imports have been controlled. Like the Wasenaar Arrangement, there is no agreement on a 'no-undercut provision' (not to export items denied by other members) and no agreement on prior notification. Taken together, the flaws in the arrangements are glaring.

The full-scope safeguards agreements as the mechanism

The NSG and Wassenaar Arrangement agreements both make reference to the full-scope (or expanded) safeguards agreements as a means of controlling imports and exports. As noted previously, one innovation in these agreements is the obligation of States to include exports and imports of trigger list items as part of their declarations. Since the declarations are to be made whenever there has been a change that should be reported, once all States are party to the Additional Protocol that sets up expanded safeguards, this could be a source of information.

The flaws in the system, described as lessons learned from the events of 2003 in the Democratic People's Republic of Korea, Iran and Libya, were set out by the Director General of the IAEA in his report to his Board of Governors in March 2004:[16]

> [It]is clear that the system in place to control the export of sensitive nuclear technology must be broadened in its reach and tightened in its controls. A system that aims to strike proper balance, between necessary controls against abuse, on the one hand, and the importance of assured access to peaceful technology, on the other, is in the interest of all, and should command global support. While many aspects of export controls are not managed by the Agency, they are clearly of direct relevance to our verification mandate, and we should put in place mechanisms to ensure that the IAEA is informed of all sensitive nuclear or nuclear related technology exports.

The question is, how is the Agency to be informed?

The chemical and biological gentlemen's agreement

In many respects, monitoring imports and exports in nuclear material is much simpler than monitoring in terms of chemical and biological weapons. In the latter, while there is some equipment and material that can only be used for weapons, most are dual-use. They could be used either for peaceful or non-peaceful purposes. It is much easier to control dual use of nuclear material.

The dual-use dilemma is that many potential weapons are similar to relatively harmless chemicals used in pesticides and herbicides. The volume of use of the harmless chemicals makes tracking exports and imports particularly problematic.

While the Wassenaar Arrangement could have elements of export control for chemical and biological weapons, this is clearly not its major focus. Instead, the gentlemen's agreement is focused on the Australia Group.

The Australia Group

In the absence of a verification mechanism in the BWC, and while waiting for the completion of the CWC and the creation of the OPCW, monitoring of trade in precursor chemicals was undertaken by an informal arrangement known as the Australia Group.

The Australia Group was founded in 1985 after it had been shown that Iraq had used chemical weapons in its war with Iran. Initially fifteen countries agreed to require export licences for a series of precursor chemicals and equipment that could be used to make chemical weapons. By requiring export licences, it was assumed that procurement of single-use chemicals would be impossible and that of dual-use chemicals could be monitored.

The group was led by Australia (and the person involved in its founding was Richard Butler who later headed UNSCOM). It is an informal group, not bound by legal obligations. It meets annually. As a press release from May 2000 states:[17]

10. Each participant in the Australia Group has introduced licensing measures on the export of certain chemicals, biological agents, and dual-use chemical and biological manufacturing facilities and equipment with a view to ensuring that exports of these items from their countries do not contribute to the spread of chemical and biological weapons.

11. All participating countries have licensing measures over 54 chemical weapons precursor chemicals. Participating countries also require

licenses for the export of dual-use facilities and equipment related to the manufacture of chemical weapons.

12. All participating countries operate controls based on lists of human, animal and plant agents as well as BW dual-use equipment developed during Australia Group consultations. Participating countries require licenses for exports of such items.

The lists include:

* Chemical weapons precursors
* Dual-use chemical manufacturing facilities and equipment and related technology
* Dual-use biological equipment
* Biological agents
* Plant pathogens
* Animal pathogens

The lists are revised regularly at the annual meetings of the Group.

The policy of the Group with regard to information is summarized in its guidelines: 'Participant states are encouraged to share information on these measures on a regular basis, and to exchange information on catch-all denials relevant for the purpose of the AG.'[18] The exchange of information, and its use, is voluntary and involves two things: information about changes in procedures and information on export licences that have been denied. There are no sanctions for not reporting on time or reporting prior to actual export and there is no way of determining whether all of the information that has been accumulated has been reported.

A 2002 evaluation of the export control regimes undertaken by the United States General Accounting Office concluded:[19]

GAO found weaknesses that impede the ability of the multilateral export control regimes to achieve their nonproliferation goals. A key function of each regime is to share information related to proliferation. Yet the regimes often lack even basic information that would allow them to assess whether their actions are having their intended results. The regimes cannot effectively limit or monitor efforts by countries of concern to acquire sensitive technology without more complete and timely reporting of licensing information and without information on when and how members adopt and implement agreed-upon export controls.

The Australia Group was particularly singled out as a mechanism where this was causing significant problems.

Existing verification organizations

The existing verification organizations, the IAEA and the OPCW, have to do their verification of exports and imports as a side-effect of their review of declarations and through inspections. They are dependent on the accuracy of the information they are given in declarations and on whether their inspections are able to detect changes in supplies and equipment that might be prohibited under their respective treaties.

The IAEA

As noted, the IAEA deals with export–import controls as a means of verification primarily through its analysis of the declarations made by States under their safeguards agreements. These, of course, are as good as the quality of the agreements. The organizations also acquire information when their inspections disclose that nuclear materials that were hitherto unaccounted for appear in a country being inspected. This is what occurred when the IAEA undertook inspections in the Islamic Republic of Iran and found equipment and materials for enriching uranium that had not been reported.

The materials from the declarations and inspections are entered into the Agency's databases and can be used – as was the case with regard to allegations of efforts of Iraq to buy uranium from Niger – to confirm whether this was likely to be true or not. The Agency can also inform both the countries concerned and the Board of Governors when it observes anomalous reports.

The OPCW

Like the IAEA, the OPCW is expected to monitor exports and imports through review of declarations and as a consequence of inspections. There is no automatic way in which information is provided, other than the information that might be reported by the Australia Group or mandatory reporting on the destruction of CW munitions.

The difficulty for OPCW is that the number of items that are of concern is considerably larger than that for the IAEA. In addition, many of its Member States have complained that export controls will impede trade in chemicals by imposing too many restrictions. This led the United States to present a paper to the Fourth Conference of the States Parties rebutting the argument[20] by claiming that only a small proportion of its total chemical trade required licensing.

In addition, the matter of whether States were obligated to report on transfers by nationals of their country to third countries was only resolved at the Seventh Conference of States Parties in 2001. The process of monitoring exports was fairly weak before that and probably not much stronger after.

Requisites for successful monitoring

The existing agreements and the evaluations that have been made of them suggest the requisites for successful monitoring of trade flows, as well as some of the difficulties in achieving them in practice.

Agreed list and classification of materials

For a monitoring system to function, there must be an agreed list of materials that needs to be monitored. Some elements of such a list are fairly clear, especially in terms of the CWC, since prohibited chemicals and equipment are included as annexes to the convention itself.

More complex are the secondary products and dual-use materials whose inclusion is less obvious. One of the functions of the gentlemen's agreements is to agree on these lists. The mechanisms have created trigger lists and updated them over the past thirty years. These have been published and distributed. However, because they have not been formally agreed upon by all States their monitoring remains voluntary, except for the members of the agreements.

For the two international verification organizations concerned – the IAEA and the OPCW – only monitoring of some materials is mandatory. This complicates the process of information exchange.

Agreement on what information should be exchanged

The current arrangements primarily exchange information on licence denials. Information on licences that have been issued are exchanged for only some classes of items. In addition, there is some evidence of underreporting even for these items. There are two issues here. First, if all licences are reported, will the volume of data be too great and the cost of reporting it too high? Second, if there is no regular monitoring of reporting, will the likelihood increase that some exports or imports will go unreported and therefore not monitored?

An important prerequisite is that all exporters agree on what should be reported and how they are to report. While many of the reporting requirements are set out in the Conventions, or have been elaborated in the context of the informal arrangements, there would have to be nearly a universal agreement covering all materials under all of the Conventions.

Method of recording movements over borders

Exchange of information requires agreement on common formats for recording the information in the first place. Only some of the arrangements involve an agreed format. And only two involve exchanges by electronic means. All of the arrangements focus on licences and are dependent on the effectiveness of the licensing processes in the respective countries. These arrangements have been opposed in some countries because they increase the cost of trade by requiring exporters to file for and obtain licences. It is possible that the increase in cost provides incentives to exporters to seek to avoid the licensing process entirely.

Alternative methods based on the normal recording of information from bills of lading do not seem to have been considered. Trade statistics are acquired from this source. However, this method would require a universal agreement to exchange information based on these bills of lading. The existence of digitalized record-keeping may make this more feasible.

Capacity to identify unusual patterns

Verification based on trade flows consists of ensuring that all prohibited exports or imports are detected; if none are detected this means that none have taken place. To be able to do this, a means has to be found to identify unusual patterns that would indicate possible cases of prohibited trade. Without this, even the kinds of action foreseen under the US-promoted Proliferation Security Initiative would likely be ineffective.

For this to happen, a credible analytical capacity has to exist in the appropriate verification organizations. Part of this depends on the ability to note when there is a deviation from 'normal' trade patterns for the respective countries. The analytical capacity is dependent on an understanding that the relevant data have been received, and processed opportunely, and that appropriate triggers are in place.

At the present time, none of the verification organizations has this capacity.

6
Verification by On-Site Inspection

For over half a century, on-site inspection (OSI) was presented by the US and its allies as the ultimate tool within a verification mechanism to monitor compliance with arms control agreements. It has formed the core of a system of mutually reinforcing elements of verification ranging from national means of detection to cooperative measures, including exchange and evaluation of information, ongoing technical monitoring and procurement control that were examined in the preceding chapters.

Because on-site inspection is so critical to the functioning of the regime and because it is the most intrusive method used, understanding how it works requires an exploration of its legal and political context. We therefore begin with an examination of this context, which shows both the potential and the constraints faced by implementation of this method.

International on-site inspection, as pioneered by the IAEA, has evolved within the Agency into a complex mechanism for compliance that provided a model of international verification to build upon, especially in the negotiations for the CTBT and the CWC. The concept of international inspection has benefited also from the breakthrough between the US and the USSR on verified nuclear disarmament.

The origins of OSI in international politics go back to the late 1950s but it was the US/USSR Treaty on Intermediate-Range Nuclear Forces (INF Treaty) that firmly established OSI as a bilateral form of intrusive verification. Although it relied entirely on reciprocity for its effectiveness, the INF model served as a source of ideas on the concept of intrusiveness also in multilateral settings. The manner and extent of intrusiveness deemed acceptable for OSI in such settings varies from organization to organization, depending upon the type of compliance to be verified and the level of reconciliation achieved by members to permit adequate access without undue harm to sovereignty rights. As the core of the verification system, OSI as a compliance instrument depends for its effectiveness on the quality and coherence of all the components and, in no small measure, on the adequacy of access with the cooperation of host States.

Recent signs of US scepticism about the efficacy of OSI deserve serious consideration since America's traditional advocacy of effective verification had been instrumental in its worldwide acceptance of the concept. This shift is largely due to the new policies of the Bush Administration to rely more on national means than on international cooperation. It is important to take this development seriously and not dismiss it merely as the reflection of an unconstructive episode of unilateralism that might pass away with a change of administration. It is essential to scrutinize the US critique on international verification for any valid aspects it might have. This can be done in the context of a comparative analysis of the functioning of existing international mechanisms under the NPT, the CTBT and the CWC. We will assess the adequacy of the OSI machinery for the task of the treaty and the effectiveness of its operation. It should be noted that each OSI system was tailor-made to verify compliance with that particular treaty, and to do so with the least intrusiveness on national sovereignty and with maximum cost-effectiveness.

International on-site inspections may be classified into three broad categories:

1. *ad hoc* inspections to set a baseline,
2. regular inspections, and
3. suspect-site inspections.

Baseline inspections include initial visits conducted as often as necessary to verify the completeness and correctness of the basic information supplied by State parties at the outset. They help to establish the structure and process for future inspections. Regular inspections, which form the bulk of the missions, are routine visits whereby the location and timing of visits are determined by prior arrangements. They are designed to monitor continuously a party's compliance with its non-proliferation and disarmament obligations under a treaty. The inspections range from data verification regarding ongoing relevant activities to on-site checking of the proper functioning of containment and surveillance instruments. Suspect-site inspections are the rarely used short-notice inspections with no right to refuse requests, at any location any time, as is the case with IAEA's special inspections and the challenge inspections under the CTBT and the CWC.

As a basis for comparative analysis of the on-site inspection functions of the IAEA, the CTBTO and the OPCW we need to abstract some common issues from the models of disarmament verification explained in Chapter 1. The three models which are based on existing systems, are: (i) the adversarial INF-type bilateral model of verification that operates on the principle of reciprocity; (ii) the adversarial international model for coercive verification in Iraq as mandated by the Security Council (UNMOVIC-IAEA); and (iii) the treaty-based consensual international model for verifying compliance by State parties, which applies to the IAEA the CTBTO and the OPCW. The common issues can also be clustered under three categories:

1. issues regarding the adequacy of authority and power for the inspectors;
2. issues about access requirements within the sovereignty rights of States; and
3. issues of effective management of the verification task.

First, as regards authority and power, although international verification cannot rely on the power of retaliation as does the INF model, or on Security Council backing as does the Iraq model, it relies on the credibility and influence generated by the legitimacy, impartiality and expertise of the inspectorate. However, its effectiveness is subject to structural constraints that vary from organization to organization, especially as regards universality of membership, the degree of cohesion that facilitates consensus on operations and the effect of loopholes in the treaty regime.

Second, as regards sovereignty and intrusiveness, international verification has to rely not on agreed reciprocity of access as in the INF or on requirements imposed by the Council but rather on practical requirements for adequate access to sites, to reliable and complete information and also access to a higher authority within and beyond the organization in cases of non-compliance.

Third, as regards effective management, international verification may not expect to attract the kind of resources available for INF operations or for special Security Council operations backed by the major powers, but is has to depend on more modest and cost-efficient use of its assets (personnel, financial resources and technology).

In this light, we may think of an elliptical model or an input/output loop of verification process. The main features are:

1. At the left end we have Member States as the source of authority and collective measures in cases of non-compliance. They are represented

by the governing bodies of organizations and ultimately by the UN Security Council.

2. At the right end we have the State parties subjected to inspection which would be judged as compliant or non-compliant.

3. From left to right we have the main elements of on-site inspection (OSI) reflecting both capabilities and challenges: mandates and powers (P), as tempered by organizational or structural constraints (lack of universality, of cohesion and/or regime loopholes); access arrangements (A), as constrained by claims of sovereignty rights of host states; cost-effective management of operations (MO), as tempered by resource constraints (personnel, finance, technology); and findings (F) of either compliance that may generate confidence or non-compliance that may call for a remedy.

4. From right to left we have two parallel lines on reports of findings (R), one on compliance that generates confidence (CC) and the other on non-compliance requiring recourse (NCR).

5. Finally, the higher authorities (boards/Security Council) decide on sanctions or other responses.

To summarize by way of acronyms, the OSI process which combines the elements of power, access, operational management and findings (PAMORF) results in either a report of compliance leading to confidence (RCC) or a report of non-compliance necessitating recourse to censure or some form of sanctions (RNCR).

IAEA inspection as a safeguard

Inspection in the IAEA is designed to provide a safeguard against the diversion of nuclear material from peaceful uses.

Legal basis, authority and constraints

IAEA's on-site inspection is the centrepiece of a safeguards system which can be described as a comprehensive set of internationally approved legal and technical measures, applied by the IAEA, to verify the undertakings of non-nuclear-weapon States not to use nuclear material for nuclear weapons. By doing so it fulfils the dual purpose of confidence-building and deterrence. It seeks to create confidence among the parties by demonstrating compliance and to discourage non-compliance by threatening detection of any diversion. According to the IAEA Statute, safeguards are 'designed to ensure' that safeguarded items 'are not used in such a way as to further any military purpose' (Article III.A.5).

The IAEA safeguards system is based on a two-tiered mandate: the safeguards provisions derived directly from the Statute just cited, and the provisions derived from the mandate of the NPT, particularly Article III of the Treaty. The former provisions, as elaborated in a landmark document known as INFCIRC 66/Rev., apply to specific nuclear activities in non-nuclear-weapon States that have not submitted their entire nuclear programmes to safeguards. The most militarily significant States in this category are India, Israel and Pakistan, which as non-parties to the NPT retained their nuclear option and eventually became nuclear weapon States.

The NPT has provided an unprecedented opportunity for the IAEA to expand its non-proliferation role within its broad statutory mandate. But, as will be explained later, this was not accomplished without introducing some problems. The Treaty prescribes for its parties a mandate for safeguards to be 'applied on all source or special fissionable material in all peaceful nuclear activities within the territory of such State, under its jurisdiction, or carried out under its control anywhere' (Article III). It was on this basis that, in 1971, the model for NPT-based comprehensive safeguards agreements were adopted by the IAEA Board of Governors under the symbol INFCIRC/153. This NPT-based model covers not only the old facility-specific verification measures but also full-scope safeguards as regards the entire nuclear fuel cycle in the whole country. The focus was on monitoring at strategic points the existence and flow of nuclear material. It covers the entire fuel cycle from source to product to radioactive waste, that is, natural uranium ore, fissionable material comprising essentially enriched uranium and plutonium and spent fuel. The approach chosen was, however, to focus the monitoring on the stocks and flow of nuclear material at strategic points.[1]

Further strengthening of IAEA safeguards took place in the 1990s, based on the lessons learned from the discovery of an extensive clandestine nuclear-weapons programme in Iraq after the first Gulf War. For the first time, the adequacy and effectiveness of international safeguards were addressed principally in terms of the capacity to detect clandestine nuclear activities rather than merely to confirm compliance with declared activities. Although the possibility of the existence of clandestine activities had always been a basic assumption of safeguards, it was previously expected that by focusing on nuclear material accountancy, safeguards would detect diversion of nuclear fissionable material for military purposes.[2]

The strengthened safeguards system broadened the focus of safeguards to include not only verification of the nuclear material being used in the cycle, but also any relevant nuclear activities. In 1997, IAEA's Board of Governors incorporated the changes in the form of a model Additional Protocol to the Safeguards Agreement, known as INF-CIRC/540, on the basis of which all NPT parties were urged to annex the protocols to their existing agreements. Even non-parties were urged to sign the new instrument and add it as a protocol to the limited INF-CIRC/66-type agreements that they had with the IAEA.[3]

The authority for on-site inspection in a Member State is thus based on a battery of legal instruments, most fundamentally on the provisions of the Statute and the NPT as elaborated in the safeguards agreements and further strengthened in additional protocol. For effective implementation, the operational details are then spelled out by the subsidiary arrangements on the objectives, scope, methods and criteria for safeguards in a particular country, with facility attachments describing the sites for inspection.

Authority for implementation

Two aspects of authority that bear upon implementation of safeguards need to be distinguished. The first, as described above, is the legal authority for inspections in a State party. It is a treaty-based delegation of authority from sovereign States to the inspecting organization.

The second represents the internal distribution involving governance and the management of inspections. The latter refers to the relative powers of the General Conference of Member States, a smaller Board of Governors that combines permanent (designated) and elected members, and an elected Director General heading the Secretariat that includes the inspectorate. A rather unusual feature of the IAEA's bicameral system is the concentration of safeguards in the Board of Governors, which relies on proposals and reports of a Director General with extensive executive powers. A limited formal role is assigned to the General Conference as regards safeguards, except as a deliberative forum.

According to the Statute, the responsibility for policy-making and for budgetary and programme decisions is shared between the General Conference and the Board of Governors. The Board prepares the programme and budget on the basis of the Director General's proposals but they must be approved by the General Conference of all Member States. It is the Board that appoints the Director General with endorsement by the Conference. However, as regards safeguards, the executive function is in effect shared by the Board with the Director General. The safeguards system is established by the Board as drawn up by the Secretariat and its technical advisers. From then on, generally, it is the Director

General who proposes and implements action while the Board considers reports and approves recommendations on behalf of all Member States.

The Director General negotiates safeguards agreements with individual States and the Board approves. Not only does he manage the implementation of those agreements but he also raises policy issues or operational problems for resolution or guidance by the Board. It is on the basis of reports by the Director General that the Board decides on issues of compliance and recourse regarding safeguards agreements. The Board has to approve the Director General's proposals on the structure and organization of the Secretariat, and on his selection of senior staff and inspectors of all ranks.

The authority and role of the Director General has evolved considerably in relation to the Board, both as initiator of recommendations and as chief administrative officer. The few long-serving and imaginative incumbents have responded to various challenges that threatened the Agency's viability by developing the post of Director General into a position of considerable authority and leadership for the Agency. With constant support by the Board of Governors, it has been the task of the Director General and his Secretariat to constitute an effective truly international inspectorate, to draft firm rules and guidelines for them, to manage the inspections efficiently and to launch special inspections in consultation with the State concerned. It is only when access was denied or obstructed that the Director General sought from the Board not mere endorsement but political support for his reports and recommendations.

Thus, the statutory delegation of authority regarding verification from sovereign States to the Agency's governing bodies has been followed by a tendency in the Board to allow considerable leeway on compliance issues to the Director General, have enabled the latter to emerge as a strong chief executive and inspection manager who acts with considerable autonomy. Support from the Board is ensured by close ongoing consultations through the Chairman of the Board.

Structural constraints of the safeguards system

There are two interrelated structural constraints on the safeguards system within the IAEA, one resulting from the diversity of IAEA membership and the other emerging from the limitations of the NPT. The NPT-based constraints in turn have two dimensions: membership-related aspects inherent to the treaty and external aspects pertaining to its limited scope relative to the non-proliferation undertakings. Of great significance are the membership aspects, as the duality of the NPT between nuclear and non-nuclear-weapon States has indeed enhanced divergences among existing groups within the IAEA.

As regards composition, the Agency was originally designed for universal membership, bringing States that had advanced nuclear technology together with those that had less or none of it. All the 130-plus States today are bound by the Statute's broad obligations designed to facilitate peaceful transfer of nuclear technology. It was inevitable that differences would emerge between the haves and have-nots over the modalities for the transfer. The interest groups were: (a) the nuclear-weapon States controlling the technology; (b) other industrialized States having civilian nuclear technology; and (c) States without nuclear technology at all. The Agency was able to reconcile the divergences by designing a non-discriminatory method of technology transfer, initially of importance only to the first two groups. This was embodied in a series of transaction-based, non-intrusive safeguards agreements (INFCIRC/66 model). However, these agreements were soon found to be inadequate for proliferation control and had to be replaced by NPT-based safeguards that enhanced the verification system but also created new conflicts.

The active non-proliferation role of the IAEA began with the incorporation of a robust verification mandate from the NPT. As a result of obligations accepted under the NPT, the vast majority of IAEA members accepted comprehensive safeguards agreements (INFCIRC/153 model), which created a new division between NPT parties and other members that remained outside the treaty. In effect, this resulted in two types of division, one between parties and non-parties to the NPT and the second largely corresponding to the old three-sided division but with a twist reflecting the differing status instituted by the new NPT safeguards. The combined result was a four-way division among the Agency's membership:

1. NPT-party nuclear-weapon States (NPT/NWS);
2. NPT-party industrialized non-nuclear-weapon States (NPT/NNWS/ ind.);
3. NPT-party developing non-nuclear-weapon States (NPT/NNWS/dev.);
4. Non-NPT party developing States (Non-NPT).

As parties to the NPT, the five nuclear-weapon States are not obligated to conclude comprehensive safeguards agreements requiring them to open their civilian nuclear programmes to international inspectors. However, in order to alleviate the criticism about their different treatment in the NPT, they have all accepted safeguards on the basis of voluntary offers to inspect a sample of their civilian facilities.

Comprehensive safeguards apply only to the non-nuclear-weapon States that have foresworn the acquisition of nuclear weapons. Comprising both the industrialized and developing country groups, they represent the vast majority of the membership of the Agency. The non-parties to the NPT have not accepted comprehensive safeguards and are subject only to limited safeguards of the INFCIRC 66-type. The most significant members of that group – India, Israel and Pakistan – have now joined the nuclear-weapon club without, however, gaining legitimacy for their unofficial status as emerging nuclear-weapon States. They have made the transition from 'threshold' or 'nuclear-capable' States to emerging nuclear powers. These divisions are a source of tension in the functioning of the IAEA.

Though all members were committed to supporting the overall purpose of the Statute to promote nuclear energy exclusively for peaceful uses, the divergent interests of these four groups often militate against finding a desirable balance among competing objectives of the Agency. The main objectives are: safeguards against diversion of nuclear material, promotion of nuclear energy with safety, and transfer of technology with assistance for development.

For the five recognized nuclear-weapon States, the predominant concern has been to prevent nuclear proliferation by applying effective safeguards to non-nuclear-weapon States, while exempting themselves from similar measures under the discriminatory provisions of the NPT. However, their attitudes are by no means identical since they are influenced by the power asymmetry within the group, by calculations of strategic advantage and by alliance loyalties. Apart from security matters, they are also concerned with nuclear safety issues. By symbolically granting 'voluntary offer' arrangements to apply limited safeguards in their civilian nuclear industry, they expect to encourage worldwide acceptance of comprehensive safeguards and also to provide the Agency's inspectors knowledge about advanced designs of nuclear plants.

For the industrialized NPT parties the dual concern is to ensure unfettered exchange of nuclear technology under improved conditions of safety, especially in the area of the former Soviet Union, and to apply full-scope safeguards with minimum infringement on sovereignty and commercial rights.

As parties to the NPT, the numerous developing countries share as a primary concern the need for adequate and sustained technical assistance as a trade-off for accepting full-scope safeguards that would have little application for most of them.

The main non-parties to the NPT – India, Israel and Pakistan – had retained their nuclear option mainly because of insecurity and tension in their respective regions. These States are determined to seek the full benefit of their IAEA membership, especially from technical cooperation programmes, while resisting pressures to accept comprehensive safeguards or any equivalent measure outside the NPT framework. The problem was not even confined to the issue of the retention of their nuclear option but involved also the risk of their acting as channels of proliferation to other States.[4]

Since all four groups are represented in the Board of Governors, the Board's deliberations on safeguards issues sometimes threaten to polarize along three lines of tension over priorities and balance among Agency activities: the NWS–NNWS line, the NPT–non-NPT line and the developed–developing country line. In addition to the legal and political constraints explained above, the deliberations exert a major impact on the allocation of adequate resources for safeguards operations.

It is remarkable that the four groups have been able to find compromises enabling the Agency to act as a cohesive political unit, both in providing adequate safeguards and in facilitating transfer of nuclear technology. A magic formula that evolved over many years balances overall budgetary allocations for technical cooperation with those for safeguards. However, this requirement of parity posed a serious constraint on the efforts to strengthen safeguards. When the budget for safeguards was increased in the 2004–5 period, there had to be a parallel effort to increase technical cooperation allocations that has proved somewhat more difficult.

Some external aspects of the NPTs limitation affect the effectiveness of IAEA's safeguards. The NPT lacked the membership of several potential nuclear-weapon States that have now crossed the threshold to become *de facto* nuclear-weapon States. In addition, the NPT does not proscribe or regulate several proliferation-related activities. The focus on preventing the diversion of nuclear material to weapons did not provide for sufficient safeguards for other aspects of nuclear-weapon development. First, it permitted non-explosive nuclear applications of fissile material (e.g. for submarine propulsion), with insufficient control. Second, it allowed unlimited, though safeguarded, research on uranium enrichment and plutonium separation and also allowed stockpiling. Third, it permitted unsafeguarded trade in various proliferation-sensitive items other than nuclear material or facilities related to the fuel cycle. This includes dual-use items and even bomb-making technology and equipment that are at present regulated only by supplier groups.

Considering the seriousness of these weaknesses of the NPT, the withdrawal provisions of the Treaty have become even more disturbing. They make it too easy for States that are determined to break away to give a 90-day withdrawal notice according to Article X, on the ground that 'extraordinary events related to the subject matter of the Treaty have jeopardized the supreme interests' of that State.[5]

Aims and limitations of safeguards

We should distinguish between the broad political and security aims of safeguards and the technical objectives of safeguards. Comprehensive safeguards aim to provide assurance that non-nuclear State parties to the NPT are complying with their undertakings not to acquire nuclear weapons or any unsafeguarded nuclear material towards that end. If a State undertakes to join the NPT as a non-nuclear-weapon State by disposing of any existing weapons (as did South Africa, Kazakhstan and Ukraine) or by renouncing any weapons programme (as did Argentina and Brazil), the aim is to verify the dismantlement and deter any attempts to revive the programme. If a nuclear-weapon State agrees as part of nuclear disarmament to release fissionable material from weapons for disposal or conversion to peaceful uses, the aim of safeguards is ensure irreversibility.

However, the technical aim of safeguards is to verify, by inspection and analysis, that a State's nuclear activities are in conformity with the legal undertaking that it has made about the nature and scope of these activities. In the context of NPT comprehensive safeguards, the technical aim has been defined as ' "*timely detection*" of diversion of *significant quantities of nuclear material* from peaceful nuclear activities to the manufacture of nuclear weapons or of other explosive devices or for purposes unknown, and deterrence of such diversion by the risk of early detection' (emphasis added).[6]

The meanings of significant quantity (SQ) and timely detection vary according to the conversion time for the type of nuclear material to an explosive device, and can range from a conversion time of one month for direct-use plutonium or highly-enriched uranium to one year for an SQ of 10-tons of natural uranium.[7] The threshold for demonstrating non-compliance has been set low: it is not required to prove positively the manufacture of an explosive device or even the physical diversion of nuclear material but simply to conclude that the Agency 'is not able to verify that there has been no diversion' of safeguarded material.[8]

This double negative formulation is intended to stress that the State remains under suspicion for non-compliance. When the outcome of inspections is positive, the good news is phrased cautiously to avoid implying a 'clean bill of health'. It simply states that the Agency 'found no indication of the diversion of nuclear material placed under safeguards'.

How does the IAEA arrive at such simple conclusions? There is a long and elaborate process involving the analysis of records and information from various sources, especially from on-site inspections. As noted above, there are three types of inspection: (i) *ad hoc* initial inspections to establish a baseline for verification; (ii) routine inspections of designated sites and activities; and (iii) special inspections to clarify inconsistencies and discrepancies in declared activities and remove suspicions about possible illicit activities.

Ad hoc inspections verify the information provided in initial declarations and any changes in the situation since then, including any transfers in and out of the country. Part of the task is to examine design information of present and planned nuclear facilities, including the type of nuclear material used and the strategic points for measuring the flow and balance of such material.

Routine inspections check the periodic reports for consistency with the records, verify the nature and quantities of safeguarded material, audit inventories for any possible discrepancies and try to determine possible causes when any nuclear material is unaccounted for. The frequency, intensity and duration of routine inspections is determined according to the quantity of safeguarded material in a country.

Special inspections come into play when inconsistencies in material balance persist after routine inspections and after the State has had a chance to explain. They are also used to verify special reports by the State about any unusual circumstances that may have caused loss or unauthorized removal of nuclear material. All inspections combine human observation and analysis as well as the application of technical instruments for calibration, measurement, sample analysis, containment (e.g. special seals) and imaging, photo surveillance and remote sensing.

The task of inspectors is never easy as they are dependent on the full cooperation of the host country to accomplish their mission. As safeguards obligations are based on voluntary acceptance of treaties, IAEA inspectors cannot compel a sovereign State to cooperate; they can only report if it does not. They have to operate under constraints that are inherent in the safeguards system. For example, in the past, the IAEA could not gain short-notice access to any facilities it wished to inspect. Timely access was difficult because arrangements had to be made with

the host State way in advance. Moreover, the Agency could not dis-
criminate between State parties by initiating inspections selectively
because of allegations of suspicious activities. It has to depend on its
regular inspections to reveal serious inconsistencies that may justify
special inspections. Finally, it cannot physically prevent an act of illicit
diversion but can only sound an alarm if it has reliable information
about it. However, these constraints have been addressed to some extent
during the recent strengthening of the safeguards system, particularly as
regards prompt access to facilities, access to reliable information from
any source and access to higher authority for sanctions against violators.

The strengthened safeguards system provides access not only to strategic points in declared facilities open to regular inspections but also routine
access to any place on a nuclear site or other location where nuclear
material may be present. Under the Additional Protocols, broader access
to locations is facilitated by the requirement of a signatory State to
provide the Agency with broader access to information – in the form of
an expanded declaration that contains information covering all aspects
of its nuclear activities. The information base is further broadened by
the use of new detection techniques, such as environmental sampling
(air, soil and water sampling at or away from nuclear sites). Finally, the
new measures provide for certain management improvements including
streamlined procedures for prompt access to an impartial, well-equipped
inspectorate.

The strengthened system is based on a commitment not only to quantitative accounting but also to qualitative assessment. In States that have
both comprehensive safeguards and an additional protocol, the Agency
will be able to implement an integrated safeguards system with an optimal combination of all safeguards procedures including the traditional
methods for material accountancy and the new measures for qualitative
assessment. Some of the new measures were implemented immediately
after the revelations about Iraq's illicit weapons programme. They are
already being fully implemented on the basis of existing statutory
authority. Notably, this includes special inspections of suspected activities, as in the confrontation with the Democratic People's republic of
North Korea (DPRK) in 1993–4. However, new legal authority was found
necessary for most of the new measures to uncover relevant undeclared
activities.

Consensus on this fundamental reform was made possible by the
Agency's successful experience in two major operations: first, in Iraq,
under a mandate from the Security Council to conduct an intrusive
adversarial investigation to dismantle its illicit nuclear programme;

second, in South Africa the Agency conducted an extensive consensual operation to verify the complete dismantlement of its nuclear arsenals and related programme. The lessons learned in both cases and also in the case of the DPRK were fully used in crafting new concepts and procedures, particularly as regards broader access to information, wider access to locations in a territory and more cost-effective techniques and technologies. More details about these and some recent other cases will be discussed in the following section.

It is significant to note that, first, the traditional tunnel-vision focus on 'strategic' inspection points and on nuclear material accountancy has now been broadened to one encompassing a qualitative assessment of all relevant nuclear activities. In a departure from the NPT-based discriminatory provisions of the comprehensive safeguards agreements as between nuclear-weapon States and non-nuclear-weapon States, the new measures are designed for universal application. They are to apply equally to all States that accept the Additional Protocol as a supplement to any existing safeguards agreement. This alleviates to some extent one weakness – the lack of universality of the NPT. Moreover, the new system is now managed within a single conceptual framework for integrated safeguards. A comprehensive State-wide evaluation approach is now used to enhance the Agency's ability to draw safeguards conclusion about both the non-diversion of declared material and the absence of undeclared nuclear activities in that State. These managerial improvements may not only improve the efficiency of safeguards but also enhance their effectiveness. Thus they may, to some extent, alleviate the weakness inherent in the NPT as a regime.

What is needed most now is to accelerate the process of ratification of the Additional Protocol to the Safeguards Agreements.

Inspections at work

The IAEA had successfully applied regular on-site inspections for over thirty years when it discovered after the first Gulf War in 1991 that Iraq had evaded detection of its clandestine nuclear-weapon programme. Since then, the IAEA has strengthened the system of safeguards to cope with undeclared activities and has applied on-site inspection in three other cases of NPT parties involved in illicit proliferation activities: North Korea (The Democratic People's Republic of Korea – DPRK), Iran and Libya. All were cases of concealment and deception where securing access to facilities and information would be a major factor for success. They will be discussed below in that order. All four cases pertain to areas of tension. In the Middle East, Iraq, Iran and Libya consider Israel as an enemy State and perceive a threat from its unrestrained WMD capabilities. Iraq and Iran remained unreconciled after their war in the 1980s when they had actually both used chemical weapons. In the Korean Peninsula, the DPRK and South Korea live in a state of military confrontation under an uneasy truce sustained by the presence of US troops backed by the US nuclear deterrent. The verification task for the IAEA is difficult in all these cases in view of the insecurities or regional ambitions that might induce resort to clandestine activities.

There are many other cases where the Agency's on-site inspection system was applied smoothly with the full cooperation of host States. They need not be addressed here since they would not be particularly useful for identifying strengths and weaknesses of the system in facing serious challenges. Suffice it to mention briefly the South African case, which is uniquely instructive.

South Africa

The South African case is significant as a benchmark for close coopera-tion with the host State that permitted maximum access for the job. In terms of scope of operation, complexity and scale of cooperation, it was an unprecedented case. South Africa was the first nation to develop and possess nuclear weapons and then renounce them.

As a non-party to the NPT, South Africa under the minority apartheid regime felt free to develop nuclear weapons and complete a few nuclear devices as a 'deterrent' against any threats from Soviet-assisted invasion by hostile African States. It had already produced six nuclear devices when the reformist government of President F.W. de Klerk took power in 1989 and embarked on the dismantlement of apartheid to end the long and punitive isolation. The far-reaching changes included a decision to dismantle the entire nuclear-weapons programme and not leave it in the hands of a possible African successor government.

Upon acceding to the NPT in 1991 and promptly negotiating a com-prehensive safeguards agreement with the IAEA, South Africa offered the Agency full access to all relevant facilities and inventories and supplied such detailed information in its declarations that the Director General was able to confirm that the weapons programme was indeed over. After a year of intensive inspections, it was possible to certify the completeness and correctness of South Africa's detailed declaration on the past weapons programme and its present civil nuclear capacity. The South African case remains a model of cooperation for situations of voluntary disarmament resulting from the reduction of regional tension. It was also the first application of on-site inspection under safeguards, covering a broad area ranging from nuclear-weapon dismantlement to the decommissioning of facilities and the conversion of fissile material to peaceful uses under the Agency's ongoing monitoring.

Iraq: operation under Security Council mandate, 1991–2003

The case of Iraq is in sharp contrast to that of South Africa. It was a case of enforced disarmament. The role of the IAEA in Iraq was based on mandatory powers entrusted to it by the Security Council in 1991, under the Gulf War Cease-Fire resolution 687(1991). Those powers were further strengthened by resolution 1441(2002) shortly before the inspectors returned to Iraq. The mandate was designed to control Iraq's armaments as a means to deter future aggression. It had a triple objective: (i) discovery of all aspects of the WMD programme, (ii) disarmament, and (iii) ongoing monitoring. Since this comprehensive action was authorized as part of the response to Iraq's aggression against neighbouring Kuwait, this action superseded the more modest verification operation under the IAEA's NPT-type safeguards. Technically, those safeguards were subsumed under the mandate given by the Security Council. A parallel mandate was entrusted to the Special Commission on Iraq (UNSCOM) which was succeeded by the United Nations Monitoring, Verification and Inspection Commission (UNMOVIC) to oversee the dismantlement of Iraq's chemical and biological weapons and long-range missiles and to monitor any attempts at reviving the weapons programme. Thus for the first time, all weapons of mass destruction and means of delivery were to be covered in a joint operation within a non-compliant State.

The responsibility in the nuclear area was entrusted to the Director General of the IAEA rather than to the Agency as such, in order to avoid any complications and delays by the Board of Governors that is often constrained by divisions, especially between parties and non-parties to the NPT as regards non-proliferation measures. At that time the Director General was Dr Hans Blix of Sweden, who later became Executive Chairman of UNMOVIC subsequent to his retirement from the IAEA. The specific mandate from the Council was:

1. To conduct on-site inspection of Iraq's nuclear capabilities, based on declared locations and designated new sites.
2. To destroy, remove or render harmless any nuclear weapons, nuclear-weapon-usable material, or any subsystems and components, or any R&D or manufacturing facilities.

3. To conduct future ongoing monitoring and verification in the nuclear area.

There was a built-in element to ensure synergy between the nuclear aspects and the other aspects of WMD and delivery means for which the Special Commission was responsible. The Special Commission was to analyze intelligence information and designate undeclared sites for both entities and also to provide logistical and any other necessary assistance and cooperation to the IAEA. These tasks were facilitated by the eventual designation of the Commission as a subsidiary body of the Security Council. The first Executive Chairman of UNSCOM was Ambassador Rolf Ekeus of Sweden who led the Commission during most of its productive years.

For the discovery phase, the principal assets to be used were credible information based on declarations and intelligence from governments; investigation based on inspections and interviews; sophisticated technical surveillance; and unbiased analysis and balanced conclusions. The dismantlement phase involved extensive physical destruction of weapons components and the destruction or disposal of any related items, including facilities and relevant activities. Bomb-grade fissionable material was to be permanently removed from Iraq. For the ongoing monitoring phase, the IAEA used both human observation and technical means for surveillance and remote sensing. The outcome of each phase was communicated to the Council in reports that formed the basis for further action.

The only power at the disposal of the verification authority was its capacity to report to the Security Council thoroughly and objectively, both on its achievements and on any obstruction posed by Iraq. Expertise and balanced judgment were the sources of its credibility and influence.

By December 1998, when the international inspectors withdrew on the eve of President Clinton's bombing of Iraq, the IAEA had completed the discovery and dismantling phases in the nuclear area and was already conducting ongoing monitoring. Thus, for the Director General of IAEA, the issue in 2002 was whether Iraq was using the absence of the inspectors to revive its nuclear-weapon programme.

After the 2001 terrorist attacks on the United States, the shock from the September 11 attacks was compounded by the fear created in its wake by the lethal and mysterious anthrax mailings. This anxiety, fuelled by growing suspicion about possible ties between a rearmed Iraq and Al Qaeda terrorists, induced the US and the UK to refocus attention on Iraq. On the basis of their own faulty intelligence assessments they claimed emphatically that Iraq had revived its WMD production during the absence of inspectors.

In a divided Security Council, the nature, legitimacy and effectiveness of any action to compel Iraqi compliance depended upon credible evidence that only UNMOVIC and the IAEA could provide. In view of Iraq's long history of concealment and deception, it was thus deemed necessary to equip the verification authority (IAEA and UNMOVIC) with the most intrusive powers. The result was resolution 1441, which was unanimously adopted by the Security Council.

The resolution demanded first that Iraq disclose everything, and submit within a month a 'currently accurate, full, and complete declaration of all aspect of its programme'. The role of inspectors was reaffirmed and reinforced in every area:

1. *On-site inspection*: to have 'immediate, unimpeded, unconditional, and unrestricted access' to all areas, facilities buildings, equipment, records and means of transport (including presidential palaces) for inspection; and have the right to 'freeze' a site by declaring it an 'exclusion zone' where Iraq should suspend any ground or aerial movement during inspections.
2. *Investigation*: to have 'immediate, unimpeded, unrestricted and private access' to all Iraqi officials involved in the WMD programme for interviews at locations inside or outside Iraq, at the discretion of the inspectors.
3. *Surveillance*: to have unrestricted use of high and low altitude airplanes, helicopters and unmanned reconnaissance vehicles.
4. *Disarmament*: to have the right to impound production facilities or equipment and to destroy, neutralize or remove any prohibited weapons or related items.
5. *Immunities*: to enjoy privileges and immunities corresponding to the requirements of the mission and to freely import or export any inspection-related items and personal luggage without any search.
6. *Non-compliance*: to report immediately to the Council any interference with inspection activities as well as any failure by Iraq to comply with its disarmament obligations.
7. *Consequences*: on the basis of such report, if Iraq still remained 'in material breach' of its disarmament obligations, including by engaging in false statements or omissions in its declarations, it would face the 'serious consequences' that it was repeatedly warned about by the Security Council.

In the parlance of the Security Council, serious consequences to material breach in the context of Chapter VII of the Charter meant collective measures, including the use of force. UNMOVIC and the IAEA were thus equipped with a powerful source of pressure to ensure Iraqi compliance.

How well did the verification authority perform? The achievement after the resumption of inspections in 2002 was as impressive as the record before 1998.

By the mid-1990s, the IAEA had already discovered and destroyed or otherwise dismantled Iraq's ambitious nuclear weapons programme. Major early discoveries in 1991 confirmed that Iraq had developed sophisticated alternative methods for uranium enrichment and had built huge facilities for producing fissile material. Later, in 1995, the discovery of a huge cache of documents revealed Iraq's advanced knowledge in weapons design and its plan to weaponize by a 'crash' programme of diverting safeguarded fissile material for bombs. Iraq was only a couple of years away from producing its first nuclear bomb when Gulf War I broke out. These discoveries enabled the IAEA to map out a virtually complete and coherent picture of the entire programme. After removing about 100 pounds of Iraq's safeguarded fissile material and completing the demolition of all 'tainted' equipment and buildings, the IAEA had only a few minor unanswered questions. All this was achieved before the inspectors left in December 1998. Ongoing monitoring was also in place, supported by strict import–export controls.

The value of the recently reinforced verification system was to enable the Director General of IAEA and the Executive Chairman of UNMOVIC to compel Iraqi officials to cooperate more actively. It worked well, as their joint team was able in just two months of on-site inspections to reset the baseline data on facilities and inventories and confirm that there was no evidence of any revival of Iraq's WMD programmes.[9] This conclusion was reconfirmed by US inspectors after the Iraq war of 2003 when their large and well-equipped Iraq Survey Group conducted an extensive nine-month search for WMD stockpiles in the occupied country.[10]

The cumulative achievement of the verification regime in Iraq is recognized to have been most effective. With a small but highly competent cadre of inspectors and a small budget, the IAEA and the Special Commission (UNSCOM/UNMOVIC) had virtually accomplished the complete dismantlement of Iraq's WMD programme, a substantial part of it having been unilaterally destroyed by Iraq. Their methodical analysis, meticulous import/export monitoring and skilful on-site investigation enabled them to build up credible evidence. Their reports to the Security Council were precise, objective, analytical and balanced. They were also imaginative in presenting concepts, categories and criteria that helped the Council to address the esoteric and seemingly intractable problems.[11]

Success of the IAEA and UNMOVIC operation was ensured as long as they received unanimous support from the Security Council, including from some members that were not parties to the NPT. Whenever unity among the five permanent members declined, Iraq's defiance increased, with detrimental effect on the access to sites and to officials that they needed to complete their task. Access to information from intelligence agencies was crucial in designating new sites for more fruitful inspections. Another favourable factor for success was the comprehensive and integrated nature of the operation. The IAEA–UNMOVIC operation was a tight regime covering all weapons of mass destruction and delivery systems, all the phases of disarmament and all the necessary controls on illicit production and external acquisition. Ironically, when the unity of the Council collapsed on the eve of the Iraq invasion, the effectiveness of the inspectorate was at its peak, with Iraq responding better in order to avoid war. The two inspection leaders, IAEA's Director General Mohamed ElBaradei and UNMOVIC Executive Chairman Hans Blix, were able to maximize the impact of their joint operation.

North Korea (DPRK): confrontation, 1992–2002

The confrontational case of North Korea was the most difficult for the IAEA, as the Agency had to operate without the benefit of much support from the Security Council. Indeed, on 31 December 2002, North Korea terminated the Agency's decade-long inspection of its nuclear facilities.

At issue was the concealment of information on the country's production of fissionable material that was subject to IAEA safeguards under its obligations as a party to the NPT. North Korea had acceded to the NPT in 1985 but waited for seven years to conclude a safeguards agreement with the Agency. When it joined the membership of the IAEA in April 1992, it had a few nuclear facilities already in operation: notably two small research reactors, one small 5-MW(e) graphite-moderated type which was suitable for plutonium production, and also a fuel fabrication plant. It was also working on a reprocessing plant to extract plutonium (called a 'radiochemical laboratory'), and had embarked on an ambitious construction of two larger reactors (50-Mw(e) and 200-MW(e)). It was believed that these facilities could eventually produce enough plutonium for five to ten nuclear warheads per year.

At the outset, the task for the IAEA was to establish a baseline of data by ensuring the completeness and accuracy of North Korea's initial declaration of all relevant facilities and inventories of nuclear material in the country. For this task the Agency began the process of *ad hoc* inspections, initially with adequate cooperation from the host country. However, the initial inspections revealed a significant inconsistency between what North Korea declared and what the inspectors began to find.

The point of conflict was North Korea's insistence that it had produced only an insignificant quantity of plutonium (90 grams), in a single experiment from damaged fuel rods. On the other hand, the IAEA determined from the analysis of samples taken at the reprocessing facility that more plutonium must have been produced on at least three occasions, although the quantity was unknown. Whether the undeclared plutonium amounted to grams or kilograms could only be determined by analysis of the waste sites. It was estimated by US intelligence agencies that enough plutonium might have been separated to equip one or two nuclear weapons. It took only a handful of initial inspections to identify the discrepancy, which Hans Blix, then Director General of the IAEA, described as 'two gloves, a waste glove and a plutonium glove, [that] don't match'. The problem began when the DPRK rejected the findings and began to deny further access to sites relevant to the investigation.

As the initial task of setting baseline inventory could not be completed, no transition could be made from the *ad hoc* inspection phase to that of routine inspection. Instead, the Agency was compelled to institute the rarely used procedures of special inspection, for the first time in a contentious case.

It was also the first time that the Director General was able to utilize some ideas from the intrusive verification in Iraq. In investigating North Korea's clandestine programme he utilized persuasive satellite information made available by the US to convince the Agency's Board of Governors to endorse his demand for special inspection and set a term of three months for it to comply. North Korea's response was completely negative. Instead, it gave notice on 12 March 1993 of its intention to withdraw from the NPT within 90 days, as provided for in Article X of the treaty.

Under these circumstances, the Board of Governors determined on 1 April 1993 that North Korea was in breach of its safeguards agreement. Thus, in accordance with the Agency's Statute, it reported the crisis to the Security Council. The result was a decision by the Security Council on 11 May 'to invite' North Korea to fulfil its obligations while it retained the issue on its agenda.

This was a textbook case of the application of almost the entire cycle of the safeguards procedures, even before routine inspections were put in place. The Director General utilized his powers under the Statute and the safeguards agreement to demand special access to sensitive sites; he utilized relevant information from all sources, mobilized the most experienced Agency inspectors for the task and persuaded the Board, with the acquiescence of some members who were non-parties to the NPT, of the necessity of appealing for political support and possibly for the application of sanctions by the Security Council. That was the first phase.

The second phase involved a supportive diplomatic effort by the United States. As a result of bilateral negotiations between the United States and North Korea, the latter was persuaded, on the eve of its announced deadline, to suspend the 'effectuation' of its withdrawal from the NPT. However, North Korea continued to frustrate IAEA inspections and even went ahead with the removal of irradiated fuel from the reactor in a manner that would undermine future prospects of retracing the history of the reactor core. The tension culminated in the suspension by the Board of Governors of all technical assistance to North Korea, which provoked an extreme response. In June 1994, North Korea gave the statutory one-year notice of withdrawal from membership in the Agency, while claiming to be in an ambiguous status as regards the NPT.

The third, more positive, phase began with intensive high-level talks between the US and North Korea, which achieved a compromise solution in the form of an 'Agreed Framework Agreement'. It was signed in October 1994 and was accepted promptly by both the Security Council and the IAEA Board of Governors. The agreement was essentially designed as a verified 'freeze' of North Korea's proliferation-prone nuclear programme, matched by a US supply of heavy oil to compensate for the energy that would have been produced otherwise, until the facilities were replaced by a less risky nuclear power programme, with assistance mainly from the US, the Republic of Korea (South Korea) and Japan but also from other members of a consortium. The IAEA's role was to monitor compliance with the freeze and to continue inspection of only declared activities. North Korea would eventually dismantle all the graphite-moderated plants under IAEA verification and replace them with two equivalent large light-water reactors funded by an international consortium. Although an unconventional monitoring task was entrusted to the Agency, its normal safeguards verification remained provisionally reduced.

To the disappointment of the IAEA, North Korea had declared that only when a significant portion of the light-water reactor was completed would it come into full compliance with its safeguards agreement. Specifically, it would allow full-scope inspections just before the delivery of key nuclear material and components for installation in the reactor core. This meant that the IAEA would have to wait for at least five years to resolve the inconsistencies that it discovered at the outset and then verify the accuracy and completeness of a new comprehensive initial declaration. This phase of continuous but restricted ongoing monitoring worked rather well at the beginning but was gradually undermined by political tension and suspicion about North Korea's illicit activities outside the frozen programme. The Bush Administration's aversion to the terms of the Agreed Framework negotiated by its predecessor was also unhelpful at a time when North Korea showed signs of backsliding.

We are now in the fourth phase. After almost a decade of effort, the whole arrangement has collapsed, leaving a half-finished project behind. The backward slide was aggravated by the DPRK's 2003 withdrawal from the NPT. The withdrawal was accompanied by its expulsion of IAEA inspectors amidst shocking claims by the DPRK about bomb-making achievements outside the scope of their monitoring. In the post-Iraq war environment, there are now diplomatic efforts under way to diffuse the crisis and to work out new permanent arrangements to create a denuclearized Korean Peninsula with appropriate security assurances and normalization of relations between the parties concerned. Rounds of talks are in progress among the countries with direct security interest – the US, Russia, China, Japan, the Republic of Korea (South Korea) and North Korea.

As with Iraq, the case of North Korea demonstrates that adequate legal authority and political support from higher bodies is essential to reinforce the Agency's capacity to conduct effective verification, and cope with a regime that is determined to obstruct inspections. Unlike Iraq, however, the necessary mandate and support from the Security Council was lacking and North Korea was able to nullify the value of IAEA's role even at the risk of war. The prospect of reversing North Korea's proliferation trend and its opposition to inspections will depend on the cohesion and commitment of the five interested States that are negotiating with it. Of these, China, Russia and the US, as permanent members of the Security Council, are well-placed to manage unified support from the Council.

Iran: cumulative inspection, 2002–2004

Iran represents a case of limited cooperation rather than open defiance against the inspection rights of the IAEA. It is a case of denial and restriction of transparency about suspicious activities in the nuclear field. Technically, Iran has failed to meet its safeguards obligation to report to the IAEA a full and accurate declaration of all its nuclear material and related facilities.

For almost 30 years, Iran was a party to the NPT and to a comprehensive safeguards agreement and had been in good standing with the IAEA until human intelligence sources revealed in 2002 some credible signs of a clandestine programme. Although Iran was suspected of having such a programme even during the Shah's time in the late 1970s, it was mainly in the context of the devastating though hardly criticized Iraqi launching of chemical warfare in the 1980s that the regime of Ayatollah Khomeini began its exploratory activities. The delays and setbacks in completing the disarmament of Iraq were also far from reassuring to Iran, which was initially receptive to the idea of more transparency when it invited the Director General of the IAEA to conduct inspection missions in undeclared suspected sites.

Iran has limited domestic technological capacity for a nuclear industry and has to rely heavily on external assistance for its legitimate civilian power and research reactors under construction.

The US, however, remained suspicious of Iran's motives and continued to campaign for restricting its external procurement even for permissible dual-use items. A US-led embargo on nuclear sales went even beyond the guidelines of the Nuclear Suppliers Group which would permit sales subject to IAEA inspection. Those restrictions have been a source of friction not only with Iran but also between the US and Russia, which had undertaken to complete Iran's large light-water power reactor with minimal proliferation risk.

It was eventually revealed that despite those restrictions on official trade, and perhaps partly because of them, the situation became even more dangerous as Iran resorted to illicit transactions conducted by shady intermediaries. The task of the IAEA thus became even more complex: it had not only to ensure thorough inspections but also to delve into investigation of the network of traffickers, with the help of Member States. There was a multiple challenge for the IAEA:

1. The periodic routine inspections were no longer enough and had to be supplemented by new *ad hoc* inspections, which needed to draw upon the reinforced safeguards system. But as Iran had not yet signed

the Additional Protocol, the inspectors were unable to insist on a right of access to undeclared sites and information.

2. The issue of non-discriminatory, safeguarded supply of legitimate nuclear items for Iraq was still a divisive issue and the Director General had to pursue a carefully balanced, objective approach based on evidence.

3. Since the issue involved not a threat from an advanced weapons programme but suspicions about an incipient one, the Agency needed to promote transparency and play a constructive role that could build on achievements in Iraq and advance the cause of a nuclear-weapon-free zone for the Middle East.

Accordingly, Director General ElBaradei embarked on a campaign to maximize access for IAEA inspectors in the spirit of a promise made by the Vice-President of Iran. In September 2002 he had stated at the Agency's General Conference in Vienna: 'Complete transparency of my country's nuclear activities is a serious commitment endorsed by my Government.' Mindful of Iraq's deception and the security environment after 9/11, few would take Iran's promise at face value. Conflicting signals about action against Iran were coming from within the US government, which were mirrored in Teheran by an internal policy confrontation about the wisdom of resorting to a nuclear option. In Washington, the strategic context involved a confrontation between the multilateralists who had secured Iranian cooperation in the war on terror and the more dominant unilateralist 'hawks' who were behind President Bush's new doctrine of preemptive action. Iran was labelled as being part of the so-called 'axis of evil' along with Iraq and North Korea. The situation was thus fraught with danger as the US prepared to invade Iraq but was not devoid of opportunities for a breakthrough with the help of constructive European diplomacy.

Paradoxically, in February 2003, even as the Iraq operation of the IAEA and UNMOVIC was about to collapse because of the US decision to put it aside for the invasion, Director General ElBaradei managed an invitation from Iran to consult personally with its authorities and lead an inspection team to visit undeclared suspected sites. Backed fully by the Board on the issue of unfettered access, he led another mission in July, which launched intensive inspections that produced findings on major violations:

1. Unreported processing of imported uranium involving conversion, fuel fabrication, and irradiation activities, including the separation of small amounts of plutonium – now acknowledged.

2. Unreported uranium enrichment by the centrifuge method for 18 years and by the laser method for 12 years, with successful production of small amounts of low enriched uranium (LEU) – now acknowledged.
3. Failure to report at least three undeclared facilities used for processing, enrichment or storage (in Teheran, Nantaz and Hastgerd) – now acknowledged and opened for inspection.
4. Continuing resistance to providing design information relating to the centrifuge and laser enrichment and plutonium production.
5. Continuing resistance to provide a credible explanation for traces of highly enriched uranium (HEU) revealed by sampling but claimed to be from contamination by imported equipment.

September 2003 was a turning point on the Iran issue, as the Board was determined to end all concealment efforts and to ensure that Iran's slow and limited cooperation should become proactive and consistent. The Board thus called upon Iran to provide 'accelerated cooperation and full transparency' in the spirit of the Additional Protocol, even as the latter tried to hasten its ratification process. It also made a request to Iran to suspend further enrichment and processing of uranium pending certification about its full compliance (resolution GOV/2003/69, 12 September 2003). The request was unprecedented, as the NPT entitles Iran as a State party to enrich and reprocess uranium and to build and operate research reactors that utilize isotope products of enriched uranium, provided that they are declared and monitored. Under the original safeguards agreements, States are also permitted to build reactors as long as they declare them six months before loading the nuclear material. Iran has to accept the new conditions provisionally and freeze the situation in order to allow some time for IAEA's inspectors to determine when, why and to what extent Iran was engaged in the violations.

It was at this point that a troika of European Union States – France, Germany and the UK – which had recently patched up their differences over the Iraq war, weighed in to facilitate Iran's full cooperation and diffuse the crisis before it was pushed up to the Security Council upon US insistence. On 21 October, the Foreign Ministers of the three countries were able to make a deal with Iran on three points. Iran promised: (a) to cooperate fully with the IAEA and to accept provisionally the reinforced procedures of safeguards pending ratification of the Additional Protocol; (b) to resolve all outstanding issues and correct any possible failures; and (c) to suspend voluntarily all uranium enrichment and processing activities, as recommended earlier by the Board. As a reward for the resolution of all outstanding issues, the three States reaffirmed Iran's right to peaceful nuclear energy and promised to facilitate easier access to supplies and technology for power generation.

The Iran situation thus entered its final phase with a positive and sustained trend towards full cooperation: Iran has now signed the Additional Protocol, provided access to all requested sites, documentation and personnel and has provisionally suspended uranium enrichment and reprocessing as a confidence-building measure. However, full transparency is yet to be achieved: its latest October 2003 declaration did not include any reference to its possession of centrifuge designs and related research and still failed to offer a credible explanation for the traces of fissile material discovered by the inspectors. The progress achieved so far is significant but may not fully obviate the need to refer the problem to the Security Council should Iran not be satisfied with the results of its negotiations with the European Union on security and technological benefits.

Libya: cooperative inspection, 2003–2004

On 19 December 2003, Libya publicly acknowledged possession of programmes, materials and equipment for the production of all types of weapons of mass destruction, not just chemical weapons as was generally known but also nuclear and biological programmes. The nuclear part of the revelation was a shock since Libya had been a long-standing member of the IAEA and a party to the NPT since 1975, subject to the Agency's comprehensive safeguards. The good news was that, after a decade of erratic informal contacts with the US, Libya was now determined to eliminate the entire programme under international verification.

The political context for the breakthrough was the interplay between, on the one hand, Libya's eagerness to end the economic sanctions and its political isolation and, on the other, the sustained pressure by the US, the UK and France to extract an admission of full responsibility for its terrorist acts, especially the bombing of American and French passenger aircraft (PanAm Flt. 103 and UTA Flt. 772). Libya was also requested to compensate the victims and renounce its policy of terrorism. For the US, Libyan renunciation of all WMD was not always a priority, as little was known about its nuclear intentions, and its earlier offer to the Clinton Administration to dismantle its chemical weapons programme was not even followed up. Libya's first concession of handing over the Libyan suspects of the PanAm flight incident for international trial did not go far enough. It was only after the September 11 shock that the two sides were able to find some common ground in fighting the new threat from Al Qaeda. Thanks to British diplomacy, two years of secret negotiations with Libya secured most of the required concessions, thus permitting the lifting of UN sanctions. However, this progress was still not good enough to persuade the US to lift its unilateral sanctions. The last issue for the US was Libya's WMD programme that the latter was now ready to resolve in all its aspects. The breakthrough has less to do with the impact of the Iraq war, as has been claimed by the Bush Administration, than with the impact of the sanctions on Libya's economy. It is the product of a 'carrot and stick' approach by the international community as a whole combined with US pressure spanning many administrations. In the end it was British diplomacy that unlocked the door for verified disarmament.

The IAEA's verification work in Libya is one of the most rapid and intense OSI operations of the Agency because both Libya and the US are eager to achieve WMD elimination as the last requirement for normalization of relations. The Director General was able to exercise fully his authority under the existing comprehensive safeguards agreement and to persuade Libya to provide unrestricted access to all requested sites, information and people in order to map out the full picture of the nuclear programme. For this task, Libya agreed to cooperate as if the procedures of the draft Additional Protocol were in force while accelerating the formalities of ratification to be completed as soon as possible. The Agency was able to deploy instantly experts not only on fuel fabrication and centrifuge enrichment, but also on weaponization and related research and development. Its teams included not only experts on fuel fabrication and centrifuge enrichment, but also on research and development related to weapons.

This operation was unique for the parallel cooperative arrangements made by Libya, with the US and the UK and with the IAEA, to achieve verified disarmament. To fulfil his regular verification mandate effectively, the Director General worked out with the US and the UK a practical arrangement for division of labour. As soon as IAEA inspectors verify the inventories of nuclear material and related items they would place them under Agency seals and then oversee US and Russian removal from Libya of all the sensitive components of the programme. Accordingly, the US has launched a major operation to ship and airlift to secure locations in America over 500 tons of centrifuge components and related items together with stocks of long-range missiles. As the Libyan stocks of safeguarded highly enriched uranium were of Soviet origin, the Russian government has, with US financial assistance, taken back the sensitive nuclear material amounting to 13 kg of uranium 235 (enriched by 80 per cent to almost weapons grade).

Thanks to Libya's full cooperation and the major logistical and financial involvement especially of the US, the IAEA predicts completion of this major verification task in only six months. In this case, collaboration has ensured smooth and rapid progress with little more to do for the Agency's Board of Governors at mid-point except to acknowledge the violations, welcome the progress made and notify the Security Council of the final resolution.

Challenges and possibilities

What lessons can we learn from these cases of verification applied by the IAEA against a variety of challenges? What are the strengths and weaknesses of the OSI system? We will focus on the main issues presented in the OSI model described at the beginning of this chapter: power and authority of the inspectorate, access and transparency, management of operations and findings and recourse. In each case of verification, the Director General had to operate within the limits set by the legal framework and was constrained in varying degrees by how Member States perceived the impact of effective action on their respective interests and relationships. In general, we may conclude that the verification operations of the Agency have been efficient and have demonstrated considerable adaptability in facing different problems. The most difficult challenge in all the cases is the weakness of the nuclear non-proliferation regime. Two basic problems of the regime are: the lack of universal regulation of nuclear trade, and the weakness of controls regarding nuclear research having possible military implications. From the IAEA's perspective, these are basically problems of inadequate mandate from Member States. However effective the on-site inspection within a State, it cannot pretend to provide a total picture of all relevant activites. It has been particularly difficult to achieve full transparency on the external procurement of sensitive technology and equipment for research reactors. This problem has been analyzed in an earlier chapter on export/import control.

Iraq, North Korea, Iran and Libya have all depended on illicit nuclear trade to develop reprocessing and enrichment capacities outside the safeguards system. Iraq's broad network of procurement through private companies in Europe and the US has been well documented by UN inspectors. This was possible because UNSCOM and the IAEA were given the mandate to collect and analyze all relevant import/export information that States were required to provide. This information supplemented significantly the information on Iraq's nuclear industry that was extracted by inspectors from the Iraqi government. The role of Pakistani nuclear scientists was not absent in Iraq but it was considered to be marginal. It has now been revealed by intelligence sources and admitted publicly in Pakistan that A.Q. Khan, the 'father' of the Pakistan bomb himself, was in charge of the secret transfer of bomb technology to North Korea, Iran and Libya. Libya's policy of full transparency has greatly helped in confirming its Pakistan connection with strong implications about possible parallel deals regarding North Korea and Iran. The most contentious outstanding issue in Iran is now whether the traces of weapons-grade fissile material detected by IAEA inspectors were from contaminated centrifuges of Pakistani origin or, more seriously, were produced by Iran itself using those centrifuges. A clear answer requires full cooperation not only by Iran but also by Pakistan.

The second major regime problem, which Director General ElBaradei has recently called the 'Achilles' heel' of the non-proliferation regime, is the poorly controlled upper end of the fuel cycle. Risks of cheating multiply with the wide dissemination of proliferation-sensitive technologies for the entire fuel cycle – fuel fabrication, enrichment and reprocessing and storage of spent fuel (reusable nuclear waste). In all the four cases, legitimate isotope production for medicine and other peaceful uses appears to have served as a cover for the acquisition of dual-use technology and equipment, as well as for advanced nuclear training. Without additional access, regular safeguards inspections are not able to detect clandestine activities beyond the safeguarded areas. The task requires access to wider territory, to borderline facilities and to more sources of information within and outside the country. The Additional Protocols would ameliorate the situation but could not make up for the loopholes. The Director General's campaign for tighter multilateral controls, possibly by forming cost-effective regional centres, is a telling reminder of the lessons learned from the four cases.

The third challenge concerns the continuing limitation of the inspectors' authority because of the delays in implementing the reinforced safeguards system. It is closely related to the second challenge about wider and deeper access. Inspectors have now to improvise by stretching the limited scope of the traditional safeguards agreements to deal simultaneously with so many cases that would require the strengthened safeguards. The slow ratification process is a handicap for inspectors in the cases studied because none of the States concerned had yet accepted the new rules. From the outset North Korea had blocked the full implementation of comprehensive safeguards and preferred to withdraw from the NPT altogether rather than seek a resolution of the problem by giving more access. However, the situation is now improving. In a precedent-setting development, both Libya and Iran agreed to permit provisionally more intrusive inspections as if the new rules were in force. It was an encouraging prelude to their subsequent formal agreement to equip the inspectors with the tools they needed to handle the unresolved issues of procurement and concealment.

Fourth, as regards the effectiveness of on-site inspections, the adequacy of personnel, technical and financial resources remains crucial. Inspections are no longer the exclusive domain of experts in the fuel cycle, especially as verification expands beyond declared items. They must now include experts with diverse knowledge and experience, ranging from energy-related science to engineering and weapon design, and from law and diplomacy to data analysis and detective work. Using the experience and insights gained from the Iraq and South African cases, a core of veteran inspectors and operation managers handled the difficult problems of concealment and deception with persistence and flexibility. Depending on the degree of obstruction in a particular case, the Director General himself found it increasingly necessary to accompany inspection teams to remove obstacles by diplomacy.

Managing the growing volume and complexity of the workload is perhaps the greatest challenge facing the IAEA today. With so many recent cases of actual or suspected non-compliance, the demand for simultaneous attention has put a stress on limited available resources. Until recently, financial resources were virtually frozen for over fifteen years, making it difficult to expand the inspectorate. There is thus a risk of spreading inspection resources too thinly in an effort to meet all demands for a timely detection of concealment. This problem is ameliorated but not really solved by the benefits of technological innovations, notably in environmental testing, imaging and remote sensing.

The fifth challenge relates to helpful information from intelligence sources. Good use has been made of such information when made available by Member States. Host States are reluctantly becoming accustomed to such use as a way to clear up false allegations. Such information is a valuable asset, when it is accurate, but it is also hard to come by, as States are normally reluctant to share it. As in Iraq, there is a risk of manipulating it to advance national goals, to the detriment of international inspections.

Finally, in confrontational situations, even the most competent inspectorate cannot expect to achieve its mission of verifying compliance if the Member States are divided over the issue. The more intrusive procedures of the Additional Protocol can be mobilized fully, with the unified support of the Member States, as represented by the Board. In Iraq, the best results were achieved when the members of the Security Council were united during the earlier years. Consensus among the major powers often rallies support from the members. Although there is no disagreement on the need to combine pressure and incentives, for example as regards Iran, there are still differences on how to do so with optimal results. In that context, States should rely on the expertise, impartiality and objectivity of inspectors who may serve as an arbiter of what is reasonably required to fulfil the treaty obligations. With those qualities intact, they are capable of discovering 'credible evidence' about compliance or non-compliance by a State without excessive infringement on national sovereignty.

CTBTO inspection as a burglar alarm

The Nuclear Non-Proliferation Treaty and the Comprehensive Test Ban Treaty form important nuclear elements of an emerging WMD control regime. They are designed as interlocking partial measures towards nuclear disarmament with verification mechanisms that would complement each other. In Article VI, the NPT states the undertaking of parties 'to pursue negotiations in good faith on effective measures relating to cessation of the nuclear arms race at an early date and to nuclear disarmament'. The CTBT was conceived as a barrier to the development or improvement of nuclear weapons. As such, the conclusion of the Treaty in 1996 was considered as a fulfilment of a preambular commitment of NPT parties to honour a pledge made in the 1963 Partial Test-Ban Treaty 'to seek to achieve the discontinuance of all test explosions of nuclear weapons for all time'. These commitments represent a linkage between the prevention of vertical proliferation by the nuclear powers and horizontal proliferation by non-nuclear-weapon States. The CTBT is seen by most States as a measure binding the nuclear-weapon States, serving as a form of reciprocation for their own NPT commitments to relinquish the nuclear option. Unlike the tripartite Partial Test-Ban Treaty, it is a universal measure that would alleviate the discriminatory features of the NPT. The relationship between the NPT and the CTBT is evident from the complementarity of their verification aspects: while the former focuses on non-diversion of nuclear material at all stages in the fuel cycle, the latter concentrates on the possibility of a subsequent illicit weaponization. In scope, the CTBT prohibition goes beyond that of the NPT, as it extends its ban to nuclear explosions used for peaceful projects and encompasses the civilian as well as the military sectors.

As regards on-site inspection, there are marked differences in the role and extent of its use. While the IAEA employs within a country technology-assisted inspections throughout the verification process, the

CTBTO system consists mostly of technical monitoring in all environments, with on-site inspection deployed only in cases of unresolved anomalies. Indeed CTBTO's on-site inspections are special measures that may be considered as the functional equivalent of the IAEA's special inspections and the OPCW's challenge inspections to be explained later.

Legal basis, authority and constraints

The legal basis to verify compliance with the Nuclear Test-Ban Treaty is embodied in Article IV of the Treaty. On-site inspection is the fourth element of the 'verification regime', which consists of:

(a) The international monitoring system (IMS) comprising three inter-dependent parts: sensors for remote seismological, hydroacoustic, infrasound and radionuclide detection; a global communication infrastructure (GCI) to transmit data from the IMS network; and an International Data Center (IDC) in Vienna to receive the data in near real time for processing and analysis.

(b) A consultation and clarification process to resolve compliance issues, which involves State parties and the secretariat.

(c) Confidence-building measures involving voluntary exchange of scientific data and other relevant information to reduce ambiguities in the signals detected by the IMS.

(d) On-site inspection, upon the request of a State party and to be carried out with the approval of the Executive Council, in order to clarify whether the detected data was indeed from a nuclear explosion.

The entire verification process is designed to detect nuclear explosions in all environments – underground, in water and in the atmosphere. To improve verifiability, the CTBT relies on the synergies among the four IMS technologies. The three waveform technologies complement one another, as the global seismological network (170 primary and secondary stations) records continuously earthquake events to provide a broad background for selection; the global hydroacoustic network (11 stations) detects sound waves made by natural or man-made phenomena in the oceans; and the global infrasound network composed of particulate and noble gas detectors (80 stations) detects low- frequency sound waves in the atmosphere made by natural or man-made events. The global radionuclide network (60 stations) is vital in narrowing down the relevant data from the waveform technologies and in identifying an event as a nuclear explosion. When these sensors identify a suspicious event, the concerns about possible non-compliance are first addressed through consultation and clarification. At this point, a State party may nevertheless request an on-site inspection, which is the final verification measure under the Treaty. The purpose of on-site inspection is to remove any ambiguity by confirming or ruling out the event as a nuclear test in violation of the Treaty.

Unlike the situation with IAEA safeguards, in the CTBTO the demands on sovereignty rights to provide access to inspectors are kept to a minimum by the heavy reliance on technological detection and by the expected rarity of on-site inspections. Nevertheless, the Treaty defines necessary access in the following manner: 'on-site inspections shall be conducted in the least intrusive manner possible, consistent with the efficient and timely accomplishment of the inspection mandate, and in accordance with the procedures set forth in the Protocol'. While a State is obliged to make every reasonable effort to demonstrate its compliance, which includes granting access to its locations for inspection, it retains the right to limit such access in order to protect national security and prevent disclosure of confidential information not related to the purpose of inspections. It is required to demonstrate its compliance by granting 'managed' access and, if necessary, by any other means deemed adequate for the task (Article IV D, paras 57–58).

As with the IAEA, the CTBTO has three main bodies. The plenary organ is the Conference of States Parties. The second policy-making organ is the Executive Council, comprising 51 members elected by the Conference on the basis of two criteria: equitable geographical distribution among six regions and adequate representation for States designated as having nuclear capabilities relevant to the Treaty. The third body is the Technical Secretariat headed by the Director General who manages the inspectorate. It should be stressed at the outset that these bodies and the verification system itself will become fully operational only after the CTBT enters into force upon ratification by all the 44 States designated as having nuclear capabilities. Seven years after the conclusion of the CTBT in 1996, only 33 of the 44 designated States have ratified the Treaty. The holdout States include India, Pakistan and North Korea, none of whom have even signed, while the US and China have signed but are yet to ratify the Treaty.

At present, the organization is still represented by provisional bodies. The Preparatory Commission for the CTBTO, composed of over 170 signatory States, continues to carry out the necessary institution-building for full implementation of the Treaty. Its focus is on the full establishment of the verification system while actively promoting Treaty signature and ratification for entry into force. It is assisted by a Provisional Technical Secretariat, headed by an Executive Secretary.

When all the organs of the CTBTO are in place they will differ significantly from those of the IAEA as regards the distribution of powers among them regarding inspections. As the highest organ, the Conference of the State Parties will be functionally comparable to the General Conference of the IAEA. Not only will it elect the members of the Executive Council and approve the programme and budget recommended by the Council but will also oversee the verification activities and take the necessary measures to ensure compliance. In a departure from the IAEA model, the Director General will be appointed directly by the General Conference without any role being played by the Executive Council. With respect to the verification process, the role of the Executive Council is also comparable to that of the IAEA Board of Governors. The main differences concern the relative powers of the Directors General *vis-à-vis* their governing bodies. While they both assist their respective policy-making organs in the performance of their functions the Director General of the CTBTO performs a strictly managerial function as the head of a technical secretariat. Unlike the Director General of the IAEA, he cannot initiate inspections. On-site inspections are indeed 'challenge inspections', which are initiated by requests from State parties on the basis of suspicious data detected by the IMS or by national technical means. It is the function of the Executive Council to assess urgently the merit of the request and decide on the inspection by a three-fifths majority (30 affirmative votes of the 51 members). In this process, the Director General is initially only a channel; he communicates the request promptly to the suspected State for an explanation and notifies all State parties of the request. His role becomes more substantive when he urgently presents the issue to the Council for action. The evidentiary aspect of his role is significant when he presents the grounds for action comprising all relevant data, including the response by the suspected State. All other State parties are also notified urgently. The Council has to decide within five days of the initiation of the request and authorize the Director General to conduct an inspection or rule out the request as frivolous or otherwise inappropriate.

The main responsibility of the Director General is to organize and manage the challenge inspection. His role is strictly operational: to draw up an inspection mandate comprising the Council's decision, the location and boundaries of the inspection area and the identity of the State to be inspected, the composition of the inspection team and the plan of activities. In a departure from the IAEA approach, the requesting State (or States) may designate a representative to join the team of inspectors as an observer, if agreeable to the inspected State. On-site inspections are short-notice inspections as only a 24-hour notification is given to the inspected State before the arrival of the team.

Aims and limitations

The aim of the inspection is to determine whether there is a violation of the nuclear test-ban. Specifically, the objective is to verify the nature of usually ambiguous events detected by the monitoring system. Its characteristics are defined by the interrelationships among the following factors: geographic area, timeliness, technological efficiency and synergy and size of mission, all within the constraints of sovereignty rights. First, the inspection area has to be large, up to 1,000 sq. km. The location estimates of certain triggering events do cover a large area. Second, since seismic after-shocks that could clarify some uncertainties tend to dissipate quickly, the inspection team needs to arrive at the site of the triggering event within a few days. On the other hand, radionuclide data that could be decisive may take weeks or even months to propagate to where they might be detectable, which explains why the Treaty permits inspections for as long as 130 days. Third, the technical sensors for seismic, hydroacoustic and infrasound detection need to be used in different combinations in order to verify the physical signatures of an event in any environment – underground, underwater or in the atmosphere. They are backed by radionuclide detectors for evidence from air, soil, water or other samples. When inspectors proceed to a suspected area for visual observation and for on-site tests they are already quipped with such data as well as with geological and above-ground imagery. Fourth, the size of the inspection team must be adequate for the extensive and complex task: a mission may comprise up to 40 inspectors at the same time.

The quality of inspections depends on the professional skills, the sophistication of technologies and the efficiency of their management. However, the effectiveness of an operation depends also on the impact of sovereignty constraints. The need for intrusive inspection has, in practice, to be balanced against the legitimate needs of the inspected State; especially the need to preserve the confidentiality of sensitive information unrelated to the Treaty. A major challenge then is how to conduct effective inspections subject to the restrictions on overflight, photography and the requirements for managed access as permitted by the Treaty.

Political constraints aside, is the CTBT verifiable from the technical point of view? Most States are confident that it can be verified effectively. The technical objective of the IMS system is to detect with a high level of confidence an explosion of one kiloton (1,000 tons of TNT) or even below, especially where deceptive methods are suspected. In theory, 'decoupling' can be used to evade detection by conducting a test in a large underground cavity to attenuate the seismic waves. It is, however, unlikely that an emergent nuclear-weapon State would have sufficient experience or resources to do successfully. Moreover, it should be noted that the task of detection is not left entirely to the international monitoring system but is greatly supported by the extensive national technical means at the disposal of the more advanced States, including satellite imagery, and may also benefit from the extensive scientific monitoring networks. In determining the verifiability of the CTBT, which was seriously questioned by the US Senate when it rejected ratification of the Treaty in 1999, it is necessary to bear in mind the combined international, national and non-governmental detection capability that can be effectively deployed to deter testing or otherwise detect events that should be inspected. The National Authority to be established by each State party is expected to coordinate national efforts with the global efforts for maximum effectiveness and not operate as a unilateral alternative.

The effectiveness of CTBT inspections cannot be fully tested until after the Treaty has entered into force when the completed IMS will be employed to detect and locate suspicious events for inspection. So far experimental tests have been conducted only to calibrate sensors and determine their capabilities.

Challenges and possibilities

The fundamental challenge for the CTBT has been the absence of key players from membership. The issue of universality in this case is even more serious than in the IAEA where NPT non-parties are not only present as Agency members, but also interact with the broader membership in seeking mutual accommodation in a two-tiered arrangement on verification matters.

The most serious setback to the treaty regime was the 1998 testing of nuclear weapons by India and Pakistan. Unless the two States can agree to accept the existing nuclear test moratorium and be persuaded to accede to the CTBT, their absence will pose an insurmountable obstacle to the full establishment of the regime. The North Korean problem is perhaps more manageable as it has not conducted any nuclear test and is engaged in intermittent negotiations for a possible resolution of the nuclear issue in the Korean Peninsula.

The second significant setback was the 1999 rejection by the US Senate of President Clinton's recommendation to ratify the Treaty.

The grounds for the narrow defeat were the questionable assumption that its mechanism could not verify evasive low-yield tests and that it could undermine national security by foreclosing the possibility of testing to keep stockpiles safe and reliable. False allegations about failure to identify a 1997 seismic event in Russia were used in Senate hearings to undermine support for the Treaty, in total disregard of CTBTO's data suggesting the contrary.[12]

In a bitterly partisan debate in the Senate, the central point was missed: it was precisely in doubtful situations such as this that on-site inspections are necessary. The Senate vote had ignored the positive assessment of verifiability given by the directors of the US nuclear weapons laboratories and most of the former US Joint Chiefs of Staff and dozens of experts.

The obstacle became more formidable under the Bush Administration, as many of the Treaty's opponents were put in charge of official policy on security and arms control. Although the US has continued to observe the moratorium and to participate in the Preparatory Commission of the CTBTO, the Administration remains hostile to the Treaty and seems determined to violate it by developing small bunker-busting nuclear devices that may require testing. The present unilateralist tendencies are diametrically opposed to the traditional multilateral approach of the US government, whose leadership was largely instrumental for the conclusion of the CTBT as a second leg for verified non-proliferation of nuclear weapons.

It is remarkable under these circumstances that the Preparatory Commission and the Technical Secretariat have quietly been able to continue their institution-building task. They have doubled the rate of ratifications by non-designated States since the US failure to ratify and have proceeded to build the worldwide monitoring system with the limited financial and personnel resources available to them. As long as the moratorium on tests continues, the CTBTO may have a chance to complete the network and demonstrate the verifiability of the system by balancing the factors of transparency, intrusiveness and cost efficiency. Hopefully, such a demonstration may eventually persuade sceptics to accept the favourable conclusions of so many experts who testified to the Treaty's verifiability.[13]

OPCW inspection as a watchguard

The Chemical Weapons Convention (CWC), which entered into force on 29 April 1997, is the second multilateral agreement (after the 1972

Biological and Toxin Weapons Convention or BWC) designed not only to prevent proliferation but also to prohibit a class of weapons of mass destruction. In contrast to the BWC, which has no formal verification measures, the CWC provides for a verified elimination of any existing stockpiles of chemical weapons and also ensures that dual-use chemical industry plants are not diverted to their production. The purpose of the CWC is to complement the non-use prohibitions of the 1925 Geneva Protocol by banning the development, production, acquisition, stockpiling and transfer of chemical weapons. As such, its scope is much broader than the combined scope of the NPT and the CTBT. Unlike the NPT, which focuses on the civilian sector, the CWC encompasses both the military and the civilian sectors, including the chemical and pharmaceutical industries and application of toxic chemicals in medicine, agriculture and research. Accordingly, the Convention equips the inspectorate with a comprehensive verification mechanism capable of performing diverse functions on a worldwide basis.

Legal basis, authority and constraints

The CWC breaks new ground in the scope and intrusiveness of its verification system. It devotes five articles to verification and elaborates detailed procedures in an extensive Verification Annex, that is an integral part of the Convention. The system is based on international monitoring of compliance with CWC obligations. It is supported by national measures, which are formally stipulated in the Convention. These include the adoption of implementing legislation and penal law to ensure compliance by relevant companies and the citizens of each State party, and the establishment of a National Authority to coordinate implementation (Article VII). At the international level, the verification system, as elaborated in Annex 2 of the Convention, consists of four elements:

(a) Initial inspections to verify the completeness and accuracy of declarations on the possession of chemical weapons, production and storage facilities, and various weapon-related and dual-use chemicals (Article III).
(b) Routine on-site inspections to observe the destruction of stockpiles and production facilities and inspect the legitimate use of permitted toxic chemicals and facilities (Articles IV, V and VI).
(c) Challenge inspection of sites suspected of prohibited activity, to clarify inconsistencies, ambiguities and anomalies (Article IX).
(d) Investigation of alleged chemical weapon use (Article I).

The Convention does not attempt to monitor all toxic chemicals, which would be too costly and impractical. Instead, inspections focus on those categories that have been assessed to pose an actual or potential threat, without exempting other chemicals.

For this purpose the Annex on Chemicals classifies toxic chemicals of particular concern into the three categories of chemicals described in Chapter 3. Categorized on the basis of their military potential and the extent of their legitimate civilian use, these chemicals comprise: twelve known warfare agents (or families thereof) under Schedule 1; fourteen high-risk chemicals (or families thereof) under Schedule 2; and seventeen lower-risk chemicals under Schedule 3. Although other chemicals are not listed, the aggregate quantities that are reported are used to organize some inspection on a random basis. The frequency and intensity of inspections at a facility is dependent on whether it produces, processes, or utilizes one or more of the scheduled chemicals; and whether the annual amount of chemicals processed exceeds specified quantity thresholds.

The CWC and the CTBT have similar institutions for the governance and management of verification because they are the product of a parallel negotiating history. They differ markedly from the IAEA's system of verification, especially in relation to the distribution of institutional authority. There are no differences as regards the responsibilities of the two Director Generals for the management of their respective organizations. The OPCW Secretariat is charged with carrying out all the monitoring, including analyzing declarations, conducting inspections and reporting the results to the Executive Council. However, the Director General, as head of a technical Secretariat, does not have the authority to initiate inspection of suspected activities. This is the prerogative of the parties, any of whom may request a challenge inspection in the territory of a State they suspected of non-compliance. The Executive Council performs standard functions similar to those assigned to the Council of the CTBTO. It oversees the verification process, evaluates compliance issues, alerts the Conference of States Parties of serious problems and may report grave and urgent cases to the United Nations General Assembly and the Security Council. It is not nearly as powerful as the IAEA Board of Governors as it is subordinated to the Conference of States Parties on matters of compliance. It is the Conference of States Parties that ensures effective implementation of the Convention. It does so in the first instance by adopting policies, implementation guidelines, programmes and budgets. It also actively oversees the verification role of the Council and the Secretariat, reserving the power to decide on measures against non-compliance. The councils of the OPCW and the CTBT differ only slightly in their relative powers *vis-à-vis* their principal plenary bodies. As regards requests for challenge inspections, for example, the OPCW Council's powers are more limited: while the CTBTO Council is empowered to consider and authorize a challenge inspection by a qualified majority, the OPCW Council can only block action by a high negative vote of its members (three-quarters), and without delaying the operation beyond a 12-hour limit.

The structural constraints of the OPCW are far less serious than those of the IAEA and the CTBTO. The OPCW is almost universal in membership. Among its over-160 members, it includes almost all militarily significant States. In addition to the five major powers, it includes States that have totally stayed away from the CTBTO – including India and Pakistan. Six States have acknowledged having chemical weapons and have declared their stockpiles and related facilities: the US, Russia, Albania, India, Libya and South Korea.

The progress towards quantitative universality has thus been impressive but there is still some way to go. There are a few holdouts, some of whom are suspected of possessing chemical weapons or weapons capabilities. This includes Israel, which has only signed, and Egypt, Iraq, Syria and North Korea, which have not even signed. However, post-war Iraq is likely to accede to the CWC in the near future.[14]

Qualitatively, however, the CWC is already universal in the sense that it covers comprehensively all chemicals with actual or potential military use, irrespective of whether the individual States possess stockpiles of chemical weapons or not. It is thus in sharp contrast to the NPT, which discriminates between the nuclear-weapons States and all others by requiring only the latter to renounce nuclear weapons.

The nondiscriminatory character of the CWC is beneficial to the organization in seeking to operate more cohesively without being seriously hindered by formal political groupings. The only groups that are formally recognized are the regional ones, which are used for ensuring geographical representation within the Executive Council. In practice, however, three informal groupings have emerged with differing interests in verification: the possessors of chemical weapons; the former possessors of such weapons and other States with advanced chemical industry; and the less developed countries interested mainly in technical cooperation to advance their chemical industry. The obligations of the first group regarding both disarmament and non-proliferation are so extensive that the success of the Convention depends on the degree of their cooperation, in the civilian as well as the military sector. The extensive non-proliferation undertakings of the second group also require extensive cooperation, spanning their entire chemical industries. Group tensions are not totally absent, especially when debates on the burden of inspections and the issue of resource allocation pit the disarmament requirements against the non-proliferation objectives of the CWC, or when developing members complain about the export control policies imposed by the industrialized States, which the developing countries claim conflict with the technology-transfer and liberalized provisions of Article XI.

The main constraint of the OPCW is not inherent in the Convention itself, whose far-reaching provisions were agreed during a brief period of post-Cold War harmony, but rather in the subsequent changing political environment that necessitated second thoughts about the security and economic implications of a strict implementation of the treaty's verification provisions. While the IAEA has been trying to cope with the inherent weaknesses of the NPT safeguards by incrementally strengthening the system, the OPCW has faced the problem of measuring up to the ambitious verification provisions written into the CWC. The experience of the first five years indicates that both the Conference of States Parties and the Executive Council have tended to water down provisions of the verification system in drawing up rules, procedures, guidelines and standards for inspections. The organization's verification task has also been complicated by advances in chemical science that pose new threats to the non-proliferation regime.

Aims and limitations of on-site inspection

The OPCW relies on on-site inspection for evidence of the compliance or non-compliance with treaty obligations. The political aim is to prevent prohibited activities and provide reassurance that disarmament and non-proliferation objectives are being met. It is done by verifying the elimination of all chemical weapons stockpiles and the destruction or irreversible conversion to peaceful purposes of former chemical weapons production facilities and by monitoring the civilian sector to deter any diversion of chemicals and production facilities to military use. The immediate technical aim is to ensure that declarations are correct and complete and that no Schedule 1 warfare agents are secretly retained or produced in the entire chemical industry.

The issue of access is carefully defined in Article VIII of the Convention, which states:

> The Organization shall conduct its verification activities ... in the least intrusive manner possible consistent with the timely and efficient

accomplishment of their objectives ... It shall take every precaution to protect the confidentiality of information on civil and military activities coming to its knowledge.

This provision balances carefully the common international interest of disarmament with the particular national interests of Member States to preserve legitimate security and commercial secrets. The concepts of intrusiveness, timeliness, efficiency and confidentiality have been elaborated in verification and confidentiality annexes of the Convention. As will be explained below, the problems emerged later as those concepts were implemented. In response to pressure from some States, the Conference of States Parties and the Executive Council watered down those concepts by elaborating rules, regulations and guidelines that would restrict the access of inspectors to sites and relevant information.

The prohibitions of the CWC are comprehensive in scope, in that they cover all toxic chemicals that could be used for hostile purposes. However, the reporting and routine verification requirements in the chemical field are mainly focused on the three schedules of chemicals contained in the Convention. Facilities that produce declarable quantities of other 'discrete organic chemicals' are also reported and inspected on a qualified random-selection basis. Thus, the verification system may monitor the possible exploitation of facilities manufacturing such unscheduled chemicals for the clandestine production of Schedule 1 and other toxic chemicals for warfare purposes. According to the General Purpose Criterion (GPC), any toxic chemical (including its precursors) is considered a warfare agent, except when it is intended for non-prohibited purposes. The type and quantity of that chemical may help to indicate the intended purposes.

Besides the issues of erosion of commitments and restriction of regime boundaries, the CWC system has been plagued by other problems that have placed limitations on the prospects for full and effective verification. Procrastination by States has been a major problem. Many States (including the US) were late in submitting their initial declarations – incomplete reporting was another problem. The high ratio of both incomplete and inaccurate declarations has thus delayed completion of the initial phase of verification of chemical stockpiles and chemical industry facilities. Initially, this backup has caused an untidy overlap with the next phase and pushed off a full-scale launching of routine inspections across the board.

Finally, as regards management, the lack of adequate financial resources due to defaults in assessed contributions and usual delays in the reimbursement of the cost for verifying the destruction operations have had a serious impact on the scope and timeliness of the verification process, and have even threatened the solvency of the organization.

Inspections at work

The general approach taken during on-site inspections is that of impartial fact-finding in accordance with an inspection mandate drawn up by the Director General for the inspection team. During the first five years after entry into force of the CWC, the inspectorate conducted over 1,300 on-site inspections in 51 States, comprising initial and routine inspections, monitoring of chemical destruction activities and verification at civilian facilities. Eighteen of those States had declared present or past chemical-weapon-related facilities.[15] This is a good beginning but far below what was envisaged when optimistic guidelines were elaborated in the verification instruments.

The rights and responsibilities of inspectors and host States are stipulated in the Verification Annex of the Convention and subsequently elaborated in the rules and regulations approved by the Executive Council. They are specified for each State in the set of Facility Agreements concluded between that State and the OPCW upon the completion of the initial inspections. For the performance of their mandated operations, inspectors are granted privileges and immunities in accordance with the Vienna Convention on Diplomatic Relations. They are designated as inspectors subject to prior acceptance by a host State, which has the right initially to reject particular individuals, or subsequently withdraw its acceptance, except when they are about to embark on an inspection. A host State is required to grant inspectors multiple entry visas and exemption for customs duties.

However, inspectors are obliged to respect the laws and regulations of the host State, especially its safety regulations, without prejudice to the privileges and immunities necessary to fulfil their inspection mandate. Although inspectors have the right of 'unimpeded access' and can select items for inspection, the host State has the right to object to a request on the grounds that it goes beyond the purposes of the Convention. A host State is required to respect the inviolability of the premises, papers, records, approved equipment and samples of inspectors. It is also required to cooperate in every way possible, particularly by facilitating interviews with personnel, inspection of records and documents, and sample-taking for analysis at the site or elsewhere at approved laboratories.

Some of the rights of inspectors have been eroded in practice by restrictive interpretations made by the governing bodies or by precedent-setting unilateral exemptions claimed by the United States. In ratifying the Convention the US Congress had approved three damaging exemptions: (a) the US President was authorized to refuse an on-site challenge inspection on the grounds that it could 'pose a threat' to national security; (b) samples collected during an inspection may be analyzed locally but could not be taken to foreign laboratories; (c) the number of industrial facilities required to declare mixtures of scheduled chemicals was narrowed.[16]

The dilution of inspector rights by the Conference of States Parties itself has also taken its toll. This involves the central issue of the inviolability of inspectors' equipment, notebooks, samples and other relevant information. For example, the Conference has permitted States to use their discretion in applying their own health and safety regulations and, if they preferred, to utilize their own environmental detectors to the exclusion of authorized devices brought by the inspectors. Secondly, if host officials claim that the inspectors had recorded information unrelated to the Convention, they can now have it deleted and may even confiscate the equipment. Thirdly, although the CWC required inspectors to provide the host State only with their preliminary findings before they left the site, along with a list of any samples, documents and other data, the Conference now permits host officials to copy all of the raw information recorded in the inspector notebooks, computers and cameras. The decisions on these issues have thus imposed new restrictions on inspections as they do tilt the balance between the rights of inspectors and the rights of host States in favour of the latter.[17]

In practice, the consequences of these restrictions have so far been modest but assessment of the full impact will require a longer period of experience. We will now focus on how the different types of inspection have been applied during the first seven years of operation.

Initial inspections and facility agreements

The baseline for future routine and challenge inspections is established after extensive initial inspections to verify the comprehensive data submitted by States in their initial declarations of all items covered by the Convention. These include all chemical weapons and related production facilities, including decommissioned ones; all industrial chemicals corresponding to the lists in Schedules 1, 2 and 3 and the related facilities, and any other activities relevant to the Convention that involve the production of unscheduled 'discrete organic chemicals' (UDOC). The specific purpose is to validate the submitted data and obtain any missing information to ensure the completeness and accuracy of the declaration.

It is on that basis that the inspectors can draw up an initial coherent picture of all existing chemical activities within a State and all relevant transactions between States. The end product of the initial inspections is the negotiation of a number of Facility Agreements for each country to regulate future verification activities.

Most of the inspectors' time is devoted to correlating the declarations on types and quantities of chemical agents with the data observed or collected on-site in order to identify those sites and activities that may pose higher risks. An important aspect of the operation is to assemble comprehensive information on weapons-related items in order to establish for each commercial facility quantitative thresholds for annual data declarations and for routine inspections. As regards chemical weapons, the information to be verified comprises: first, the aggregate quantity of each toxic chemical, associated munitions and other relevant equipment; second, detailed data on each facility for weapons production, storage and destruction; third, data on decommissioned or abandoned chemical weapons or production facilities; and, fourth, information on any commercial site that had previously been involved in weapons production. The inspections assist in preparing plans for verified destruction of stockpiles and the dismantlement of facilities without delay. The initial verification of peaceful activities is done along the following lines:

- *Warfare agents*: All the stocks of highly-toxic chemicals that are retained at declarable Schedule 1 production facilities for research, protective purposes, medicines and other legitimate uses must be verified by an initial inspection. Any facility producing more than 100 grams of such agents is subject to inspection. The task of the initial inspection is to ensure that the facility complies with restrictions set out in the Convention, and that the aggregate annual amount of such chemicals produced by the State (and acquired from dismantled weapons) remains within the limit of one metric ton. Another aim of initial inspection is to prepare the facility agreement for future inspections.
- *Industrial chemicals*: Verification of industrial chemicals is done according to thresholds of annual production set for each category. For Schedule 2 chemicals, the inspection thresholds per facility range from 10 kilograms to 10 metric tons (ten times the reportable thresholds). For Schedule 3 chemicals, the corresponding inspection threshold for each facility is 200 tons per year. Unscheduled discrete organic chemicals are treated similarly to Schedule 3 chemicals when

they contain any of the building blocks for chemical weapons – phosphorus, sulphur or fluorine (PSF).

The delay problem has greatly affected the phase of initial inspections. It was largely due to the failure of most States to submit timely, accurate and complete initial declarations. Although States were required to submit declarations not later than a month after becoming parties, it took months and, in some cases, years for them to do so, thus delaying onset of initial inspections to establish arrangements for routine verification. Moreover, the burden on the inspectors was increased by the lack of a standard model for State declarations, which magnified the task of clarifying inconsistencies and of completing the baseline information. In many countries, this has resulted in numerous unresolved issues as regards permitted industrial activities.

Routine inspection of disarmament

So far the main achievement of the OPCW has been in the area of verified destruction of chemical weapons. Under the Convention all possessors of chemical weapons are required to achieve verified destruction of their stockpiles and associated facilities within ten years, and to reach the 20 per cent benchmark five years after entry into force. The magnitude of the verification task is formidable: to monitor the destruction of over 72,000 metric tons of chemical-weapons stockpiles and related facilities (US, 31,000 tons; Russia, 40,000 tons; others, about 1,000 tons). However, by the 2002 deadline, it was possible to destroy only 11.2 per cent of the aggregate stockpile, the bulk of which belonged to the US, the only party that has now almost met its quota. Russia was unable even to start, due to economic hardships, as was Albania. India, Libya and South Korea have started destruction and are on track. Libya has destroyed unfilled munitions, but may need assistance when it comes to destroying its stockpiles of agents. These delays have made it necessary to extend the overall completion deadline for some States, in certain cases by as many as five years, thus pushing it from 2007 to 2012.

This uneven progress has serious implications for the inspection system. The sudden US progress after a long initial delay in processing its national legislation has sucked in disproportionate inspection resources into the comparatively large number of CW destruction facilities readily available in the US. Two-thirds of all inspections of the new organization have been dedicated to a systematic verification of the US weapons-destruction programme. Only one-third of the resources could then be devoted to the civilian sector of State parties, with heavy emphasis on the chemical industries of European Union States, China, India, Japan, Russia, as well as the US. A timely commencement of the US destruction programme would have spread the task over a longer period permitting a more balanced and equitable distribution of inspection missions. The first problem then is how to reorder priorities so that balanced progress can be made in both the military and civilian sectors, in a manner that is fair to all inspected States.

The monitoring of chemical destruction also raises a serious financial problem. Even though a part of the verification costs of destruction is chargeable to the possessor States, timely reimbursement of expenses has been lacking. Furthermore the formula adopted for this reimbursement is such that the OPCW ends up bearing as much as 60 per cent of the actual costs. This had a major impact on the financial resources of the OPCW that are available for all other inspections. Unless this problem is solved, the capacity to increase inspections in the chemical industry might not improve, and might even decline as disarmament monitoring intensifies in other CW posessor-States, especially Russia.

The monitoring of disarmament is as complex as it is costly. Upon verifying the declared weapon stockpiles and facilities for production, storage and other related activities, inspectors must first ensure that production is halted and that all facilities are sealed. These are subjected to continuous instrumental monitoring and periodic inspections until the phased destruction is completed under international supervision. Another component of the weapons-related verification is focused on monitoring the conversion to peaceful uses of former chemical weapons production facilities, as well as inspecting previously converted ones.

Routine inspection of peaceful facilities

The magnitude of the task of routine inspections in the chemical industry of State parties is enormous but can be managed in a strategic manner to provide reasonable assurance of the non-diversion of scheduled and other chemicals to weapons. The First Review Conference of the Convention has confirmed that, during the first five years, all facilities containing Schedule 1 chemicals have been initially inspected and that routine inspections of other scheduled chemicals were well under way. However, it also confirmed that this was achieved without a systematic plan to ensure a coherent approach to verify the absence of chemical warfare agents at inspected sites. There is still a need to finalize guidelines on the optimal frequency and intensity of inspections in each category of declared chemicals, and to mobilize and distribute resources equitably across the board to deter proliferation, even as progress is being made on the disarmament aspect.[18]

The declared Schedule 1 chemical warfare agents pose the least problem, as they are small in volume, restricted to a few small-scale facilities and subjected to intensive short-notice inspections. Indeed, as long as the declared quantities are accounted for, the diversion potential in those facilities is minimal. The potential of a breakout to produce illicit warfare agents resides rather in the chemical industry as a whole, stemming from the Schedules 2 and 3 chemicals and the broader field of unscheduled chemicals when potentially 'CW capable' facilities are involved in the production.

As regards modalities, while the Schedule 2 chemicals require no more than two long annual inspections per site, the less risky Schedule 3 chemicals are subject to shorter inspections in a relatively few selected facilities. The selection is done randomly, using weighting factors to ensure a fair distribution and to minimize inconvenience and cost. Other facilities dealing with unscheduled chemicals including those producing organic chemicals containing atoms of phosphorus, sulphur and fluorine are inspected on a similar basis as facilities for Schedule 3 chemicals. In most cases inspectors are satisfied about compliance by just reviewing the documentation and plant records, interviewing facility personnel and conducting visual observation–inspection of plant equipment, pipe-work, storage and processing areas and waste disposal areas and facilities. It is only if they discover inconsistencies with the annual declarations that they resort to more intrusive methods involving measurements and sampling, followed by analysis at the site or elsewhere in order to clarify whether any controlled chemicals have being diverted or whether undeclared scheduled chemicals have been produced.

Routine inspections in the chemical industry had a good start in many countries, with the active cooperation of private commercial facilities. However, late in 2000 when the US welcomed inspections to industrial facilities, it insisted on a narrow interpretation of the term 'plant site', with a possible threat to the scope of access permitted to inspectors. For the first time it challenged the general understanding about the Convention's guarantees of 'unimpeded access' to the entire declared plant site to verify the absence of chemical warfare agents. The issue was whether inspectors may have automatic access to all facilities within a Schedule 2 plant site or, initially, only to designated parts of the larger plant. The US would grant broader access only after inspectors had identified a specific 'ambiguity' from a preliminary inspection activity at the designated sites. The wider inspection would then be conducted under procedures of 'managed access', involving precautionary measures by a State to protect national security information and trade secrets by limiting or controlling access to specific areas, items and documentation considered sensitive or unrelated to the purpose of the inspection. Access is negotiated between the inspection team and the representatives of the State party.

Those procedures were indeed not designed for routine inspections but were elaborated in the verification annex for challenge inspections and foreseen as legitimate procedures for escorted access to those parts of a plant site beyond the boundaries of the declared plant. It is disturbing that other countries are following suit by imposing similar restrictions of this questionable practice regarding the perimeter of the plant site.[19]

The random inspections of Schedule 3 chemicals and other discrete organic chemicals, including those containing some weapons-relevant elements (PFC plants) has so far not caused any serious problems. However, there are some technical issues yet to be fully tested. The method of selection and the nature of inspections at industrial facilities carry a potential for disagreement. It is the OPCW verification division that selects the sites for inspection on the basis of equitable weighting of factors such as geographical distribution, characteristics of the site and the nature of the activities. Industry officials often maintain that a review of the published report of annual output followed by a 'walk-through' or 'talk-through' tour should be sufficient to show that no Schedule 1 chemicals are being produced. However, inspectors need more detailed documentation and access to undeclared parts of a facility to have more confidence in their findings. Moreover, to maximize the short duration of the inspections, the 24-hour limit should permit a breakdown in segments to stretch the period in accordance with working hours – say, eight-hour segments over two or three days – rather than requiring continuous inspections as some hosts have demanded.[20]

Issue of challenge inspections

No challenge inspection has so far been undertaken to verify any suspected weapons activities at declared or non-declared facilities of a State. The focus of attention of the OPCW has been on the development of procedures and the preparation of staff. Mock exercises have, however, been taken in a number of countries to test and improve the system. The main characteristics of challenge inspection are: (a) prompt launching of an operation by the Director General, after a request by a challenging State, unless it is blocked by the Executive Council within 12 hours on grounds of frivolity, abuse or irrelevance of the request; (b) strict timelines with short-notice arrival by inspectors and access for them 'anywhere without delay'; (c) procedures of managed access to sensitive areas by balancing the need for intrusive methods against the need for protecting unrelated confidential information; and (d) urgent completion of the operation (within eight days) with a report to the Executive Council to consider any necessary compliance measures.[21]

Challenge inspections are generally regarded as a method of last resort and have been described as a 'safety net' underneath the monitoring system, coping with three potential problems: deterring the abuse of declared activities; deterring prohibited activities at undeclared sites; and enabling States to demonstrate that the suspicions are unfounded. In case the mechanism is abused by a State party, the challenging State would be held accountable for the charges.[22] The greatest potential use for such inspections is in the wide area of unscheduled chemicals, which is a fertile ground for risky scientific advances while being subject to minimum international control. Yet this is also an area where a challenging State would have the greatest difficulty in obtaining credible information on possible non-compliance. The reluctance of State Parties to resort to this mechanism even as some of them make unsubstantiated public accusations about other States (e.g. by the US about Iran) may tend to marginalize this useful tool and weaken the whole verification system. Even though a challenge inspection may not discover a 'smoking gun', it may still reveal a pattern of anomalies or discrepancies in a State that may indicate cheating. It is thus worth applying, even if rarely, as the IAEA has done with its special inspection procedures.

Challenges and possibilities

Although the history of CWC verification is relatively short we may still draw some useful lessons on the strengths and weaknesses of the inspection system as it faces present-day challenges. We will do so in terms of the issues presented in the model of on-site inspection described at the beginning of this chapter: power and authority; access and sovereignty; management and resources; and recourse to non-compliance.

There were high expectations for the CWC verification system when the convention entered into force on 29 April 1997. This was so not only because of its completeness as a regime, both as regards its near-universal membership and its comprehensive coverage of the chemical field, but also because of the unprecedented convergence of post-Cold War disarmament policies of States. The Convention's provisions and the annexes on verification and confidentiality provided an elaborate and balanced legal framework, with considerable power and authority for inspectors. With the subsequent changes in US foreign policy and the erosion of its multilateral commitments, it became difficult to sustain the high benchmarks set for the inspectorate.

The greatest challenge for the OPCW has thus been the shift in US disarmament policy from one of leadership advocating effective international verification to a unilateralist defensive approach that would restrict inspections. The US was not alone in its effort to weaken inspections, but was the most influential in the governing bodies where the industrial States watered down the agreed principles of access to sites and to all the relevant information on grounds of national security or commercial interests. However, despite such erosion of the powers of inspectors, the impact on at least the monitoring of the disarmament segment of the mandate seems to have been minimal. As the bulk of that process was conducted in the US, initial confrontations with host country officials did not deter significant achievements. The problem for the future might be more in the civilian sector where the inspection procedures as elaborated might prove inadequate to cope with a determined violator. It is, of course, within the authority of the governing bodies to reverse the decisions that have been taken and strengthen the verification system as it is tested more fully in suspicious cases.

Besides the challenge posed by policy shifts, the OPCW has to cope with the difficult task of determining when dual-use chemicals are deemed to pose a proliferation threat. The General Purpose Criterion focuses on the intended end-use of the chemicals rather than on the presence of specific agents or technologies. The effort of inspectors is geared to resolving inconsistencies or anomalies by assembling and analyzing as much information as possible on chemical inventories and activities. Since only six States have declared chemical weapons stockpiles, inspectors need to determine whether more States should have declared weapons or warfare agents that would place them in the category of former chemical-weapon possessors. Inspectors also need to have a full picture of the scientific advances in chemical research and in the chemical industry for signs of proliferation threats at the outer limits.

To ensure credible reports on compliance or non-compliance in doubtful cases, the inspectorate needs to exercise the full extent of the inspection rights, especially as regards 'unrestricted access' to entire plants, the inviolability of inspector equipment and information, with safeguards against an abuse of the confidentiality provisions.

Management challenges have also been considerable. Given the monumental task of the initial years, inspection management has on the whole been adequately efficient, with ups and downs caused largely by pressures from Member States. The designation of the Secretariat as 'technical' had removed from the OPCW Director General's mandate the broader aspects of authority as enjoyed by the Director General of the IAEA. Efforts by the first OPCW Director General, José Bustani, to exercise political discretion to promote universality of membership, for example by encouraging Saddam Hussein's Iraq to accede, fatally conflicted with the policies of the Bush Administration. Even his justified efforts to strengthen the credibility and independence of the Secretariat, by improving the remuneration and other conditions of service of his staff, tended to aggravate the divisive friction. At the same time, the OPCW found itself in the midst of a financial crisis that led to significant cuts in programme delivery. For months the crisis had paralyzed the organization and set back its inspection efforts that were already way behind schedule. Although the crisis was eventually resolved in the governing bodies by replacing the Director General, the new leadership has for now to operate cautiously within boundaries defined painfully by the recent experience.

Finally, ambitious deadlines and costly operations have posed the challenge of underestimation of the verification mandate under the CWC. As shown above, the ten-year time-frame for the verified destruction of all chemical weapons and associated facilities is too short, if an adequate simultaneous monitoring of the chemical industry is to be ensured and an allowance to be made for delays in national legislation to implement the Convention. The heavy cost of chemical destruction has also had an impact on the extent and pace of the inspections. Whenever reimbursements of funds advanced for monitoring chemical destruction were delayed the industrial inspections were bound to feel the impact. Achieving balanced progress in both the disarmament and non-proliferation segments of the regime requires a plan not only for more financial resources but also for considerable budgetary reform, including possibly a separation of the funds for verification of disarmament and non-proliferation. In the meantime, the recommendations of the First Review Conference of States Parties need to be promptly implemented with respect to the adjustment of priorities and the broader and more equitable distribution of inspection operations. It would be ironic if chemical warfare agents remained concealed or newly-discovered agents escaped detection for lack of fuller deployment of inspections even as major strides were being made in the monitored destruction of declared chemical weapons.

Conclusion

The verification systems of the IAEA, the CTBTO and the OPCW share similarities in their broad objectives of confidence-building and deterrence by assuring members that rigorous inspection would detect non-compliance. They are up against various constraints and sometimes defiance by States, both internal and external to the treaty regime. These constraints pose major challenges to the effectiveness and reliability of the verification operations. In the nuclear and chemical fields, these organizations have the dual mandate: to verify the completeness and correctness of vast declared information on peaceful activities and on any relevant events; and to detect any concealed activities in violation of the non-proliferation and disarmament obligations of Member States. The concepts and methods employed are basically similar while differing in their scope and complexity, depending on the nature of the treaty obligations, the negotiating history and the inspection experience.

In the nuclear field, the IAEA safeguards process was the first to evolve incrementally from modest Statute beginnings to a robust verification system. The nuclear non-proliferation regime is now supplemented by a technology-intensive verification system of the CTBT, a product of three decades of negotiation. However, there still remain fundamental gaps and loopholes in the regime, which tend to diminish the combined effectiveness of the IAEA and the CTBT verification capabilities. At least three major problems can be identified. The most intractable is the lack of universality of membership, essentially because of the boycott by India, Pakistan and Israel of both the NPT and the CTBT. The second problem concerns the reversal in US nuclear policy: its failure to ratify the CTBT, its reluctance to advance disarmament negotiations and its tendency to apply double standards based on selective threat assessment. The third problem is the failure to conclude a fissile material cut-off treaty. The world is already awash in fissile material and is increasingly threatened by the possible consequences of illicit trafficking in such material.

The current verification issues faced by nuclear inspectors in North Korea and Iran demonstrate the negative impact of most of these regime problems, especially the aspect about nuclear trafficking, on the capacity and effectiveness of on-site inspections. The lessons from an only recently cooperative Libya can now be put to good use.

The chemical field poses fewer problems. The ban on chemical weapons is a virtually complete post-Cold War regime, with state-of-the-art concepts and procedures of verification resulting from decades of negotiation. The concept of challenge inspections, as adapted from the bilateral INF model, is far-reaching but needs to be tested in an international setting. Compared with verification problems in the incomplete and fragmented nuclear non-proliferation regime the inspection challenges for the chemical ban regime seem to be less formidable. They have to do mainly with the subsequent erosion of inspection authority as State parties interpreted the provisions of the Convention in elaborating operational procedures. The absence of North Korea and some key Middle Eastern countries from the OPCW diminishes the universality of the Organization. Operationally, however, the US tendency to apply double-standards is perhaps more damaging, particularly its decision to secure precedent-setting exceptions for itself while expecting other States to allow greater access to inspectors. Although all transfers and trade in declarable chemicals is subject to OPCW monitoring within a State, there is not yet a universal mechanism transcending group arrangements to prevent illicit trafficking in warfare agents. This defect has therefore had some impact on the effectiveness of on-site inspections in detecting concealed violations.

The detection of prohibited materials and activities is the common goal of the nuclear and chemical regimes for which the most intrusive and intensive procedures are activated by the three organizations. The special inspections authorized by the Director General of the IAEA are not so difficult to initiate. In the context of the strengthened safeguards, the new procedures have now a better prospect of discovering undeclared activities, particularly at the upper end of the fuel cycle where weaponization of enriched uranium and plutonium is within reach. In the CTBTO and the OPCW, requests for challenge inspections are within the domain of State parties. They are expected to be relatively easy to initiate once a State manages the difficult task of assembling credible evidence to justify its request and decides to proceed with the inspection request. There is insufficient experience to judge conclusively about the relative merits of the two types of special measures. The IAEA has used some leverage from its capacity to mount special inspections; the probability of such action enhances the authority of the Director General. Indeed, special inspections were attempted in North Korea, the blockage of which enabled the IAEA to establish an important precedent. There, denial of access induced the full application of non-compliance procedures all the way to the Security Council. The OPCW, however, has not yet launched a challenge inspection, despite some public allegations of non-compliance that have fallen short of a request for action. A case in point is the occasional US charge against Iran, which has never been followed by a request for challenge inspection, nor by a formal request for clarification through the Executive Council. There is some concern that such inaction may degrade the value of this measure as a usable tool and may deny the suspected State a chance to disprove the allegations. For the CTBTO this is not yet an issue, as the treaty is yet to enter into force.

Accounting for the strictly peaceful application of dual-use items constitutes the bulk of the work of the inspectorates at the IAEA and the OPCW. A common challenge for both fields is the advance of science and technology in the vast nuclear and chemical industries and the ingenuity of some determined proliferators to deceive by concealing illicit activities under legitimate ones. Inspection procedures and technologies need to keep up with the requirement for flexibility and adaptation to change. This approach calls for reviewing the validity of criteria for selecting sites for routine inspections and for greater randomness in the selection of sites outside designated locations. Technological advances in detection technology such as environmental sampling and remote sensing and imagery do enhance detection while also reducing the need for large human presence. However, only greater transparency by inspected States through greater opportunities for physical access to entire sites, for sampling operations and for interviews with personnel can be expected to remove inconsistencies. The recent case of Libya has set a positive model of transparency where adequate access was given to the inspectorates of both the IAEA and the OPCW. Another benefit from this case is the revelation about the role of rogue nuclear scientists in Pakistan, and possibly elsewhere, as proliferators of weapons technology to Libya, Iran, North Korea and probably to other countries. Libyan cooperation has provided leads that IAEA inspectors can utilize in investigating other countries subject to safeguards where similar illicit activities may have taken place. We may also be aware that the shady network of illicit nuclear trafficking may well overlap with that of warfare agents. The problem may call for a coordinated approach by the IAEA and the OPCW.

The effectiveness of verification in the three organizations depends heavily on the leadership of the Director General, and the integrity and independence of the inspectorate. It also depends on the efficient management of the inspections, which involves a balancing act – to meet the high expectations from on-site inspections with the increasingly limited resources available to them. Often, the inspectorates of the IAEA and the OPCW operate without the full benefit of all the assets provided for them in the agreed procedures, especially as regards, legal authority and rules for access and transparency. This occurs when an inspected State insists on its own interpretation of sovereignty rights and confidentiality needs. In situations of proliferation, cases of full cooperation and transparency such as South Africa and Libya are the exception rather than the rule. It has thus been necessary for the inspectorate to compensate for any diminution of access rights by imaginative and flexible management, combining the various components of on-site inspection to minimize intrusiveness while achieving optimal results.

The common objective of the three organizations is to assemble and analyze all relevant information in order to conclude reliably whether a State is or is not complying with its treaty obligations. This task is perhaps easier for the CTBTO that relies mostly on technological monitoring, with challenge inspections as a last resort. For the IAEA and the OPCW, the management of verification is more complex, involving a combination of issues: (i) priority-setting for better allocation of inspection resources between high-risk and low-risk facilities; (ii) planning for inspections with adequate coverage and intrusiveness; (iii) optimizing the combination of human and technology assets for such inspections; (iv) ensuring efficient and cost-effective management of operations; and (v) reporting findings with thoroughness, objectivity and impartiality.

The issue of priority-setting and resource allocation is a greater challenge for the OPCW than for the IAEA, which has a longer history of pragmatic adjustments in personnel and technological resources within the limitations of a virtually flat (zero real-growth) budget. The former is yet to meet the challenge of dismantling chemical weapons and facilities within set deadlines without unduly diminishing the resources available for routine inspection of the chemical industry. Both also face the challenge of balancing between, on the one hand, routine inspections in the vast area of declared facilities to build confidence about compliance, and on the other, inspections focusing on detection of possible undeclared facilities where a higher risk of illicit activities may exist to cause compliance concerns. As will be elaborated in Chapter 9 an additional challenge for the OPCW is to manage its policy of limiting service time of its professional staff (including inspectors and most verification personnel) to a maximum of seven years, leading to an annual turnover of some 15 per cent.

The issue of an adequate operational plan for each inspection is important in setting the basis for meaningful findings. The operational mandate determines the technical objective of the mission, the size and composition of the inspection team, the scope and level of intrusiveness required and the precautions to respect legitimate sovereignty rights. The IAEA has progressively fine-tuned its missions to establish an adequate system which is paying dividends in difficult current cases such as Iran. The OPCW is yet to overcome the challenge from the US and some other States to its effort to ensure sound operational plans, which must include the unrestricted use of designated equipment, the inviolability of information gathered by inspectors and the unrestricted access to entire plant sites. Inspectorates should be given much leeway in judging the level of intrusiveness required for their task strictly in terms of technical necessity. The solution is not to regulate access by acquiescing inappropriately to the procedures of managed access but rather to keep the integrity of the system. As the different elements of on-site inspection are mutually supportive, fuller access to documentation and to interviews with plant officials may narrow down the questions that may require clarification by extensive physical inspection and sample analysis. This understanding may, in practice, help persuade States to refrain from tendencies to impose unnecessary restrictions.

The optimal combination of human and technological assets is a dynamic issue that benefits from innovations; it can enhance transparency while alleviating the necessity for intrusiveness. Technological innovations help also with cost-effectiveness, as greater reliance on state-of-the-art techniques for remote sensing, environmental monitoring, and sample analysis may keep the more expensive and intrusive human inspections to a minimum.

The positive experience of the IAEA offers useful lessons and may serve as a standard for evaluating the cost-effectiveness of on-site inspections for the elimination of weapons of mass destruction.

Part III

How to Make the Regime Effective

Part III will focus on possible ways to stem the erosion threatening each verification system and close any existing loopholes as a foundation for further building the broader regime for the elimination of weapons of mass destruction. The following chapters will first address the main compliance issues and assess the available recourse measures, and then focus on the broader political and security issues in repairing and further developing the regime, as well as on the specific issues in enhancing the management of the regime.

7
Compliance Issues and Recourse

We have earlier explained that verification is a means to determine whether a State is complying with its disarmament or non-proliferation obligations under a particular agreement. Compliance issues are, therefore, our first area for specific attention. Compliance measures become necessary only if the verification process detects significant violations. They result from a thorough evaluation of information at different stages: the analysis of information from declarations and other sources, from ongoing technical monitoring, from import/export monitoring and, ultimately, from on-site inspections.

Tightening of compliance measures

A compliance process enables parties to address all types of compliance issues and to recommend remedial action. It should enable organizations to:

(a) distinguish genuine allegations of non-compliance from politically motivated false information;
(b) differentiate between technical and substantive non-compliance, which often corresponds to minor versus significant non-compliance;
(c) determine whether non-compliance has actually occurred; and
(d) determine whether the non-compliance is deliberate or unintentional.

The processes employed by the IAEA, the CTBTO and the OPCW are meant to ensure that minor violations, ambiguous situations, unfounded suspicions and frivolous allegations are sorted out in consultations so as not to escalate to major political issues. The goal of the system is to take firm and effective action against any significant violations. Seen in hierarchical terms, the combined process should help to discard false allegations, remedy minor infractions, and remove technical or procedural obstacles in order to focus on any substantive problems.[1]

The verification and compliance processes are mutually reinforcing. Together they may give States confidence about the continued commitment of other States to fulfil their obligations. A system that combines effective verification with a credible compliance process may not only maintain a robust regime but may also provide hesitant States with an incentive to join the treaty. The importance of compliance measures can thus hardly be overestimated.

At the outset we need to stress that the concept of compliance relates to two factors: the nature of the commitment requiring compliance and the level of cooperation from the State concerned. By combining these factors we may classify violations into technical and substantive non-compliance since they would require different types of response. Technical non-compliance occurs when a State demonstrates a commitment to the objectives of the treaty but for some reason fails to implement its obligations as prescribed. The reason may be lack of technical or financial resources or may be bureaucratic obstacles. Substantive non-compliance occurs when a State seeks to deceive by providing false documentation, concealing an illicit programme, obstructing verification, or otherwise circumventing the spirit of the treaty. A State may appear to be technically compliant while acting in a manner that undermines the goals of the treaty.[2] In this regard, it is instructive to refer to the experience of the IAEA and UNMOVIC preceding the US-led invasion of Iraq in 2003. The executive heads of both institutions, IAEA's Director General Mohamed ElBaradei and UNMOVIC Executive Chairman Hans Blix, combined the two dimensions in stressing the significant distinction between procedural or technical compliance and substantive compliance. The operative terms they used were 'cooperation on process' as against 'cooperation on substance'.

They both reported to the Security Council that Iraq's response to the intrusive verification efforts under Resolution 1441 was to acquiesce passively instead of cooperate actively. The cooperation was satisfactory as regards process. Iraq was technically in compliance since it had restored the inspection infrastructure and was providing access to requested sites, although not very helpful in facilitating private interviews with its officials. The major substantive problem was its persistence in withholding some significant information on its prohibited weapons, and its deception about the fate of the rest of its chemical, biological and missiles programmes. The precision and objectivity of the approach used was unsurpassed as a model for deciphering levels of non-compliance in international verification. The arrangement succeeded in presenting clear findings for appropriate action by the Security Council.[3]

How are non-compliance issues handled by the three organizations, and how effectively? We need to distinguish between the practice regarding technical non-compliance that weakens the verification system, and substantive non-compliance, ranging from sustained non-cooperation to violations amounting to 'material breach' of the treaty. The final question is: how effective are the remedies in the latter cases?

In multilateral agreements, compliance issues are handled by the executive bodies that oversee implementation of the treaty as a whole. It is the responsibility of the Executive Councils of the CWC and the CTBT and the Board of Governors of the IAEA. In the case of the IAEA, the statutory mandate was enhanced by a special mandate from the NPT and from regional arrangements applicable to nuclear-weapon-free zones. At the OPCW and the CTBTO, the Conference of States Parties becomes involved if the Executive Council is unable to agree about the existence of a significant violation, or if the problem is considered so politically important that the views of all the parties should be sought. In all three organizations, after all the internal processes have been tried, any obstacle to resolving the compliance problem is brought to the attention of the United Nations. In the case of the IAEA and the OPCW, both the Security Council and the General Assembly are explicitly mentioned as the organs to receive a report on the crisis.

Handling technical non-compliance

Once a State has ratified the treaty, it may be held responsible for two types of technical non-compliance: a failure to meet deadlines for various aspects of treaty implementation and a failure to cooperate fully with the preparation and conduct of verification missions.

Technically, the first type involves the failure to meet reporting and notification deadlines, but it may reflect domestic problems causing neglect, or delays in the national processes to implement treaty provisions. The IAEA has a long-standing problem from the failure of over 40 NPT parties to conclude the required safeguards agreement. But since these are mostly small States with little or no nuclear material, the impact has not been serious. The OPCW faces more serious problems since many States have missed important deadlines: on the adoption of implementing legislation and the establishment of a national authority to coordinate operations; on the designation of points of entry and exit for inspection teams; and on making arrangements for diplomatic clearance for inspectors. Progress is being made but the delays may still affect the pace and smooth functioning of inspections. Evidently, non-compliance is not an issue with respect to States that have signed but not yet ratified the CTBT or the Additional Protocol to the Safeguards Agreements of the IAEA because they have not yet made a legal commitment. However, the remedies are similar: a redoubling of effort by the governing bodies and secretariats to persuade governments to complete the legal process.

Technical non-compliance that bears directly on the verification process may slide into a substantive one, depending on the degree of transparency and cooperation permitted by the inspected State. For example, as regards initial declarations, missing deadlines or the failure to provide full information may be due to technical problems or to differing of interpretations about the requirements. In such cases remedies may be found through consultations, clarifications or practical assistance from the secretariats. The role of the Director General is important in the first instance, as supported by the governing body, which provides a forum for helpful diplomatic initiatives. Most of the cases at the IAEA and the OPCW are handled successfully in this manner. However, as the cases of Iraq, North Korea and now Iran have shown, the problem can become one of substantive non-compliance, if the reporting State shows signs of stonewalling, deliberate omission of important information or posing other obstacles to verification.

The risk of escalation should be a warning against underestimating the issues of technical compliance. Indeed, persistent disagreement between the verification organization and a State party may signal the possibility of a serious breach of treaty obligations. The governing bodies should therefore pay attention to any process-related problems highlighted in the inspection reports in order to seek early remedies through diplomacy.

Handling substantive non-compliance

In the preceding chapter, we analyzed the extensive experience of the IAEA on compliance issues regarding Iraq, North Korea, Libya and Iran. The first two involved serious cases of non-compliance that the IAEA managed to detect, without however being able to resolve them. In Iraq, because of the combination of Security Council sanctions and an effective inspection/disarmament regime, success was within sight when it was thwarted by a preemptive US military action. North Korea was a case of effective *ad hoc* inspections that showed a significant contradiction between facts as declared and the evidence from sampling. When North Korea blocked any possibility of special inspections to confirm the evidence, the case was brought to the Security Council, which was unable to take effective action. Without a credible threat of sanctions, the Council allowed itself to be sidelined by an initially promising but ultimately counterproductive bilateral arrangement between the US and North Korea.

By contrast, Libya was a case where international inspections had no role in the discovery of deception and concealment, but became an essential instrument in reversing the state of non-compliance. The discovery of Libya's illicit nuclear trafficking was made by US interception of shipping, made under President Bush's Preventive Security Initiative. A combination of factors facilitated Libya's full cooperation: the impact of the long-standing economic sanctions by the Security Council and the embarrassment of the discovery at a time when progress was being made towards normalization of relations encouraged by British diplomatic initiatives. Libya's admission in all areas of its clandestine programme, and its grant of unrestricted access to IAEA and OPCW inspectors, have set a high standard of cooperation for any non-compliant State. Iran is presently falling short of this standard.

The Iran case is one of incomplete declaration of facts over a long period of time. By withholding significant information on declarable nuclear material, enrichment technologies and associated facilities, Iran has committed acts of concealment that constitute substantive non-compliance. At present, the challenge for the IAEA is to secure the abandonment by Iran of its current proliferation policy and proceed towards full cooperation with IAEA. The OPCW has so far managed to cope with many cases of technical non-compliance. A notable example is the Russian failure to begin destroying its chemical arsenals on schedule for lack of funds and perhaps also lack of priority. Russia is now a few years behind schedule and has negotiated an extension from the OPCW.[4]

Of similar nature is the three-year delay in implementation legislation by the US. But there are also more serious issues concerning the two powers.

The US has adopted legislation to exempt itself from some of the verification requirements of the Convention. The exceptions, which go to the core of the verification regime, are: granting the President the right to refuse on-site inspections on grounds of 'national security'; preventing samples collected by inspectors from leaving US territory; and narrowing the number of industry facilities required to report chemical solutions containing scheduled agents.[5]

The issue should not be underestimated. Perhaps it should not be condoned but regarded as a form of substantive non-compliance and be subjected to resolution by consultation within the governing bodies of the organization.

As regards Russia, there has been some speculation that the actual size of its chemical arsenals might be larger than what it declared. Several experts have also expressed suspicion that it is engaged in the development of a new generation of CW agents. However, no request has been made by any government for an investigation by the OPCW to determine the facts.[6]

China and Iran are also often mentioned among the few States suspected of non-compliance. The concern is whether their declarations on past chemical-weapons programmes were accurate and whether they are still withholding information on some aspects. Iran had omitted from its baseline declaration the fact that it possessed chemical weapons during its war with Iraq in the 1980s. It subsequently admitted the omission and explained that any remaining stockpiles were destroyed and that the related production facilities were converted to peaceful uses subject to inspection. However, US intelligence officials continue to make allegations that Iran still possesses several thousand metric tons of weaponized and bulk chemicals, including nerve, blister, choking and blood agents.[7]

Persistent allegations are not helpful unless they are followed by a call for challenge inspection to clear up the issue, or dropped until actionable information can be obtained.

As regards China, despite its technical compliance with the requirements of the Convention, US intelligence sources have expressed allegations that it retains 'moderate' stockpiles of chemical weapons and has not acknowledged the full extent of its chemical weapons programme. China has declared that it had destroyed all its CW stockpiles along with three former production facilities, but is reluctant to reveal the full nature and scope of its past programme.[8]

At present the issue is lack of transparency, which may or may not represent concealment. As similar allegations could easily be levelled at the US itself, a constructive approach might well be to attempt bilateral diplomacy for greater reciprocal transparency. A deal by both sides to welcome challenge inspections might help not only to remove ambiguities but also to set a precedent on applying an instrument that may otherwise atrophy.

Findings and recourse

In both the OPCW and the IAEA, the determination of non-compliance is a complex issue. Suspicions and allegations by individual States may help to flag an issue. But consultation and verification are essential to determine the nature of the problem and decide on appropriate remedial action.

The ultimate verification tool for the IAEA is special inspection, authorized by the Director General to resolve major inconsistencies or serious allegations of possible material breach. It is designed for problems that cannot be resolved by *ad hoc* or routine inspections, or consultations with host countries. This confrontational tool has rarely been used. When special inspection was attempted in North Korea, access was denied without repercussion from the Security Council. In the case of Iran, the IAEA refrained from using special inspection, as the level of cooperation has been sufficient for the Agency to rely on a new set of *ad hoc* inspections supplemented by political pressure to encourage full transparency. At present, it is at a delicate stage where the Board of Governors needs to weigh the benefits and risks of referring the situation to the Security Council. Both positive incentives and the threat of referral to the Council have been used with good effect to induce further cooperation from Iran. But benchmarks and deadlines are necessary to evaluate the progress and determine when to report to the Council. Access to the Council should not be unnecessarily inhibited. It should be perceived not only in terms of sanctions but also as an opportunity for diplomatic initiatives at a higher political level, in the context of broader peace and security concerns.

For the OPCW and the CTBTO, the ultimate verification instrument is the challenge inspection. In the chemical field, despite signals of suspicion and allegations about non-compliance by certain States, no State party has so far requested a challenge inspection or supplied the OPCW with information to justify the allegations. The OPCW has by now sufficient institutional capacity and experience to try challenge inspections in the few cases where allegations have been made; those who make them should either press for employing the procedure or refrain from making unsubstantiated charges.

If the findings confirm non-compliance, what are the options for a treaty organization? There are essentially three courses of action that might be taken, depending on the nature of the problem, the extent of cooperation by the host State and the level of consensus among

Member States:

(a) resolution by consultation;
(b) internal measures – suspension of rights and privileges of membership, suspension of assistance and return of any previously granted material and equipment; and
(c) reporting the crisis to the Security Council for supportive action, ranging from political appeal to diplomatic and economic sanctions.

Any compliance concerns can be raised bilaterally through diplomatic channels between State parties. This traditional method for consultation and resolution of differences has been incorporated in the CWC (Article IX) and the CTBT (IV.C) as a means for clarification of any matter that may cause doubt about compliance with the treaty. A State may also request the Executive Council to obtain clarification from another State. If the clarification received is unsatisfactory, it may request a challenge inspection or request the Executive Council to consider any appropriate measures to redress the situation. There are no comparable provisions in the IAEA Statute, but evidently Member States are free to use any bilateral channels to resolve issues by consultation.

Each organization has some form of sanctions against a non-compliant State that fails to fulfil the request to comply within a specified timeframe. In the OPCW and the CTBTO, it is the Conference of States Parties, upon the recommendation of the Executive Council, which restricts or suspends the rights and privileges of membership until the State concerned takes remedial action. In cases of material breach of the disarmament or non-proliferation objectives of the treaty, the Conference may also recommend to the State parties 'collective measures – in conformity with international law'. The types of measures are not spelled out but may obviously include the suspension of material or technical assistance. In the IAEA also, the rights and privileges of membership may be suspended by the General Conference upon determination by the Board of Governors that the State concerned had failed to take corrective action as requested. However, it is the responsibility of the Board itself to take collective measures comprising curtailment or suspension of assistance and even to call for a return of material and equipment made available in the past to the non-compliant State.

Recourse to United Nations organs

The statutory link of the three organizations with the political organs of the United Nations are formulated succinctly and somewhat vaguely, consistent with the emphasis on the autonomous nature of each organization. This may also imply caution against too much closeness in order to avoid politicization of difficult issues under their jurisdiction. There is no rush to refer them to the United Nations before the specialized technical bodies have exhausted their own remedies. This attitude is reinforced by lessons from the history of the Security Council. The usual lack of unity among the five permanent members of the Council on non-proliferation issues has sent signals that consideration of a proliferation issue by the Council may not necessarily result in effective action. The combined effect of these factors has kept an important component of the compliance mechanism underutilized. As a result, the enforcement dimension has been the weakest link in the WMD control regime. Prompt access to and response by the Security Council remains a problem to be resolved.

The constituent instruments of the three organizations mention two kinds of reporting to the United Nations: (a) general reporting of activities of relevance to one or more agenda items of UN organs, especially the General Assembly and, when appropriate, the Security Council; and (b) specific referral of compliance issues to the main UN organ, especially the Security Council.

Relations with the General Assembly

As regards general reporting, the process has functioned smoothly in the context of reciprocal arrangements made as part of the relationship agreements concluded between the United Nations Secretary General and the Directors General of the three organizations. The Director General of the IAEA is required to present an annual report to the General Assembly on the work of the Agency, which is debated and acknowledged in a supportive resolution. The executive heads of the CTBTO and the OPCW do not have a similar privilege, though they may report on an *ad hoc* basis, depending on the Assembly's agenda. However, they have regularly addressed the Assembly's Disarmament and Security Committee (First Committee) once a year, under subjects of special relevance to their organizations. As a statement of the UN Secretary-General is also delivered at annual plenary sessions of each organization, the attention given to broad issues of common interest is satisfactory.

Reporting to the Security Council

The weakness of the link is at the level of the Security Council, where issues of the three organizations of relevance to the Council are rarely raised, unless reports are requested or the organizations formally report a compliance issue to the Council. Let us briefly focus on the two aspects.

As regards general reporting to the Council, the IAEA Statute is permissive: the Agency may report to the Security Council 'when appropriate' (Article II.B.4). But this channel has not been used often. The CTBTO and the OPCW do not have a comparable arrangement though the possibility cannot be totally excluded. To benefit from the potential, a clear encouragement is needed from the Security Council. The prospects are promising in the post-September 11 era as the Council has been broadening its proceedings to include not only crises between States, but also potential threats, especially from States suspected of proliferation designs and non-State actors with suspected access to WMD.

The Security Council should consider ways to receive and utilize regular reports from the IAEA, the CTBTO and the OPCW on relevant aspects of their work, particularly on proliferation-related issues in the nuclear and chemical fields. One possible approach would be for the Executive Heads of the IAEA, the CTBTO and the OPCW to brief the Security Council once a year. It could preferably be done sequentially within the same week, or under a common agenda item in order to highlight inter-relationships among issues. The ideal time might be in the autumn when all of them would be available in New York to report to the General Assembly or its Security and Disarmament Committee. A *tour d'horizon* on WMD issues might serve as a broad context for a debate on trends and impacts as they relate to peace and security issues before the Council.

More problematic is the issue of referral of compliance issues to the Security Council. The IAEA's experience regarding North Korea and Iran is instructive. The North Korean case of 1993–4 was classic. Within a period of five weeks the case within the IAEA escalated from detection of traces of undeclared plutonium, to denial of access to designated facilities, then from rejection of mandatory special inspections to a determination by the Board of Governors that North Korea was in breach of its treaty obligations. By 1 April 1993, when the Board referred the case to the Security Council for possible action, North Korea had already given notice of its intention to withdraw from the NPT by 12 June and was not disposed to respond to the Council's decision inviting it to fulfil its obligations.

Although as a result of direct talks between the US and North Korea tension was reduced and North Korea's NPT withdrawal was suspended on the eve of the deadline, the resumed routine inspections were again restricted if not totally blocked. It was not even possible to preserve the evidence of past violations. When the IAEA Board suspended technical assistance to North Korea as a sanction, the latter gave notice of withdrawal from IAEA membership. A parallel US-led attempt for economic sanctions by the Security Council was blocked by the threat of a Chinese veto, followed by intensive negotiations within the Security Council for economic sanctions. This second round of pressure diplomacy at the Council was allowed to subside as a private démarche by former President Jimmy Carter facilitated a successful resumption of dialogue between the US and North Korea which brought about a deal – the 'Agreed Framework' arrangement to freeze the latter's nuclear programme under IAEA's monitoring, but without access to information on the past violations. After half a decade of calm monitoring, North Korean duplicity has once again undermined the provisional arrangement, with mute response from the Security Council.

The lessons for the future are both positive and negative. All the statutory and political assets were effectively deployed by the IAEA against a recalcitrant non-compliant State. Moreover the Security Council had tried in two phases to exert political pressure and threatened sanctions, while a second track of bilateral diplomacy diffused tensions to allow provisional measures for progress. On the negative side, North Korea was not amenable to any pressure, as it did not hesitate to retaliate militarily and could also count on China's veto for support. Nevertheless, the Security Council's role, which was judicious and effective for a while, faded away as the US made a promising though faulty bilateral deal with North Korea.

Placing the issue on the agenda was a useful precedent. Although the issue has been dormant within the Security Council while multilateral initiatives are attempted outside the Council, it still remains on the agenda and can be revived if there is a determination to do so. In view of the crucial role of China, which tends to abstain on most proliferation issues, a consensus among the five major powers is necessary for coordinating effort toward a solution consistent with NPT obligations. The challenge is how to balance the three parallel tracks of diplomacy and pressure: multilaterally among the concerned States, at the levels of the IAEA Board of Governors, and at the Security Council. At all levels China's diplomatic role remains important for balancing interests to ensure a peaceful resolution.

These lessons are pertinent to a case like Iran. Although Iran has not openly defied the IAEA inspectors, the pace of its cooperation to resolve inconsistencies and ambiguities concerning its nuclear programme has been too slow. The likelihood of a finding of non-compliance and the threat of referral to the Security Council have induced joint diplomatic initiatives by European States, with good initial results in Teheran. However, since pressures and positive inducements have been insufficient to bring about full compliance, further delays to refer the issue to the Security Council may be counterproductive and may even weaken the credibility of the IAEA's safeguards system. On the other hand, placing the issue on the Security Council agenda might generate different dynamics in addressing the non-compliance problem in the context of more basic political differences and their relevance to international peace and security. A debate may not necessarily trigger economic sanctions but might allow consideration of Iran's own issues in a search for a constructive solution.

If no further progress is made the IAEA Board should not be discouraged by the North Korean experience to bring the matter to the attention of the Security Council. It should be left to the Council to assess the significant progress made so far and decide how best to reinforce the role of the inspectors. Iran appears to be among the easier proliferation-related cases and might lend itself to a precedent-setting, unified approach by the Council in the post-Iraq rapprochement among the major powers.

8
Building an Effective WMD Control Regime

The history of the WMD control regime began in the early years of the United Nations with the most ambitious plan, the Baruch Plan, to create an international authority responsible for the development and peaceful use of nuclear energy. It would take custody of all fissionable material and technological information essential for producing nuclear weapons. It would also verify the freeze on weapons production and the destruction of existing stockpiles of nuclear weapons. Although the plan was not accepted, it launched a process that broadened the arms control objective to include chemical and biological weapons and classified them all together as weapons of mass destruction, a concept used to distinguish them from conventional weapons. All the proposals that evolved during the first decade were then pulled together to form a comprehensive model for General and Complete Disarmament (GCD). The model was then considered to be unrealistic as a basis for negotiating a convention for phased across-the-board disarmament to be implemented by a single international disarmament and verification organization. However, it established a firm conceptual foundation and an outline of partial or collateral measures that would be separately negotiated as building blocks towards verified disarmament in all areas. The long-term objective was to achieve comprehensive disarmament through the coordinated implementation of the components, all under effective international control.

Effective control meant strict verification of compliance by States with the commitments they made in the various treaties. Effectiveness would depend on various factors, especially the following: the security concerns of States and their willingness to cooperate with inspectors; the capabilities entrusted to a verification system, including authority for access; the capacity for impartial and efficient verification operations: and the credibility of the process to cope with non-compliance issues.

Disarmament was recognized by the international community as one of the pillars for promoting international peace and security. From the outset, the emphasis was on the elimination of nuclear and other weapons of mass destruction, without neglecting conventional weapons. We should bear in mind that it is in this context that the various partial measures were negotiated – notably, the Nuclear Non-Proliferation Treaty, the Chemical Weapons Convention, the Comprehensive Test-Ban Treaty and the Biological Weapons Convention. They represent a major step forward, but the WMD control regime remains flawed and incomplete. The problem at present is not merely the loss of momentum towards the ultimate goal of GCD but, more seriously, the multiple challenges that threaten the integrity of each treaty regime. Thus, the focus of this chapter is first on how best to strengthen each treaty regime and enhance synergies among them to face the new challenges more effectively and, for the long-term, how best to resume progress towards a more complete WMD control regime. Recent events have confirmed that the two levels are interrelated, especially in the context of regional crises that may threaten international peace and security.

We recognize that there are experts with serious reservations about the value of WMD as a concept combining nuclear, chemical and biological weapons in order to devise a common strategy to control them. The reservations are mainly based on the fact that nuclear weapons are the most difficult to build, most devastating to use but also least likely to be used, except as a deterrent; thus, arguably, necessitating a special military doctrine and disarmament strategy. Chemical weapons, they add, are the least devastating but most usable in the battlefield to gain tactical military advantage, while biological weapons stand somewhere between chemical and nuclear weapons in destructive potential and likelihood of use, either for war or deterrence or political blackmail.[1]

These notions may serve arms control strategists well if the purpose is to design effective military doctrines for defence but, for our purpose, it is the package of the WMD weaponry in relationship to international security and the potential for trade-offs and relationships between the different components that justifies the WMD perspective. This is particularly true today with the blurring of doctrinal boundaries with preparations to use mininukes against perceived CW threats or use of any available weapons by terrorist groups.

Current threats

These and other dangerous developments call for urgent action in strengthening each treaty regime and its verification mechanism and in building a comprehensive WMD control regime in the long-term. The dangers have increased since the high water mark in arms control was reached in 1995 when the NPT was made permanent. A stringent bargain was then made by 173 States pledging to give up permanently the option of acquiring nuclear weapons in return for an explicitly reaffirmed commitment by the five nuclear-weapon States to eliminate eventually their nuclear weapons. There was good reason for optimism: the Cold War had just ended, Iraq's aggression and its violation of the NPT were vigorously handled, the CWC was concluded as a non-discriminatory convention for the elimination of all chemical weapons, the CTBT was finally within reach and the need for a verification mechanism for the BWC was widely recognized.

Since then, however, dramatic events have occurred. The looming dangers have been summarized in a special report by the Carnegie Endowment for International Peace focused on a strategy for future nuclear security. Below, we have adapted and broadened key points in order to include the chemical and biological dimensions of the threat.[2]

First, India and Pakistan went beyond merely refusing to sign the recently concluded CTBT but actually crossed the nuclear threshold by dramatically conducting a series of nuclear tests in 1998. The new moratorium on testing was thus broken by States outside the NPT, with reverberations within and beyond the nuclear proliferation regime.

Second, the danger of unconventional weapons in the hands of terrorists became evident when the Al Qaeda attacks on 11 September 2001 revealed that shadowy movements, not under the control of any State, were capable of committing catastrophic attacks and were presumably willing to use unconventional weapons, if they were able to acquire them.

Third, the imminent danger of nuclear trafficking was demonstrated by the revelation in 2003 that Pakistan's nuclear scientists and engineers had for years sold nuclear bomb designs and equipment to North Korea, Iran, Libya and perhaps other States. The network was connected by shady middlemen and front companies in various countries. This time, the centre of the 'proliferation bazaar' was Pakistan, which had itself acquired nuclear weapons without violating any treaty, but failed to control the conduct of its experts in violating its political commitments to respect the non-proliferation objectives. The risk of similar leaks from India and Israel appears to be less, but their nuclear capabilities remain a source of regional tension and uncertainties that might further undermine the NPT regime.

Fourth, a lingering dangerous problem has been the wide availability of fissile material and chemical and biological warfare agents in countries with poor security arrangements, especially in Russia and some other republics of the former Soviet Union. Some disgruntled or rogue States with terrorist links may be tempted to exploit the inadequacies and loopholes in existing non-proliferation regimes to acquire the material for illicit purposes.

Fifth, there is a serious concern about the policies of the five major powers. As veto-wielding permanent members of the Security Council they have failed too often to act with unity to halt the trend towards proliferation, regardless of their respective alliance connections. Their failure or reluctance to act in cases of non-compliance deprives the non-proliferation regime of its enforcement possibilities and undoubtedly weakens it. As nuclear-weapon States, they have retreated from their end of the bargain, mainly to proceed irreversibly towards the final goal of nuclear disarmament.

Sixth, the US and the Russian Federation, as the powers most heavily armed with weapons of mass destruction, bear a special responsibility to reduce their WMD stockpiles and generate momentum for the whole process of disarmament. They have, however, not even abandoned their Cold War nuclear force postures; they still have not stepped back from their 'hair-trigger' state of readiness to launch a nuclear war under the doctrine of mutual-assured destruction (MAD).[3]

They have virtually halted their bilateral efforts towards strictly verified, irreversible nuclear disarmament. Moreover, they both now rely on a policy of nuclear deterrence, which undermines the long-term goal of complete disarmament. Even more disturbing is the recent shift in US policy concerning WMD proliferation. While the Clinton Administration considered the weapons themselves as posing a threat, President Bush has framed the issue differently: 'the gravest danger facing America and the world, is *outlaw regimes that seek and possess nuclear, chemical and biological weapons*' (State of the Union Address, January 2003; emphasis added). Regime change was to be sought, if necessary with unilateral 'preemptive action', rather than relying on disarmament in cooperation with the international community.

Paradoxically, the international community seems to be less safe today than during the bipolar world of the Cold War. Then there was a modicum of stability with effective restraints applied by the US and the USSR on potential disruptive actions by their allies. Now, however, global instability and power struggle make it essential to recognize the urgency of the current threats to the integrity of the disarmament regime, and to aim for more than cosmetic changes. The new challenges to international peace and security call for bold initiatives for WMD control.

In its perceptive report on 'Strategy for Nuclear Security', the Carnegie Endowment identifies five types of commitment that must be made by States:[4]

(a) No new nuclear-weapon States: to deter North Korea and Iran and any other State from crossing the threshold.
(b) Secure all nuclear materials: to establish high standards of protection, monitoring and accounting for fissile materials everywhere, especially in vulnerable sites in the former Soviet Republics.
(c) Stop illegal transfers: to establish enforceable prohibitions against clandestine trade in sensitive material and technology and to criminalize illicit transactions.
(d) Devalue the political and military currency of nuclear weapons by honouring the nuclear test-ban, abandoning obsolete doctrines and resuming nuclear disarmament.
(e) Reinforce commitment to conflict resolution: to resolve regional conflicts, with active leadership or support from the nuclear-weapon States, in order to facilitate the eventual establishment of WMD-free zones.

Although the proposals were focused on nuclear security, these commitments would form the core of a universal WMD compliance system that would complement the existing obligations to eliminate chemical and biological weapons as well. They would significantly broaden the scope of the WMD control regime. In this context, we will focus on specific strategies for strengthening the existing disarmament schemes and for building a broader regime that may integrate them all.

Strengthening the treaty regimes

The executive heads of the IAEA, the OPCW and the CTBTO have been pioneers in the effort to identify new challenges to their respective organizations posed by the changing political environment. They have themselves taken initiatives to persuade governments to maintain the integrity of the verification system as envisaged in the respective treaties and to seal any loopholes that undermine its effectiveness. There is also a wealth of proposals made by governments in different forums and by outside experts. The following suggestions are therefore not entirely new but are selected for their salience, timeliness and consistency with the current perspectives of the leadership within the three organizations.

IAEA: greater control of nuclear material

When Hans Blix, then Director General of the IAEA, launched the last reform of the IAEA safeguards system in the 1990s, the aim was to enhance the verification capacity of the Agency to detect any secret, undeclared nuclear material, installations and clandestine activities such as those uncovered in Iraq after the second Gulf War. The strengthened safeguards had a number of essential elements to detect non-compliance with greater probability and make access to the Security Council more likely. The three main elements were: increased access to information about a State's nuclear activities; broader access to sites and facilities within a State; and maximum use of new and available technologies to improve detection. Blix had warned that no verification system can 'give 100 per cent guarantee' about the absence of research effort and of small facilities or equipment. The objective was to reduce uncertainty as much as possible without incurring high costs and imposing high intrusiveness.[5]

It took five years of intensive work by the IAEA Secretariat and the Board of Governors to complete the improvements in 1997 as a Model Protocol to be added as an integral part of the existing Safeguards Agreement. As more than two-thirds of the NPT parties are yet to conclude an Additional Protocol, persuading them is a top priority while the Agency explores further reforms.

Mohamed ElBaradei, the current Director General of the IAEA, has launched a campaign to gain wider acceptance for the procedures of the Additional Protocol. He has embarked on a new campaign to alert all States of the new threats from loopholes in the procedures to control the nuclear fuel cycle. His main proposals are described below, with some comments:[6]

- *Conclusion of additional protocols*: The effectiveness of the inspections in Iran and Libya demonstrates the value of broader access, even if it is only based on a provisional acceptance of the procedures. A more intensive campaign is needed in various forums to gain universal acceptance for the Protocol, especially at NPT-related conferences and in the UN General Assembly. As universality of adherence is also a major goal of the CWC and the CTBT, such a campaign would be an ideal subject for a joint effort.
- *Control of fissile material and nuclear waste*: Under the current non-proliferation regime the controls provided over the sensitive reprocessing and enrichment portions of nuclear material are inadequate for timely detection. Serious consideration should be given to the

suggestion to limit the production of new fissile material, possibly by restricting operations or by placing them under multinational controls. However, new limitations would be unfair and unworkable unless a reliable assurance is given for an adequate and affordable supply of such material. The approach is consistent with the NPT principles. These bold ideas, which go back to the Baruch Plan and the founding of the IAEA, may now be ripe for action. The case for developing multinational approaches to the management and disposal of spent fuel is a strong one. The experience of EURATOM in Europe and of the Argentina–Brazil Agency for Accounting and Control of Nuclear Materials (ABACC) suggests that two or more contiguous States can cooperate successfully in running a joint operation on fuel cycle facilities.[7]

- *Radioisotopes*: Research reactors in about forty countries use weapons-usable nuclear material (highly-enriched uranium (HEU) and plutonium) to produce radioisotopes for medicine and other purposes. As reactors can be adapted to use low-enriched uranium, this is another area where international cooperation may help to reduce the risk of diversion.

- *Conversion*: Building on the Russia–US model of down-blending stocks of weapons-usable uranium (HEU) to low-enriched uranium. Such conversion worldwide could become a significant source of fuel for civilian reactors that generate electricity while reducing the risk of proliferation.

However, the last three proposals are complex and costly. They involve issues that require balancing a diversity of interests of an economic, scientific, security and political character. Their value in reducing the risk of proliferation is indisputable, but they may become negotiable only in a broad non-proliferation framework that alleviates rather than perpetuates the discriminatory character of the NPT. Progress towards a verified production cut-off of all fissile material might be a good catalyst.

OPCW: overcoming teething problems

The main problems of the OPCW are related to the uniqueness of the CWC as regards the complexity and scope of its implementation provisions. As Jonathan Tucker has clearly explained, the CWC contains a large number of 'affirmative' obligations that are key to effective implementation. Parallel sets of obligations must be implemented synchronously at the international, governmental and industry levels. Unlike the NPT, which entrusts to an existing institution – the IAEA – the task of implementing only some of the obligations undertaken by State parties, the CWC created its own independent implementing body, a model that was later used by the CTBT. As the first international agency devoted to the verified elimination of an entire category of weaponry, the OPCW's implementation experience is important for the positive or negative precedents that it may establish. At the national level, governments are required to engage in multiple activities: establishing a National Authority to communicate with and assist the OPCW, enacting implementing legislation and chemical export controls, submitting a declaration and annual reports, hosting inspections, and conducting weapons destruction or conversion under supervision. Significantly this involves regulated access to present and past military facilities. Finally, the depth and breadth of engagement by the private sector, especially by the chemical industry, goes far beyond the experience of the IAEA in the nuclear field. Here, too, the experience of OPCW might set precedents on how far the international community may go in controlling the military applications of dual-use technologies.[8]

The lessons from the OPCW's experience of implementation are likely to be valuable for the CTBTO as it prepares for regular operations after the treaty's entry into force and also helpful to the IAEA in its effort to expand its control over the production, transfer and use of fissile material.

In previous chapters we tried to identify the main problems that have been analyzed by the various experts cited. Some of the problems were addressed by the First Review Conference of the CWC, that was held in March 2003,[9] but the remedial actions taken are still inadequate. In general we may cluster them as follows:

(a) The Conference of State parties and the Executive Council tend to accommodate interpretations that might create a gap between the intent of the Convention and the practice, especially in setting limitations on verification activities.

(b) Many States have been too slow in taking the required action to fulfil the four notification requirements: action on the implementing legislation, on the establishment of a National Authority, on points of entry for inspection teams, and on diplomatic clearance arrangements for inspectors.

(c) Some States have insisted, with the acquiescence of the governing bodies, on limiting the ability of inspectors to cover entire sites or to collect and retain all information. Worse still, the US has formally approved precedent-setting exceptions regarding access that might undermine the spirit of the Convention. States have also tended to misuse the confidentiality clause of the Convention by citing excessively their own health codes.

(d) There has been an inhibition on the part of States to request challenge inspection to clear up allegations of non-compliance by others and give the organization an opportunity to test its adequacy in real cases.

The way forward for the OPCW is to follow a two-track strategy: to ensure full implementation of the CWC as intended by the founders of the Convention and to adapt the process of verification to meet new challenges caused by scientific discoveries.

As regards the first track, it is necessary to speed up the process of resolving the long-standing issues without further diluting the verification procedures. It is also essential to study the impact that restrictive interpretations have made so far on the outcome of inspections. An objective review of the experience may suggest whether and how the process can be strengthened back to the original intent of the Convention. These are not routine matters but deserve a close look by the Executive Council with high-level representation assisted by the advisory bodies and outside experts. Secondly, the OPCW should focus on establishing uniform declarations, reports, facility agreements and access procedures. It should build on the considerable progress made so far in establishing its institutions and information bases and in performing much of the required verification work.

In the light of the new threats, especially from terrorists, the governments and the chemical industries of the more advanced countries need to recommit themselves to the obligations that were already made and assist in resolving the outstanding issues about rules rather than complicate them by new interpretations.

The second track is even more difficult to navigate. As the sources of chemical or biological threats shift away from the States that are now dismantling chemical weapons, the threat from terrorist organizations and the few States that support them has increased. There is a risk that clandestine production facilities might manufacture toxic agents from chemical precursors not monitored under the CWC control system. Although the solution has to depend on more effective intelligence work and domestic law enforcement, the trend of technological developments that might indirectly feed know-how into those facilities should be a priority concern to the OPCW. The technical aspects of this problem are beyond the scope of our study, but we need to emphasize that commercial technologies could be misused for the development of 'novel' chemical weapons.[10] The General Purpose Criterion (GPC) was drafted broadly enough to accommodate any trends in scientific and technical research that would have a significant impact on the development of chemical weapons. For example, new toxins developed for medical applications that can be misused as weapons may not be among the scheduled chemicals, but they are still banned for such use under the GPC. The important issue is thus how to adapt and update the CWC procedures. In this regard the role of the Director General and his secretariat is vital, as well as that of the Scientific Advisory Board of the OPCW.[11]

CTBT: removing obstacles to full implementation

The process of establishing a comprehensive test-ban regime has been seriously blocked by two developments of the late 1990s: the US failure to ratify the CTBT followed by President Bush's revival of certain weapons programmes that might require testing and, more seriously, the decisions by India and Pakistan not merely to boycott the Treaty, but to undermine it by conducting a total of eleven nuclear tests. It is remarkable that the Preparatory Commission and the Technical Secretariat have not been deterred from virtually completing the technical infrastructure and the institutional mechanisms while waiting for the remaining designated States to ratify the Treaty.

There is no shortage of imaginative proposals on how to overcome these obstacles in the long run. The most compelling proposals have been recently issued by the Carnegie Endowment for International Peace.[12] The present US counter-proliferation policy includes counterproductive elements. Research is already proceeding for the development of new 'low-yield' nuclear weapons. Ostensibly, the aim is to have effective weapons that could conceivably penetrate deeply buried bunkers containing chemical or biological weapons hidden by terrorists or their State supporters. Unless this policy is reversed, there is a risk of defection by some State parties that might use the same logic or might feel threatened by the new weapons. The likely result is to weaken further not only the CTBT but also the NPT.

The resumption of US positive leadership is what the CTBT needs to move forward. It may indeed be the essential catalyst to bring about a reduction of tension in South Asia, to open a dialogue on freezing the nuclear arms race. Under such circumstances, the possibility of rollback by India and Pakistan cannot be ruled out, thus opening the door to joining the CTBT and the NPT as non-nuclear-weapon States. However, if this possibility is too remote then perhaps the CTBT should be amended to allow entry into force without them, while their nuclear status is reviewed in the context of the broader issue of nuclear disarmament.

Completing the biological weapons regime

In Chapter 2, we referred to the evolution of the earlier negotiations to ban chemical and biological weapons under a single treaty, with an effective mechanism to verify compliance. When the negotiations failed, biological weapons were singled out for a total ban, without a mechanism to verify compliance. The BWC was concluded with the understanding that it would be the first step in the search for a comprehensive ban in the interrelated biological and chemical areas, with an appropriate mechanism for verification. Two decades of intermittent negotiations resulted in another separated convention devoted to chemical weapons, but one with exemplary procedures for verification. The idea of an integrated chemical/biological convention was not actively pursued, but a parallel effort was made in the 1990s to equip the BWC with a verification mechanism. At the last phase of a promising process, the effort collapsed because of serious US doubts about the verifiability of the BWC.

In the light of the current threats of bio-terrorism since 9/11, especially since the postal anthrax attacks by an unknown terrorist in the east of the United States, it is irresponsible to abandon the search for an effective verification mechanism for the BWC. Without going into the details of the discontinued negotiations, we may identify three options for progress.

The first option is to convert the UN Monitoring, Verification and Inspection Commission on Iraq (UNMOVIC) to serve as a verification instrument covering biological weapons and also missiles applicable to all WMD. This constructive idea, proposed by UNMOVIC Chairman Hans Blix in his last report to Security Council, deserves special attention by the Council.[13] If it is acceptable, the linkage with the BWC can be carefully considered. One option would be to use the converted commission as a provisional arrangement to fill the gap until the BWC can be equipped with its own mechanism. It could thus serve both the Security Council and the Convention. It may be timely to consider the proposal as the future of this valuable commission is yet to be determined. However, this will require a change of attitude in Washington. In the aftermath of the 2003 invasion of Iraq, there is wide recognition that the pre-war international inspections were effective, contrary to the dismissive previous judgments by key US officials.

The second option is to resume negotiations on the rolling-text on BWC verification to address the US reservations with a fresh perspective.

By now it should be obvious from the post-war US experience of weapons search in occupied Iraq that exclusive reliance on national means is no substitute for effective international verification. This might induce sober reflection to allow a reviewing of the issue of verifiability of the BWC from a pragmatic rather than a dogmatic perspective. It should be understood that no verification mechanism can provide 100 per cent assurance about the absence of some prohibited weapons.

The third option is to expand the scope of the CWC verification system to include an additional dimension covering the requirements of the BWC. The draft proposals from the earlier negotiations for a BWC verification mechanism can serve as the basis for the expansion. Such an integration would not be easy but would fulfil the sound original intention of keeping together these overlapping weapons areas, with benefits in synergy, cost-effectiveness and capacity for detection. If there is a will a way can be found. It would, however, call for bold and imaginative approaches.

Linkage between the two conventions might be accomplished by parallel amendments of the two conventions or by a joint protocol. By now, the OPCW may have accumulated sufficient administrative and technical skills and experience relevant to subsuming the verification task of the BWC. However, it is important to take precautions so that new responsibilities assumed by the OPCW will not distort the balance of work within the organization. Some useful ideas may be borrowed from studies done previously when negotiators considered whether the CTBT verification should be assigned to the IAEA.[14]

For example, until the discrepancy in membership between the CWC and the BWC is removed by the accession of some key States to the former convention, it may be necessary in the first instance to install an autonomous verification unit for the BWC within the OPCW. This might include a special sub-committee of the Executive Council to oversee implementation of the BWC, and a provisionally separate fund for the new verification responsibilities. However, it would be useful to maintain a common inspectorate from the outset, a new secretariat department being added to cover the biological area.

The last proposal, if successfully implemented, could serve as an important experiment in selective integration of elements of the WMD control regime.

Integrative initiatives

In the 1960s, the concept of a single disarmament organization was actively negotiated in Geneva to serve as the verification mechanism for

General and Complete Disarmament. However, governments soon recognized the formidable obstacles to serious negotiation at the peak of the Cold War and settled for a more pragmatic approach. They thus decided to concentrate on separate but interrelated partial measures, leaving open the possibility of eventually integrating the whole system. Since then, suggestions have occasionally been made to consolidate existing institutions or merge into them newly created mechanisms to benefit from synergy and enhance cost-effectiveness. It was in this spirit that the NPT refrained from creating a new implementing organization but entrusted the verification function to the IAEA. When the CTBT was negotiated in Geneva a similar idea of linkage with the IAEA was considered, but there were objections and a separate verification mechanism was established. It was located next to the IAEA in Vienna, with the expectation of close collaboration between them.

There are formidable difficulties to merging existing organizations, as they operate on the basis of separate treaties, without built-in procedures for harmonization. Furthermore, it is politically difficult to do so because of differing memberships, competing interests in national bureaucracies and resistance by international secretariats with obvious vested interests. Yet the current threats are so formidable that we need not shy away from bold initiatives. The experience gained by the international community in dismantling Iraq's WMD capacity with the effective joint operation of the IAEA and the UN Special Commission (UNSCOM/UNMOVIC) may serve not only as a source of inspiration but also of practical ideas to move forward. The cause of disarmament may now benefit from the well-grounded voices of Hans Blix and Mohamed ElBaradei, who, as the leaders of that operation, have extended their valuable contribution by articulating many ideas of particular relevance to further building the WMD control regime. Many of those ideas were used in earlier chapters and others will be reflected below.

In the following sections, we will focus on possible initiatives towards consolidating the regime: first on ways to enhance coordination and synergy among the existing organization, an achievable short-term goal; and, secondly, on the long-term necessity of adding the missing components to complete the WMD control regime.

Coordination and synergy

The following ideas for enhancing coordination and synergy can be accomplished within the existing legal framework of the IAEA, the CTBTO and the OPCW. The three organizations have bilateral relationship agreements with one another and with the United Nations.

However, cooperation among them is rudimentary and needs to be built for mutual benefit, as well as for strengthening their compliance process. It will only require parallel initiatives by the executive heads to obtain the blessing of their governing bodies for a process of regular cooperation.

Coordination body

The first proposal is to arrange regular coordination meetings among the executive heads of the IAEA, the CTBTO and the OPCW. Basically, the purpose would be: to exchange information and experience; to identify problems regarding treaty implementation that can benefit from close cooperation (e.g. campaign for ratifications or accessions); to discuss common substantive and management problems and seek cooperative solutions; to synchronize the nature and timing of reporting to the United Nations in order to draw the attention of the Security Council as well as the General Assembly; and to explore possibilities for strengthening the WMD control regime as a whole.

A good model for the meetings would be the committee of executive heads of the organizations of the UN system, known now as the Chief Executive Board for Coordination, which is chaired by the UN Secretary-General. The meetings could be held annually at the headquarters of each organization by rotation, with the benefit of gaining a deeper understanding of each other's institutional and technical problems and possibilities. They would also be useful for identifying regime-related issues for possible consideration by their policy-making organs.

Ideas emerging from their respective internal reviews and from their thematic scientific forums could be combined with the many proposals being made by outside experts and non-governmental research institutions. In this context, we present the following suggestions for consideration.

Trade information. As was discussed in Chapter 5, the IAEA and the OPCW have procedures to receive information on exports and imports of sensitive information regarding the nuclear and chemical industry. But the system has proven inadequate, as the cases of Iraq, Iran, Libya and North Korea have shown. The illicit trafficking by Pakistani nuclear scientists in all the cases had escaped reliable detection. It was particularly difficult since it had involved unknown intermediaries, some of them in countries belonging to the Nuclear Suppliers Group. The story is yet to be told as regards the domain of the Australia Group covering the chemical and biological fields. It would be extremely useful for the IAEA and the

OPCW, within the limits of their confidentiality rules, to share experiences and coordinate their investigations, as it is likely that some citizens or companies of the same countries may be involved across-the-board.

As explained in Chapter 5, sensitive global exports are currently controlled by four coalitions: the Nuclear Suppliers Group, the Australia Group, the Wassenaar Agreement and the Missile Technology Control Regime. But they have many shortcomings, including their limited membership and lack of common standards. Their cooperation with the relevant verification organizations is insufficient and sometimes problematic. These organizations need to strengthen their internal capacity to supplement information reported by governments and to follow up with investigations. In serious cases of proliferation involving non-State actors, the Security Council has adopted unanimously Resolution 1540 (2004) forbidding States from assisting such groups in acquiring WMD and their means of delivery and also requiring them to establish and enforce legislation on export controls and to criminalize illicit trade in this area. Thus there is a new opportunity for the IAEA and the OPCW to use the Security Council more effectively. However, they need to strengthen and refine their information systems in order to distinguish legitimate from illegitimate trade and report the latter to the Council.

Satellite information. The IAEA has greatly benefited from the use of satellite pictures and other images, sometimes made available by Member States, but more often by commercial arrangements. This source of information will be important for the CTBTO and may also benefit the OPCW in some respects. Exchange of experience among the organizations may help in deciding the modalities for cooperation. It may provide the first opportunity to reconsider some aspects of the old French proposal to establish an International Satellite Monitoring Agency which was widely supported in the General Assembly but was postponed in 1982 because of Soviet opposition and US abstention.

Confidentiality issue and rules of access. This is a sensitive area where the rules are tailored to fit each treaty's requirements with a minimum of intrusion. It is closely guarded by Member States. However, confidentiality rules are not intended to restrict access to relevant information; yet they are often challenged by certain States, threatening the integrity of the verification regime. The OPCW and the IAEA may therefore need to exchange experiences to identify positive precedents on safeguarding the rules.

Compliance process. The IAEA has a long experience of combining inducements and diplomatic pressure by Member States to assist the inspectorate when the host government is not cooperative. The diplomatic role of the Director General has been sparingly but effectively used on some occasions before referring the issue to the Security Council. Even though the compliance procedures of the OPCW and the CTBTO have not yet been tested, IAEA's experience may serve as a good basis for clarifying the entire process, from the point of discovering a substantive infraction to the point of referral to the Security Council.

In this respect, full advantage should be taken of current trends in the Security Council to make itself more accessible. In 1992, the Security Council announced in a 'Presidential Statement': 'The proliferation of weapons of mass destruction constitutes a threat to international peace and security.' The Member States pledged to take appropriate action in case of any violations that would be reported to the Council. This policy has now been reinforced by Resolution 1540 on WMD proliferation, cited above. It is thus up to the organizations concerned to report without much hesitation any serious compliance problems for political support and possibly for some sanctions.

Completing the WMD control regime

The second set of proposals concerns further regime building on the basis of previously agreed principles. The basic principles for the elimination of weapons of mass destruction were adopted by consensus at the first Special Session on Disarmament (SSOD I). The session was convened by the UN General Assembly in 1978 to plan for General and Complete Disarmament. A master plan for a WMD control regime would thus be based on principles already agreed over 25 years ago. The main elements for a master plan can be extrapolated from the Principles and Objectives for Nuclear Non-Proliferation and Disarmament, also adopted by consensus, at the 1995 Review and Extension Conference of the Parties to Nuclear Non-Proliferation Treaty.[15]

In this light, a complete WMD control regime would resemble a model with seven dimensions comprising thirteen components, as presented in Table 8.1 entitled 'State of WMD Control Regime'. They are annotated with comments to indicate the present status of each component and what needs to be done to complete constructing the regime as a whole.

Two interrelated issues are of crucial importance in the effort to remove the current threats to the integrity of the existing treaty regimes, to ensure complementarity and facilitate consolidation among them. These issues are: universality of membership, at least as regards the

Table 8.1   State of WMD Control Regime

A. Nuclear weapons
1. Nuclear Non-Proliferation Treaty (with Review Conferences) and IAEA Safeguards Verification. *In place.*
2. Comprehensive Test-Ban Treaty: CTBTO for implementation and Verification. *Needs ratifications for entry into force.*
3. Fissile Material Cut-off Treaty (FMCT). *Negotiations stalled at CD (Geneva).*
4. Nuclear Disarmament: US–Russia reductions. *Progressing.*
   China–France–UK reductions. *Yet to begin.*
   Israel–India–Pakistan. *No commitment to begin.*
   Ultimate elimination. *Hindered by deterrence doctrine.*

B. Chemical and biological weapons
5. Chemical Weapons Convention: OPCW for implementation/verification. *In place.*
6. Biological Weapons Convention. *Lacks verification mechanism.*

C. WMD delivery vehicles
7. Missiles Technology Control Regime. *Merely voluntary with limited membership.*

D. Demand/supply regulation
8. Assurance of supply for peaceful use. *Guaranteed by treaties.*
9. Export Control Regimes. *Not universal, discriminatory, inadequate.*

E. Regional dimension – WMD-free zones
10. Nuclear-weapon-free zones: Treaty of Tlatelolco for Latin America & Caribbean; African NWFZ Treaty; South Pacific NWFZ Treaty; Southeast Asia NWFZ. *In place.* Central Asia NWFZ Treaty. *In progress.* NWFZs for the Middle East, for South Asia and for East Asia & the Korean Peninsula. *Missing.*
11. Consolidated WMD-free zones. *Long-term possibility to add chemical/biological components to existing nuclear-weapons-free zones.*

F. Security assurances and reduction of tension
12. Binding Security Assurances. *Only negative assurances under NWFZs and as volunteered by the five nuclear-weapons States (not to threaten NPT parties with nuclear weapons), without any positive assurance of protection.*

G. Compliance enforcement
13. Security Council Action. *The declaration to act on proliferation is too vague. A veto-free procedure is needed, with a commitment to cope firmly with threats of withdrawal from treaty.*

---

militarily significant States, and multilateralism with effective leadership by the major powers. Unless multilateral solutions are actively sought under the leadership of the US as the most powerful nation, we cannot reasonably expect the holdout States to consider acceding to the treaties. Without it, the prospect of strengthening and consolidating the treaty regimes will remain poor.

The main problem of universality revolves around India, Pakistan and Israel, as new but unrecognized nuclear-weapon States, and North Korea as a prospective one. Their nuclear policies have an impact on the universality issue in the chemical field as well. All of these States have stayed away from the NPT, a situation that affects cohesion within the policy-making organs of the IAEA when they deal with NPT verification. The same four have also stayed away from the CTBT. Israel went as far as signing the Treaty, as did Egypt, Iran and Indonesia. However, these States are waiting for Israel to make the first move towards ratification. Without all of them and a few smaller States joining, and without decisive action by the US and China to ratify the Treaty, it cannot even enter into force. The situation is much better with respect to the CWC, since, of the four, only North Korea and Israel have stayed away, joined by Egypt, Lebanon and Syria in protest at Israel's nuclear policy. In the biological field, the problem is minimal, as all except Israel are parties to the BWC, which bodes well for any verification mechanism that might eventually be created.

There is no magic bullet for resolving the universality issue, as it is caused by fundamental security concerns in South Asia, the Middle East and East Asia. However, a reversal of the current unilateralist and proliferation-oriented policies of the US could make a major difference in alleviating those concerns and in reviving negotiations to strengthen the WMD control regime. Before focusing on the crucial regional issues, let us attempt to outline the requirements for a progressive strengthening, enlargement and consolidation of this regime.

Nuclear policies: resumption of US leadership

The lessons from the 2003 Iraq War and its aftermath are instructive. They have revealed the danger of relying on a basically unilateral approach to resolve WMD problems, particularly by national counter-proliferation measures, rather than relying on the traditional multilateral approach of the United States. The pendulum of US foreign policy under the Bush Administration may well have struck the limits of unilateralism to swing back towards judicious multilateralism. As the Carnegie Endowment

Report has recently proposed, there is an urgent need to de-emphasize the value of nuclear weapons for US national security, particularly by:[16]

(a) reducing the risk of nuclear war;
(b) renouncing the development of new types of nuclear weapons and halting research on such weapons;
(c) reaffirming the ban on nuclear testing and pursuing ratification of the CTBT.

Such changes would restore the credibility of the US in persuading other States to roll back their nuclear arsenals or refrain from acquiring the weapons.

Defusing regional crises

The nuclearization of South Asia, the Middle East and the Korean Peninsula did not come about suddenly but was a consequence of deteriorating regional disputes and rising insecurity at a time of diplomatic complacency and laxity in proliferation control. The key to disarmament is peaceful resolution of the major disputes in each region – the Kashmir dispute, the Arab–Israel crisis over the status of Palestine, and the crisis involving North Korea. Unless a sustained and balanced diplomatic effort is made by the US and other influential powers to assist the protagonists, progress in arms control is not likely to happen. Even-handed diplomatic engagement might eventually help in promoting common security interests in each region and thus facilitate arms control as part of a broad agenda for peace. The disarmament agenda should include: nuclear risk reduction, a halt in fissile material production, respect for moratorium on testing, agreement on conditions for accession to the CTBT, and the creation of a nuclear-free zone in each area. The task is very difficult but the necessary steps are evident and urgently needed.

The way ahead

It is difficult to propose a road map for building an expanded WMD control regime but we can briefly attempt to outline the logical steps to future negotiations.

Future measures

Enforcing existing agreements.   Efforts should be intensified to ensure not only essential ratifications of the CTBT but also successful negotiations by the IAEA on wider acceptance of the Additional Protocol to the NPT Safeguards Agreements. The Secretariats need active diplomatic help from the nuclear-weapon States.

BWC verification. In view of current threats from well-organized terrorist groups, new initiatives are urgently needed to equip the Biological Weapons Convention with an effective verification mechanism. As mentioned earlier, the current loophole might be provisionally closed by adapting UNMOVIC for the task, but all options must be considered for a permanent mechanism. The idea of aligning the new mechanism with the OPCW or of even entrusting it to that organization would have the additional merit of reversing the fragmentation trend in arms control.

A Fissile Material Cut-off Treaty (FMCT). The nuclear non-proliferation regime, currently based on the NPT and the CTBT, needs to be completed by adding a Fissile Material Cut-off Treaty applicable to all States. US leadership is essential to jump-start the stalled negotiations on this item at the Geneva Conference on Disarmament, especially as this will require bringing along all nuclear-weapon States, including India and Pakistan. As in the case of the NPT, the IAEA's mandate and experience is suitable to perform the verification task. Negotiators should therefore seriously consider entrusting the task to the IAEA, with the additional benefit that it might catalyze a higher level of collaboration between the IAEA and the CTBTO.

Missile Technology Control Regime (MTCR). Over 33 States, mostly industrialized countries with active export control policies, belong to a group set up to limit the proliferation of missiles capable of delivering weapons of mass destruction. Although they include Argentina, Brazil, South Korea and South Africa, the group's membership criteria are so strict as to exclude many countries involved in the missile trade. This is an area where exporters and importers need a serious dialogue about rules of trade in dual-use missiles in order to develop a genuine international regime.

Coordinated import–export control. UNSCOM and the IAEA had a successful joint unit to control sensitive WMD-related items imported by Iraq. The unit was responsible for receiving and analyzing notifications from all suppliers as well as from Iraq. Inspectors had also the right to monitor the borders of Iraq and to conduct investigations abroad. It is understood that this single-country model may not be feasible in the complex multilateral setting of the IAEA and the OPCW, given their differing reporting procedures and technical requirements. However, they might benefit not only from strengthening separately their information gathering and evaluation capacity but also from regular collaborative arrangements to investigate suspicious cases. This approach might commend itself, since the sources, the channels and the pattern of the illicit trade may be part of the same network.

Creating WMD-free zones. The creation of nuclear-weapon-free zones has already made a major contribution to the cause of nuclear nonproliferation in five parts of the world. At the regional level it was possible for States to go beyond the requirements of the NPT in excluding any deployment of nuclear weapons within the zone and also to receive binding security assurances from the nuclear-weapon States. The next task is to create similar zones in other regions, especially the tension zones of the Middle East, South Asia and the Korean Peninsula. For the Middle East, there has long been a consensus in the UN General Assembly to create a nuclear-weapon-free zone as part of the peace process. Beyond that, the Security Council has launched the idea of creating a zone free of weapons of mass destruction in the Middle East. A successful disarmament of Iraq was expected to be a step towards the creation of such a zone. Now that Iraq has been disarmed, the time has come to study the modalities of a WMD-free zone for the Middle East beyond the studies done already on the nuclear aspect.

Such a zone in the Middle East might serve as a valuable framework for a joint regional verification mechanism run jointly by the IAEA, the CTBTO and the OPCW. Successful negotiation might also provide a model for an integrated approach for the other areas of tension.

Political agreements

Over the years, negotiators and scholars have explored possibilities to build a coherent process of disarmament. A quarter of a century ago, the international community agreed at the first Special Session of the General Assembly devoted to Disarmament (SSOD I) on a comprehensive framework for General and Complete Disarmament. A great deal was achieved since then, especially in the 1990s, in strengthening the NPT verification system, in agreeing on the long-awaited Comprehensive Test-Ban Treaty, in establishing a complete disarmament regime under the Chemical Weapons Convention and in initiating nuclear weapon reduction by the two superpowers. However, the decade ended with major setbacks threatening the entire arms control system. Major initiatives are therefore needed to restore the integrity of the system and resume the task of strengthening and consolidating the WMD control regime. A promising strategy would be for Member States to engage in consultations at four levels:

- *Among the major powers.* As permanent members of the Security Council, the five nuclear-weapon States need to hold intensive consultations on a range of disarmament issues in the context of current threats to international peace and security. The priority issue should be to establish a 'code of conduct' for dealing with cases of serious violation of WMD treaties, with a commitment to take automatic response. This idea as suggested by Germany in April 2004 implies reaching a fundamental agreement in advance on a veto-free process to handle non-compliance cases.[17] Other important issues for a deal are: joint security assurances to all NPT parties, verified implementation of the BWC, and progress towards nuclear disarmament. Within the P-5 Group, the US and Russia have begun to reduce their nuclear weapons, but need to speed it up and be followed soon by China, France and the UK. The G-8 Summits are also a useful forum for giving impetus to priority issues for negotiation, with the participation of all economically significant States, including Canada, Germany, Italy and Japan.
- *Between the P-5 and India, Pakistan and Israel.* A serious dialogue is necessary between the two groups to reach an understanding on the issue of nuclear status and to negotiate the possibilities for a freeze on the nuclear programmes of the three States and the conditions for a roll-back in the context of reductions by all the P-5. Such a dialogue may also help in resolving the stalemate on fissile material control. However, China and the US would need to demonstrate their sincerity by at least ratifying the CTBT.
- *Geneva negotiations.* Consultations at the two levels mentioned could greatly assist disarmament negotiations at the Conference on Disarmament, not only in concluding a Fissile Material Cut-off Treaty but also in selecting other negotiable issues.
- *Special plenary conferences.* The periodic review conferences for the NPT, the CTBT, the CWC and the BWC will remain useful for strengthening each regime and for considering concepts about building linkages with one another. The review conferences for the NPT and the BWC are particularly important in advancing the completion of their respective regimes. However, none of them can address all the possibilities for long-term consolidation within a broad WMD control regime.

It is therefore necessary to convene a fourth Special Session of the General Assembly Devoted to Disarmament (SSOD IV). It is time to take stock of the progress made so far and lay out a road map towards the verified elimination of WMD.

When all is said and done, the basic fact is that Member States, especially the most powerful of them, will act according to what they will see as serving their national interests. How that is defined then becomes the key issue. In the face of the new threats, which demand cooperation among States, the pursuit of narrow self-interest may jeopardize the common interest of all and may run the risk of a catastrophic use of weapons of mass destruction. In reaching a global consensus, every effort should be made to encourage rather than inhibit active participation by the smaller States that are keenly concerned about the negative trends, and equally by non-governmental organizations as a useful channel for public opinion.

9
Building Effective Management for the Regime

The regime for the verification of the elimination of weapons of mass destruction is only as good as the organizations that have been set up to implement the agreed procedures to verify compliance. The question has to be asked, and has been asked: are the international organizations up to the job?

Part of the answer, as has been discussed, is political. The various States have to provide the necessary support and cooperation with the organizations. But, as was especially noted in Chapter 6, part of the answer is administrative: can the organizations be managed effectively?

The link between the two has been demonstrated throughout the half-century in which international organizations have been major players in international politics. Political problems have often been expressed as management issues, as when States have withheld assessed contributions under the guise of 'efficiency' of international organizations.

The first major United Nations financial crisis was political. The Soviet Union, unhappy with the General Assembly's vote to authorize (and fund) the Congo operation in the 1960s, withheld its assessed contribution. The argument was based on a legalism: only the Security Council could authorize a peacekeeping mission and therefore the increase in assessment was illegal. Thereafter, whenever a State encountered something funded from the assessed contributions with which it disagreed, it could (and often would) withhold payment on that amount. This was a tactic used consistently by the United States starting in the 1970s.

A more apposite case is the removal from office of José Bustani, the first Director General of the OPCW in 2002, to which reference has already been made in Chapter 6. This was apparently the first case in history when an elected head of an international organization was removed. Previous cases had been solved by the resignation of the head (as happened with Trygve Lie, the first Secretary-General of the United Nations). The vote, at a special meeting of States Parties to the convention, was 48 to 7 with 43 abstentions, indicating that less than half of the States favoured removal.[1]

Bustani had been in many ways a normal choice for head of a new programme. He had overseen the negotiations leading to the creation of the OPCW. As such he was a 'known quantity' and presumably understood the nuances of the agreements reached by the negotiators over the long period between the agreement on the Convention in 1992 and its entry-into-force in 1997. It was assumed that he would understand the constraints under which he would have to operate.

This kind of choice is not unusual in international organizations, as was shown by the appointment of Ambassador José Ayala Lasso as the first High Commissioner for Human Rights. Ayala Lasso had led the negotiations creating the post and, as the head of the United Nations' liaison office of Amnesty International wrote a few months later: 'the fact that Ambassador Ayala Lasso himself presided over the tortuous process of creation means that he personally understands the expectations of him and some of the gaps the post is supposed to fill.'[2]

Bustani's first five years, during the Clinton Administration in the United States, were politically acceptable, and he was re-elected to a five-year term in 2000, again during the Clinton Administration. The Bush Administration had a serious political problem with Bustani, although it is not clear whether this was due to Bustani or to a marked hostility that the Administration had towards any international organization.

What is instructive, however, is that the political problems that the United States had with Bustani were expressed as administrative and management issues. The Nuclear Threat Initiative's Newswire stated:[3]

> U.N. sources have said, however, that Bustani has drawn the ire of the United States on two major issues. For one, he is resisting an attack on Iraq if investigators prove that Baghdad is still producing chemical weapons. In addition, he insists on adhering 'literally' to the OPCW's mandate, which calls for inspections not only on 'hostile' countries but also on nations such as the United States.

Both issues were within the authority of the Director General of the OPCW. As he stated in his final speech to the Special Session of the Conference of Parties just before he was voted out of office:[4]

> I am blamed for seeking Iraq's membership of the CWC, even though this effort is in full accordance with the decisions of the UN Security

Council, and with the mandate issued to me by all of you, to ensure the Convention's universality WITHOUT EXCEPTION.

On the second charge, Bustani stated:

> I insist on measures that will ensure that OPCW inspectors verify those weapons and equipment that the OPCW must verify, rather than merely those which might be volunteered by a State Party for verification. In other words, I trust, but I also verify, everywhere, in full accordance with the Convention. I do criticize attempts to water down the verification regime. I do criticize the continuing attempts of a small number of States Parties to stonewall long-awaited solutions to critical issues out of perceived national preferences.

Because it would be difficult to criticize Bustani for, perhaps imprudently, adhering to his duties as set out under the convention, the argument for removing him turned on management issues. In fact, had Iraq become a party to the CWC, the on-going issue of removing Iraq's assumed weapons of mass destruction would have been made more complex by injecting another institutional actor into an already difficult situation. The second reason is more obscure.

The management problems about which Bustani was accused were those with which most international organizations have to cope. According to Robert Matthews, there were disputes about whether the Technical Secretariat was making decisions that should be made by Member States through the Executive Council. There were also concerns that financial controls were inadequate and that Member States were not being told enough about how costs were being incurred or calculated.[5] These were presented under the general heading of lack of transparency. In his defence before the Conference of States Parties, Bustani disputed all of the allegations, but to no avail.

Management issues can also become political. UNSCOM had built a large proportion of its staffing on inspectors who had been seconded from national civil services and the military. In part this was to reduce the cost of UNSCOM, by keeping the regular establishment size small. It was also to provide for flexibility in meeting what were perceived as varying needs for different types of inspectors. One consequence of this was that the inspectors were not considered to be United Nations staff, subject to the normal rules on secretariat performance.

This management choice became an issue in 1999, when investigative journalists found that many of the inspectors, especially those from the

United States and the United Kingdom, had been reporting back to their national intelligence agencies. What was worse, they were not reporting all that they were finding to UNSCOM itself and were installing additional monitoring equipment without UNSCOM's knowledge.[6] This provided a further excuse to the Iraqi authorities to reject accepting United Nations inspectors.

This chapter looks at the management issues that must be solved if the political issues are to be controlled. These issues centre on the key administrative functions that any organization must perform:

- Human resources management
- Finance and budgeting
- Information management
- Accountability and oversight.

The leader in all of these is the IAEA, which is widely considered to be the best managed of all the international organizations. It served as the model for the CTBTO and for the OPCW, so its experience can be instructive for those organizations as well.

Human resources policies: the problem of rotation

Without question, the staff of international organizations constitutes its greatest asset. Not only are personnel costs the largest element of the organizations' budgets, but the staff represents the visible presence of each organization. Obtaining, retaining and using good staff is a central management question.

When the United Nations was established, it had the experience of the League of Nations, where the concept of an international civil service had been developed. Under that experience, the idea of an independent, politically neutral, career civil service had emerged as an alternative to the notion of staffing international organizations with seconded personnel from national services.

The United Nations Charter is, in many ways, a curious document. In terms of the functions of its principal intergovernmental organs, like the General Assembly, the Security Council or the Economic and Social Council, it is very specific about duties and responsibilities. In contrast, its articles dealing with the United Nations Secretariat are essentially silent about what the Secretariat is supposed to do, but is very explicit about whom the Secretariat is and how it is supposed to do what it does.

Two elements are clear: the Secretariat is supposed to be politically neutral, and it must be above reproach. Article 100 clearly states the neutrality issue, both from the perspective of the individual staff members and of the Member States:

1. In the performance of their duties the Secretary-General and the staff shall not seek or receive instructions from any government or from any other authority external to the Organization. They shall refrain from any action that might reflect on their position as international officials responsible only to the Organization.

2. Each Member of the United Nations undertakes to respect the exclusively international character of the responsibilities of the Secretary-General and the staff and not to seek to influence them in the discharge of their responsibilities.

The standards to be met in recruiting international civil servants are also clearly stated in Article 102:

3. The paramount consideration in the employment of the staff and in the determination of the conditions of service shall be the necessity of securing the highest standards of efficiency, competence, and integrity. Due regard shall be paid to the importance of recruiting the staff on as wide a geographical basis as possible.

Underlying this agreement was an understanding that the credibility and independence of the international civil service was its most important characteristic. Hans Blix (2004, p. 264), reflecting on UNMOVIC's role in Iraq expressed the importance of perceived independence and neutrality of staff:

We had the advantage, compared to some of the national intelligence services, of being less exposed to pressures from the outside and from above. Our loyalty was to the Security Council, with its many member states and diverse opinions ... Another advantage was the important international civil service tradition that normally prevails in the UN System. On no occasion did I find that staff members, whether of American, British, French, Russian or any other nationality, were influenced by positions that the governments of their home states had taken or could be expected to take.

UNMOVIC's exercise of independent critical judgment was, I believe, the main reason why our analyses and assessment were respected and accepted.

How to achieve this impartial, competent civil service has been one of the major administrative issues that have been discussed in the rather arcane precincts of the administrative committees of international organizations. It has focused on how to recruit, train, pay and discipline staffs of organizations so that they will be truly independent.

When most United Nations system organizations were established in the 1940s, the civil service tradition was clearly in the mind of the Member States who were negotiating. They foresaw a civil service which, like the British and French services on which the Staff Regulations and Rules were based, was a combination of career officials and technicians brought in for short periods.

The underlying logic was that career officials, whose loyalty would be to the organization, would provide the institutional memory and cultural continuity to the service, while the short-term people kept the organization up-to-date with technical expertise.

The IAEA experience

By the time that the IAEA was founded in 1957, the original innocence about an international civil service had been lost in the Cold War. The Agency was clearly seen in that context and, moreover, it was felt by many of the negotiators that a critical factor was to ensure that the organization would be able to obtain staff versed in the latest technology. As a result, the Agency Statute's Article VII on staff included the UN Charter's standard criteria of 'highest standards of efficiency, technical competence and integrity', the idea of due regard to geographical distribution and the admonition to not accept instructions from any country. Article VII also made an unusual provision:

C. The staff shall include such qualified scientific and technical and other personnel as may be required to fulfill the objectives and functions of the Agency. The Agency shall be guided by the principle that its permanent staff shall be kept to a minimum.

This was the principle of rotation. No staff member hired by the Agency should expect to stay and make a career. In practice, this meant that after an initial three-year contract, staff should normally only expect one two-year extension, and only exceptionally a further two years. Longer-term contracts, in effect permanent, would be granted only 'to provide the necessary continuity in essential functions or for other compelling reasons in the interests of the Agency'.

While this was never written down, Agency lore says that a key reason had to do with the Safeguards Department. When the Agency was founded, it was assumed that most inspectors would have to be recruited from the intelligence or military services of the nuclear powers. There was a fear that without rotation, the Safeguards Department would become mini-KGBs or mini-CIAs. In fact, this assumption turned out to be completely erroneous.

As the Agency's safeguards programme evolved it became clear that if competent inspectors were to be obtained and maintained, the Agency would have to train and develop them itself. There were no other places where that type of inspection would take place and the only employer of nuclear inspectors would be the Agency. Moreover, if the objective of having a politically-neutral inspectorate was to be achieved, inspectors who came from non-nuclear states would have to be employed. These would have to be trained within the Agency itself and the high cost could not be justified if the rotation principle were to be applied.

Over time, the proportion of staff on long-term contracts grew. In 1998, a report by the External Auditors that focused on personnel policy noted that 40 per cent of the professional staff of the Agency held long-term contracts.[7] The largest proportion of these contracts was held by staff in the Safeguards Department, consistent with the view that the inspectorate, to be effective, had to be a career service.

Safeguards professionals receive training within the Agency. In addition, there is a form of career development, where professional staff may move between the operational divisions, the Division of Technical Support, the Division of Safeguards Information Technology and the Division of Concepts and Planning.

With the exception of the Deputy Director General in charge of the Department, most of the division directors and section chiefs are career staff, who have emerged through the ranks. This reflects an understanding that in management of the inspection function an ability to navigate the complex political environment in which inspections take place is more important than the technical skills, which are also essential but can be acquired more easily.

The second largest proportion of long-term contracts is found in the management department. This also reflects an understanding that internal management of international organizations is qualitatively different from management of national public or private organizations. Understanding the history, reasons for procedures and political context for administration is an essential element of maintaining the credibility of the organization.

The OPCW variant

When the CWC came into force on 29 April 1997, it was the first new international verification organization to have been created in almost 40 years. The States Parties to the Convention were conscious of the problems that were perceived to have arisen in the United Nations Secretariat and other secretariats of the United Nations System, including increasing costs and a high percentage of staff with permanent contracts. This was a period in which legislatures of major contributors to the organizations, including the United States, the European Union states and the Russian Federation, were imposing zero-growth budgets on the organizations.

After the Convention was agreed in 1992, a Provisional Technical Secretariat was set up to undertake the tasks that needed to be accomplished before the entry-into-force. These tasks included setting the basis for a permanent organization.

Defining the detailed structure of the OPCW was one of the tasks, as was determining the Staff Regulations to apply. The regulations for the Provisional Technical Secretariat were drawn from those in force in the organizations of the United Nations System, with the exception of a provision that 'Recruitment shall be guided by the principle that the staff shall be kept to a minimum necessary for the proper discharge of the responsibilities of the Secretariat.' The other guidance to the Executive Secretary of the PTS was that 'In filling staff positions, the Executive Secretary shall bear clearly in mind the transitional character of the Commission.' This left undetermined whether there would be a permanent core staff or not.

In negotiating the OPCW staff regulations after entry-into-force, the concerns about finance and permanence continued to enter into play. When the staff regulations were adopted they included the same language as the Charter regarding independence of the secretariats and the criteria of competence, integrity and efficiency in hiring.

In 1999, in adopting the final Staff Regulations, the rotation principle was graven in stone, completely prohibiting the creation of a permanent career staff. Regulation 4.4 explicitly stated that:

(a) The OPCW is a non-career organization. This means that no permanent contracts shall be granted. Staff members shall be granted one of the following types of temporary appointments: short-term or fixed-term. The initial contract period shall not normally exceed three years. Contract extensions are possible; however, contracts, including extensions, carry no expectation of renewal or re-employment.

Contract extension will become progressively more difficult, and shall be assessed upon, inter alia, the staff member's performance measured in accordance with a rigorous performance appraisal system. Any contract extension will be based on a continuing need on the part of the Organization for the specific skill and knowledge of the staff member.

(b) The total length of service of Secretariat staff shall be seven years.

The negotiators clearly felt that by restricting the size of the Secretariat, costs could be contained, and that by prohibiting permanent contracts, rigidity could be avoided. Smithson suggests an additional motivation:[8]

> Worried that the Technical Secretariat would become a warehouse for below-par or unsuitable personnel, the CWC's early signatories created a plan to ensure that fresh blood would enter the inspectorate. The inspectorate's 'tenure' policy would limit employment at the Technical Secretariat to seven years. The worthy intent of this policy is to sustain a vibrant, state-of-the-art, trained inspector corps over the lifetime of the treaty, not to have the Technical Secretariat saddled with political appointees who grow comfortable and stale in their jobs.

How they developed this concern is not clear, since it had clearly not been the case with the IAEA, the only comparator organization. More likely, it reflected a perception on the parts of governments that the organizations of the United Nations System had that problem, although even in those cases there was no evidence of it.

Exceptions were only to be given for locally-recruited clerical staff and linguistic staff. In the first case, this was based on the assumption that clerical staff were not important, and in the second case, that obtaining and retaining good linguistic staff was difficult because they were in short supply.

The rotation principle was the same logic that had been applied when the IAEA had been created, but did not take into account the IAEA's experience, which was directly contrary to the assumptions made that rotation was desirable. It created the likelihood that the organization would not be able to develop and retain a cadre of competent inspectors and other key staff. It assumed that the main factors in successful verification were technical rather than political. This, had the IAEA's experience been applied, would have been highly questionable.

During his first four years, one of Director General Bustani's problem areas was personnel. First, staff had been hired for the PTS based on an assumption that once the organization became permanent, job classifications would be revised to make them consistent with United Nations system classification practice. (For example, a Director in most United Nations organizations was graded at D-2 level, while in the PTS, a director was graded at the Principal Officer or D-1 level.) The Executive Council of the OPCW, made up of Member State representatives, did not agree to implement the re-classification that had been proposed by an outside consultant. Given the Executive Council impasse, the Director General resisted implementing the re-classifications until some eighty professional staff members appealed the decision to the ILO Administrative Tribunal and won.

As Maurizio Barbeschi, a former Senior Policy Officer in the Verification Division of the OPCW, recounted in one of the few articles on the internal workings of the organization:[9]

> The reassessment exercise generated considerable resistance among some states parties, which expressed their dissatisfaction both overtly through the Executive Council and the CSP, as well as covertly through their delegations. Bustani stood firm in his belief that he had the mandate to decide such issues, which led to mounting frustration as states tried to assert their power as the final authority of matters concerning the management of the OPCW Secretariat. A number of states claimed that the reassessment exercise was more a question of status and 'self-promotion' than of fair treatment for Secretariat personnel. There were also strong concerns regarding the financial implications for the organization.

> This experience illustrates how an element of the technical dimension (budget authority, a part of control systems) is inseparable from the political/cultural dimension. The fact that the Director-General decided to undertake the post reassessment exercise notwithstanding the opposition of members of the Executive Council became a powerful symbol to the Secretariat of having a leader that was willing to stand up to states parties to defend the integrity of the Secretariat staff and independence of the organization.

The second personnel issue had to do with when the rotation principle was to apply. Many of the professional and managerial staff had begun work with the organization during the PTS period. By 2000, many were already reaching a seven-year point from the date they were first hired. Without a clear instruction about when the rotation was to start, Bustani proceeded to permit extensions. This also brought him into conflict with the Executive Committee.

In the aftermath of Bustani's firing, a second special session of the Conference of States Parties had to be convened on 30 April 2003, with the tenure policy of the OPCW as its only agenda item. The Conference met in private session for exactly 18 minutes and adopted a tenure policy recommended by the Executive Council.[10] The decision was detailed and unambiguous:

1. Decides that:

   (a) The average rate of turnover beginning with the calendar year 2003 with respect to turnover of Secretariat staff subject to tenure, other than those falling under the provisions of Staff Regulation 4.4(b) (i) and (ii), shall be one-seventh per year.

   (b) As an exceptional measure so as not to compromise the financial stability and operational effectiveness of the Organisation, the Director-General shall be authorised to grant contract extensions or renewals which would result in a total length of service in excess of the seven-year limit provided for in Staff Regulation 4.4(b).

   (c) This exceptional authority of the Director-General to grant contract extensions or renewals beyond the seven-year total length of service provided for in Staff Regulation 4.4(b) shall expire effective 1 January 2009. At that time, not more than 10% of the number of staff subject to tenure that were incumbent on 2 July 1999, other than those falling under the provisions of Staff Regulation 4.4(b) (i) and (ii), may remain on staff, and by 31 December 2009, no member of Secretariat staff, other than those falling under the provisions of Staff Regulation 4.4(b) (i) and (ii), who has served more than seven years shall remain on staff.

2. Reaffirms that:

   (a) the nature of the OPCW as a non-career organization with limited staff tenure, and the Staff Regulations, in particular Staff Regulation 4.4, require the Director-General, when considering contract extensions or renewals, to take fully into account the need for decisions on contracts to contribute to, and be consistent with, the faithful implementation of overall tenure policy; and,

   (b) when implementing the Staff Regulations and the decisions of the Council and the Conference in this matter, the Director-General's authority includes at any time to extend or renew or not to extend or renew contracts for Secretariat staff who have served less than seven years.

The difficulties inherent in implementing that policy were reflected in the statement of the new Director General, Rogelio Pfirter, to the First Review Conference of the Convention on 28 April 2003, just two days before this decision was ratified.[11] After referring to the year following his predecessor's ouster as a trial by fire, he stated that:

> I will implement this measure as mandated by the Policy-Making Organs in a fair and transparent manner. This will not be easy, as it will require the introduction of a phasing-in mechanism that will have to reconcile the turnover rate defined by Member States with the operational requirements of the OPCW and the financial resources available to it.
>
> This was no easy decision for Member States to take, and it will certainly not be any easier to implement it. Rotation means that new talent joins the OPCW, but inevitably it also means that some of our highly esteemed colleagues will leave it.

Among those leaving were some of the key staff who had developed the organization and who had carried out its initial verification efforts that had often been fairly successful in the face of financial and political adversity (see below).

As Smithson's analysis puts it, there were two immediate consequences of implementing the tenure policy. There was an immediate decline in the morale of the Technical Secretariat staff, whose career options were now severely constrained. Second, since the original staff are all leaving or have left, so has the institutional memory. Smithson states: 'Future generations of inspectors and key support personnel must be able to benefit from the experience and knowledge of their predecessors. Otherwise, all of that wisdom just goes out the door.'[12]

There was a third consequence. The management of the Technical Secretariat had not anticipated either the number of separations it would have to sustain or the cost of recruiting replacements. As a consequence, there was an immediate drain on finances. The Director General stated in his introductory statement to the Eighth Meeting of the Conference of States Parties that funds had not been set aside for that purpose and he had to request a budget increase. This was granted, although very reluctantly.

The OPCW has opted for a personnel structure based on a 'non-career secretariat' that, if experience is a guide, will undermine its ability to function effectively. Clearly the experience of the IAEA was not properly considered; instead, States were motivated by a general image of how secretariats in international organizations function. Time will tell whether the systematic loss of key staff will seriously affect the organization's capacity.

The CTBTO's staffing problem

The Test-Ban Treaty section on the Technical Secretariat was consciously guided by previous organizations, especially the OPCW, where negotiations had just been concluded. It specifies: 'The paramount consideration in the employment of the staff and in the determination of the conditions of service shall be the necessity of securing the highest standards of professional expertise, experience, efficiency, competence and integrity.' The addition of the criterion of 'experience' implies that professional staff will mostly not be brought in at the entry-level. The Treaty makes the usual reference to seeking equitable geographical distribution among States Parties.

The CTB Treaty has the same condition as the CWC that 'Recruitment shall be guided by the principle that the staff shall be kept to the minimum necessary for the proper discharge of the responsibilities of the Technical Secretariat.'

Because the Treaty has not yet entered into force, the organization is run by a Provisional Technical Secretariat, placing it in the same situation that was faced by the OPCW. It is by definition a temporary organization, although it has the expectation of becoming permanent. The negotiations in the CTBTO worked in parallel with those in the OPCW and it also took several years for the organization to agree on its Staff Regulations.

There were two major problems. First, a number of countries, including the Russian Federation, did not want the new organization to join the United Nations System's Joint Staff Pension Fund, for reasons that are not really clear. The second was that a number of countries wanted a strict rotation policy applied: no one should have a contract longer than seven years. After some difficulties in achieving agreement on adapting the United Nations Staff Regulations for the CTBTO, the Executive Secretary proposed a modification: 'No staff member will be granted a permanent appointment and only temporary contracts for a fixed term will be granted.'[13] The situation is slightly different from that faced by the OPCW, where the treaty entered into force rather quickly. It was only then that the debate on tenure took place. In contrast, the issue of tenure is affecting the CTBTO during the preparatory phase that is likely to continue for some time.

The consequence of limited tenure policy is that the professional staff that set up the International Monitoring System will have all left the organization before the system is fully constructed and the Treaty enters into force. The staff that set up and trained the inspectorate will also all have left. In 2004, all of the initial staff reached the mandatory rotation point. Whether this will affect the stability and credibility of the organization remains to be seen.

However, unlike the OPCW, the entry-into-force could lead to a more serious consideration of the consequences of trying to maintain a credible verification organization without a career staff.

Finance: the problems of cash flow

Unlike national governments, almost all international organizations are financed from assessments of their Member States. This means that States have to agree on the formula for dividing assessments among themselves and about the total amount to assess. The first agreement is one that is made when the organization is formed and usually only revised occasionally. For most organizations, the assessment is determined for the United Nations and then applied to the other organizations. This has been the case for the three verification organizations.

The assessment system used in the United Nations is based on ability to pay. The largest economies bear the larger portion of the assessment, while poorer countries pay the rest. Population size is used as a modifying factor. Thus, while China and India both have large economies in the aggregate, their very large populations mitigate this and neither has a large assessment. Under this system, the largest single contributor is the United States, which currently contributes 22 per cent of the United Nations budget. Japan is the second-largest contributor, but the European Union, taken as a whole, is in fact the largest contributor. These States have historically tried to ensure that the United Nations budget process does not lead to what they would perceive as a raid on their treasuries by the developing countries, whose total contribution to the budgets is much less.

National contributions to international organizations' budgets have to be built into national budgets and appropriated, usually, by national legislatures. This has a beneficial effect and a difficulty. The beneficial aspect is related to the fact that most national budgets (like most international ones) are incremental. That is, each succeeding budget is built on the base of the previous budget. For international organizations that means that once a contribution is built into a national budget base, it is fairly secure, at least in nominal terms. International organizations can therefore budget with a reasonable expectation that the previous budget period's level can be maintained in a new budget. This provides stability to the organization and ensures that a staffing structure can be maintained.

The downside is that any increase in an international budget requires either an increase or a redeployment within the budgets of all national contributors. The increases would affect all Member States and would require each to obtain additional functions from all of the national legislatures. Moreover, contributing to an agreed assessed budget is a treaty obligation for Member States. This is not an easy task and most major contributors accordingly resist increasing the total budget of the organizations. It is one reason why, for over 20 years, most international organizations have been required to live within zero real growth (which allows increases for inflation and currency fluctuation) or, more recently, zero nominal growth (the total dollar amount from one year to the next is unchanged).

For most organizations, working under this system, needs for additional resources have been met by convincing interested Member States (which have more flexibility in the use of public funds) to provide extra-budgetary, voluntary contributions. This has been possible because the total amounts of international contributions within public budgets have been proportionately small. In periods of economic growth this has worked with some success, but in periods of economic recession this has been less viable since one of the easiest elements of public expenditure to eliminate is voluntary contributions to international organizations.

Arrears constitute an additional factor in finance. Not all States pay their assessments on time (or at all). Smaller developing countries often have difficulties paying their assessments, since these must be paid in foreign exchange. The only sanction for non-payment is loss of vote, and then only after a State is over two years in arrears. As a result, by the end of most fiscal years, a relatively large number of States risk losing their vote and only contribute enough funds (sometimes borrowed from or granted by wealthier patron States) to retain their vote in the General Assembly, general conferences or conferences of State parties.

In addition, while most large contributors pay their assessments at or near the beginning of the organizations' fiscal year (almost universally a calendar year), the United States for historical reasons only pays its assessment in October of the current year, and only if it has adopted a national budget.[14] A consequence is that all international organizations have a systemic cash-flow problem. The amounts contained in budgets are almost never really available. Some organizations solve this problem from transfers among accounts, but most simply cope by underspending, which has negative effects on programme delivery.

Of the three organizations, the IAEA has been most successful in solving the cash-flow problem, although it has had difficult periods as well. For the OPCW, the finance has been one of the most difficult problems the organization has had to face.

The IAEA experience

The IAEA General Conference in September 2003 approved a budget of $268,534,000 for 2004. Of this $102,278,000 was for nuclear verification. Although the Agency programmes on a biennial basis, for historical reasons it has an annual budget. The 2004 budget constituted a significant increase. It foreshadowed an increase of $25 million over a four-year period, and the first $14 million would be included in 2004. The Agency was the first organization of the United Nations System to obtain an increase in real terms in many years, and it was the first time in 16 years that the Agency had received an increase.

As the budget document puts it:

> The proposals for an increase above zero real growth do not represent an abandonment of the principles of responsible financial management that the Secretariat has always strived to follow. Rather they should be seen as an attempt to establish an updated budget level that could act as a revised baseline for budget formulation in future biennia once the final elements of the proposed increase have been phased in 2007.

The process by which the Agency reached this point demonstrates the interaction between substance and finance. Zero real growth levels had been imposed by the major contributors in 1984. In 1991, the Agency faced a major financial crisis when the Russian Federation announced that it would not be able to pay its assessed contribution. This resulted in an immediate 4 per cent cash shortfall that had to be met by deferring equipment purchases. For the following year, the budget had to be reduced by 13 per cent.

The Agency's budgeting has always been complicated by the bargain between nuclear and non-nuclear States that was struck at the outset. In exchange for agreeing to a programme that emphasizes nuclear security, the developing country members of the Agency have been granted a technical cooperation fund, financed from extra-budgetary sources. When the regular budget would change, there would be an equivalent change in the technical cooperation fund.

In the wake of the Gulf War and the discovery that the Agency inspection process had not detected Iraq's undeclared programme, the Agency worked to develop what became the Additional Protocol on enhanced Safeguards. The adoption of enhanced Safeguards had financial implications that would have to be met if the Agency was to implement them as designed.

The Agency approach has always been to find a way to achieve its objectives within its political constraints. Since it was difficult to fund the increased costs of Safeguards through increased assessments, the Agency chose to do two things. First, they used efficiency saving techniques, to show how much additional work could be absorbed within the existing budget. Then, they sought voluntary contributions for some of the costs, including a new laboratory to analyze specimens. Only after the increased tasks flowing from the Iraq, North Korea, Iran and Libya cases did the Agency propose an increase in the assessed budget.

The negotiations were difficult. The United States, having appreciated the role of the Agency in Iran, for example, was supportive of increasing the budget. It had been a major contributor of voluntary funds for the implementation of enhanced safeguards. Japan and the European Union, even larger contributors in the aggregate, were less enthusiastic. In the end a compromise was reached in which the increase in the assessed contribution would be agreed, although it would be implemented in stages. As the programme budget document put it, the increases would be contingent on:

- A review of the modernization, flexibility and cost-effectiveness of the safeguards working methods;
- A review of the needs of Major Programme 6, Management of Technical Co-operation for Development;
- The Medium Term Strategy 2006–2011.

In other words, the increase had to be justified on the grounds that the safeguards programme was efficient, that there was a corresponding increase in the technical cooperation programme and that both programmes would be developed in a strategic context.

OPCW: getting the kinks out

The OPCW budget was designed like those of other international organizations, with the bulk of resources to come from assessments of States Parties. The assessment rates were based on those applied in the United Nations proper, adjusted, of course for those States not party.[15] Under this formula, the United States was assessed at 27.4 per cent of the total, Japan at 17.2 per cent and Germany at 9.9 per cent. The assessment rates in the United Nations have been one of the issues subject to the most complex negotiations. They are essentially based on a five-year moving average of national income and are expected to reflect an equitable ability to pay criterion. Under that criterion, the United States would be expected to pay an even larger proportion of the assessment, but a cap was placed on contributions some years ago. Ostensibly it was to prevent a single State from dominating an organization, but in practice it reflected a United States reluctance to absorb substantial costs of international organizations.

Because it is based on the United Nations formula, the OPCW budget has also been hostage to changes in that formula. Thus, in 2000, when the United States negotiated lowering the cap on the contribution to 22 per cent, that affected the OPCW as well.

All international organizations have been affected by a defect in the assessment system: not all States pay their dues and many, if not most, do not pay them on time. In each of the annual reports made by OPCW to the Conference of States Parties, the Director General reports that receipts are below the budgeted amounts. In 2001, for example, there were expenditures of 55.9 million Euros against a budget of 60.2 million Euros, with the deficit due to non-payment of assessments. The situation was similar, although a bit less, in 2002, where there were expenditures of 58.9 million Euros against a budget of 61.9 million Euros.

There is, additionally, the problem that if enough States do not pay their assessments on time (and they are due on the first of the year), the organization can face cash-flow problems. This problem occurs for each international organization, as noted earlier, because the United States only makes its annual contribution in October. The matter is further complicated when an organization's financial rules require that any unexpended funds at the end of a fiscal year need to be returned to the contributors.

Most international organizations have means to overcome both the deficit and the cash-flow problems in a given year. The United Nations is able to borrow among accounts and, for example, traditionally taps peacekeeping accounts when there is a cash-flow problem in the regular budget.[16] Other organizations borrow against voluntary funds that have not yet been expended, but very few have the authority to borrow on commercial markets.[17] In some cases, including the United Nations, a 'working capital' account can be set up as a buffer. And, in other cases, States agree to roll over unexpended funds from one fiscal year into the next.

The OPCW experienced the deficit and cash-flow problems but lacked the means to compensate for them by borrowing using a working capital account or using savings. The only alternative, especially during the problems faced by Bustani, was to curtail the work programme. As the annual report said: 'A projected cash deficit in the amount of EUR 4.3 million resulted in the decision of the Secretariat to reduce the level of implementation of the 2001 programme of work. Neither supplementary funding, nor changes in the Financial Regulations, could be agreed to by the States Parties in 2001.'

A second complicating feature was a decision in establishing the Convention to seek a form of cost-recovery for chemical weapons inspections – the 'possessor-pay principle'. These inspections were to be paid for by the States in which they took place. This was unusual, since the IAEA and other United Nations organizations were not permitted to charge for or be reimbursed for their services. Presumably the charge policy was done to relieve developing countries, which would have few facilities to be inspected, of the financial burden of inspections related to CW disarmament. The problem with this arrangement became quickly apparent. States that were expected to receive inspections (and pay for them) were reluctant to do so, and the income estimated was higher in every year. In 2000, for example, the annual report showed, that only EUR 2.8 million was invoiced during the year to those States Parties that received inspections under Articles IV and V in 2001. This was approximately EUR 1.2 million less than the estimated income that had been contained in the 2001 OPCW budget. The report said that the reduction in projected income for this item was the result of the lower than planned (and budgeted) level of chemical weapons destruction activities, as well as of fewer inspections during the year.

Moreover, payment of invoiced amounts was also very slow. The annual report

> showed that as of 31 December 2001, less than 2 per cent of the invoiced amount had been received by the OPCW. Bosnia and Herzegovina, India, the Russian Federation, the United States of America, and Yugoslavia, were all in arrears.

The annual report drew two conclusions:

> (a) The monitoring of chemical destruction also raises a serious financial problem. Even though the verification costs of destruction are chargeable to the possessor States, timely reimbursement of expenses

has been lacking. This has had a major impact on the financial resources of the OPCW that are available for all other inspections. Unless this problem is solved, the capacity to increase inspections in the chemical industry might not improve, and might even decline as disarmament monitoring intensifies in other CW-possessor States, especially Russia.

(b) The heavy cost of chemical destruction has also had an impact on the extent and pace of the inspections. Whenever reimbursements of funds advanced for monitoring chemical destruction were delayed, the industrial inspections were bound to feel the impact. Achieving balanced progress in both the disarmament and non-proliferation segments of the regime requires a plan not only for more financial resources but also for considerable budgetary reform, including possibly a separation of the funds for disarmament and non-proliferation. In the meantime, the recommendations of the First Review Conference of State Parties need to be promptly implemented with respect to the adjustment of priorities and the broader and more equitable distribution of inspection operations. The lack of a sound financial footing, or arrangement that would allow the organization to cope with cash-flow issues without curtailing programmes, means that the OPCW remains fragile.

CTBTO

The CTBTO faces similar problems, perhaps aggravated by the fact that the Convention has not entered into force. Any State contribution to the organization's budget is, in a legal sense, voluntary. However, the CTBTO has been able to avoid the problems that have afflicted the OPCW.

First, the Executive Secretary and the Secretariat staff have followed the IAEA's model of developing a reputation for fiscal conservatism. Budget increases have been few and slow in coming.

A major part of the CTBTO budget has been allocated for the construction of seismic and other remote sensing stations. While construction has been steady, funding has been obtained in advance and can be used to cover cash-flow problems of the organization. Moreover, the Preparatory Commission has been willing to allow carry-overs from year to year.

Finally, the CTBTO monitoring system, because it can be used to track non-nuclear seismic events, already provides a service to signatory States and thus can help justify the use of funds.

Information systems: the problem of information flow

All three verification organizations function on the basis of information. All have expended considerable effort to ensure that they use information technology that is appropriate. All have state of the art equipment and, it can be argued, have the infrastructure necessary to process information needed for verification purposes.

The problem is not the systems, but rather ensuring that information flows to the organizations. If, for example, trade data – even in the form of licences granted – were to reach the international organizations concerned, they would be able to track movement of precursors, raw material and equipment.

Leadership: the key to management

The experience of the IAEA shows the importance of a particular leadership style. The last three Directors General of the IAEA have covered almost the entire life of the organization. They have been quiet, technically competent and politically adept in their relations with their Member States. This type of leadership, in which the Director General works almost seamlessly, is particularly effective in international organizations. The contrast with the problems of Director General Bustamante in this sense is striking. It can be argued that the same problems can be seen in the United Nations proper, where contrasts could be made between Secretary-Generals Perez de Cuellar and Annan, representing the same style that has been achieved in the IAEA, and that of Waldheim and Boutros-Ghali.

But the issue of leadership goes beyond that. Unlike national governments, international staff cannot be led by command. Leadership in international organizations implies that staff would be willing to follow their top managers. The IAEA, consciously through its management training, as well as through its culture, has sought to inculcate a participative leadership style and has largely achieved it. In part this is because, despite the formal rotation policy, many of the key managers are long-termers. The longer-term means that the staff who cannot exercise this kind of leadership are less likely to reach management levels.

At the top, the current Director General, like the current United Nations Secretary-General, is a career official. The extent to which this explains their effective leadership style remains to be examined, but the authors, who have worked with both, believe that their experience with them suggests that the hypothesis is correct.

In the OPCW, leadership problems have hampered efforts to create a more successful organization, and the rotation policy will undoubtedly work against it. It remains to be seen whether the CTBTO will be immune to the same problems.

10
Conclusion

The goal of non-proliferation and eventual elimination of weapons of mass destruction is not just a wish of idealists aspiring to a better world but is an anxious expectation of humankind for a realistic solution to ensure survival. Today's rapid changes in the strategic environment are being met by inadequate – and sometimes detrimental – policies of arms control. In the past, doctrines of balance and deterrence were used to maintain equilibrium in a disciplined bipolar world. The post-Cold War asymmetry in power distribution and the emergence of new threats from disgruntled smaller States and from well-organized terrorist organizations outside State jurisdiction have unleashed new threats requiring new solutions. In this context, the existence and accessibility of the lethal weapons has become part of the problem, which necessitates more and not less control of the weapons of mass destruction in the possession of the major powers. During the past decade, the two Gulf Wars against Iraq and the crises in the rest of the Middle East, in the Korean Peninsula and in South Asia have shown that despite over 40 years of effort, there is a clear perception that weapons of mass destruction are not under control. There exist enough chemical, biological or nuclear weapons, or the capacity to produce them to pose an immediate risk of their falling into reckless hands.

There are four approaches to controlling weapons of mass destruction. The first is a basically unilateral use of coercion, where a powerful country like the United States imposes control by force with the help of a few allies, as was done in Iraq in 2003. The second is a multilateral use of coercive force, as was tried by a broad-based UN-authorized coalition, combined with UN disarmament, also in Iraq, in the 1990s. The third is the use of cooperative measures by single countries or groups of countries, assisted by international verification with the blessing of the

United Nations, as was attempted in the mid-1990s with North Korea through the Framework Agreement. And finally, there are cooperative measures on a global scale.

It is the last approach that has been evolving for the last forty years, built around an edifice of arms control treaties and their verification arrangements, particularly the Nuclear Non-Proliferation Treaty (NPT), the Comprehensive Test-Ban Treaty (CTBT), the Chemical Weapons Convention (CWC) and the Biological and Toxin Weapons Convention (BWC). The US Iraq experience of 2003 has shown not only the limitations of preemptive unilateral military action but also of the exclusively unilateral approach to disarmament known as counter-proliferation. This experience has also shown that the international inspections, supported by sanctions, have worked well and may now help to remove doubts about the efficacy of properly supported verification mechanisms under these treaties. It may indeed have a long-term beneficial effect on efforts to preserve and strengthen the existing verification systems.

In this book, we set out to test a central question about the global edifice of arms control: Can the agreements be verified effectively? Put differently, can the treaty-based organization provide effective verification to ensure compliance by Member States with their non-proliferation and disarmament obligations? In order to answer these seemingly simple questions, we have undertaken a detailed comparative analysis of the verification issues faced by the IAEA, the CTBTO and the OPCW in the nuclear and chemical fields. We have found them well-disposed to deliver the expected services if they are provided with sustained support from Member States. Their challenges are considerable: they have to cope with internal regime weaknesses, as does the IAEA; resist the attempts of Member States to backslide from commitments that they had made in the treaties, as is being faced by the OPCW; and overcome handicaps caused by lack of universality, even when they are spared the formidable membership problem of the CTBT that is preventing its formal launching.

The US current attitude has been particularly unhelpful. Not only has the US been inconsistent about its support for established norms, but its persistent doubts about the efficacy of multilateral verification has inhibited others from sustaining the momentum of the early 1990s. So far only three of the four WMD control treaties provide for such international verification – the NPT, the CTBT and the CWC. The BWC has no verification mechanism, and efforts to create one through a Protocol have ceased due to opposition from the United States. It may sound paradoxical that it was because of the determination of US President

Richard Nixon three decades ago that the prolonged efforts of the UK and others to ban biological weapons became a reality. It was right then not to delay the ban by the lack of consensus on how to proceed in tandem with a chemical weapons ban and on a verification mechanism jointly for both. The purpose was to expand and formalize the norm banning any use of biological weapons, and it was met.

The detailed examination of the existing verification regime reveals several truths. First, the existing mechanisms can adequately verify compliance if certain conditions are met. Cohesion among the Member States is essential, especially among the P-5 nuclear-weapon States. An important aspect of this is to remove, or at least minimize, double standards on nuclear policies to facilitate cooperation by recalcitrant States. A common fair approach by them is also bound to have a positive impact on the major weakness of the treaty regimes, which is lack of universality. Regional tensions and security problems are at the core of the universality issue, and they call for special attention by P-5, both individually as major powers and collectively within the Security Council where they have special responsibilities in the maintenance of peace and security. We have made some suggestions in Chapter 8 regarding this set of issues.

We have devoted most of the chapters to a detailed comparative analysis of the verification systems of the IAEA, the OPCW and the CTBTO, with a focus on the adequacy of their legal authority, the nature of their objectives and mandates, the efficiency of their verification operations and their handling of technical and political challenges to ensure an effective compliance process. We have critically examined the functioning of the four methods for verifying compliance as practised in the three organizations: first, the setting of baseline information by assembling and evaluating all relevant data, especially from original declarations and any updates for their value in constructing a true picture of the compliance situation; second, the continuous monitoring of relevant events and activities by technical means without tampering by the inspected States; third, the monitoring of procurements to ensure that illicit trade and trafficking in prohibited or dual-use materials is detected; and, finally, on-site inspection to verify the facts on the ground.

Each method, as developed today, has advantages and weaknesses. However, in combination, they have generally worked well in identifying inconsistencies, anomalies and gaps in information that needed to be resolved to avoid more intrusive special inspections or challenge inspections at the request of other States. All the verification operations have to cope with at least three substantive issues to seek an equilibrium in practice between the rights of inspectors under the treaties and the sovereignty rights of States: adequate intrusiveness to guarantee access to relevant locations; sufficient access to relevant information while respecting the confidentiality requirements of a State; and reasonable controls over the transfer of sensitive technology without unduly restricting the benefits that State parties are entitled to. The dynamics of the relationships are complex but the IAEA and the OPCW have managed to draw the line to sustain the integrity of their verification tasks. In all cases the main weakness has been in the insufficiency of governmental support to the inspectorates, especially in taking firm measures in cases of noncompliance. The credibility of the whole process of verification ultimately depends on how Member States respond to the inspectors' reports on non-compliance. Strengthening the links between the three organizations and the UN Security Council is therefore essential.

Effective management is, of course, indispensable for the success of verification operations. It is also the basis on which the heads of the secretariats, as general managers, can assess the weaknesses of their verification systems to come up with proposals to strengthen the treaty regime. As custodians of the common interest of Member States in properly verified treaties for arms control, the 'agencies', as represented by the international secretariats and their inspectorates, need to maintain the 'highest standards of efficiency, competence and integrity'. This requires special expertise and skills and behaviour consistent with the international character of their work: objectivity, impartiality and independence from government influences. The basic management of all of the verification organizations is sound. All of them now function with independence, transparency and efficiency, which are critical elements of credibility for the verification process.

However, the effectiveness of the staff is often diminished by pressure from various governments. Quite often, management problems are indeed political in nature. They are largely based on an unwillingness of key States to provide the political and financial backing necessary to do the job. Except for the IAEA just recently, they are underfunded, and thus understaffed, for what they are required to do. As their budgets are not allowed to grow, they are threatened with possible deficits even as they struggle with current cash shortfalls.

Another serious problem refers to the ill-advised personnel policies that governments have imposed on the secretariats. For a combination of historical and financial reasons, the verification organizations have not been set up to develop a career-based professional staff that could provide the kind of competence and credibility that an effective verification machinery will need. Experience has already shown that verification by a career service is much more credible than that based on either seconded staff or staff who lack loyalty to the organizations. The staffing of the organizations was based on the original model of the IAEA that called for a non-permanent staff. This reflected the perception that Cold War rivalries would make the creation of a career staff impossible. Despite the fact that the Agency itself, in practice if not in formal policy, has developed a career inspectorate, the OPCW and – in its rules prior to entry-into-force – the CTBTO have opted for the non-career model. This would seem to be an unwise policy that should be reviewed when the final staff rules of the CTBTO are negotiated and revised in the case of the OPCW.

For the long term, the credibility and stability of the existing treaty regimes will depend on the nature and momentum of the progress made towards the elimination of weapons of mass destruction. We have therefore attempted to chart a possible course from an existing but neglected road map in a 'back to the future' exercise. There is no better time than now to dust off proposals and guidelines already agreed by all States twenty-five years ago, at the peak of the Cold War. The goals, principles and steps adopted by consensus at the first Special Session of the UN General Assembly Devoted to Disarmament are still valid today.

The WMD control regime still remains incomplete in critical respects, due not to the inherent design of the envisaged plan but rather to lingering political obstacles posed by retrogressive policies of the major powers. A political malaise has affected the emerging regime for the elimination of weapons of mass destruction. This malaise is a combination of left-over policies from the Cold War about the role of multilateral institutions, and an unwillingness to see the elimination of nuclear, chemical and biological weapons and the means of their delivery as a package in which elimination in one area is linked to disarmament in the others. Basically, this is a reflection of the persisting unwillingness to suspend some of the dysfunctional elements of State sovereignty even in the face of common threats requiring cooperation in today's interdependent world.

How can we move forward? The Conference on Disarmament is still the sole truly representative negotiating forum available, but it has been unable even to agree on an agenda for its work. This reflects the depth of the problem facing the international community. The problem then is what can be done to gain acceptance for the various items already proposed for its agenda, and more. These include the conclusion of: a fissile material cut-off treaty; a missile technology control treaty; an international export/import control mechanism for WMD; a security assurances treaty applicable to all WMD; and a plan for progressive nuclear disarmament, beyond the bilateral agreements between the US and Russia, to include the other six nuclear-weapon States. The task is very difficult but there is no time to waste.

In the meantime, the most urgent task is to equip the Biological Weapons Convention with a verification mechanism. Several options have been suggested in Chapter 8: to adapt UNMOVIC for that purpose, thus creating a direct link between the convention and the UN Security Council; to revive BWC negotiations to add a verification arm to it; or to add a biological component to the CWC verification system. The absence of such a mechanism leaves a wide loophole in the WMD control regime and also makes it difficult to agree on cross–weapon verification issues such as export–import control.

Creating an effective export–import control system is an urgent task. The case of Iraq has shown how it can be particularly effective when a common approach is adopted for reporting and analyzing trade in sensitive materials across the board. To be fair and effective, a con-solidated system would have to be universal in application and not just restricted to voluntary reporting among a limited group of countries. In the existing 'gentlemen's agreements' it is the prerogative, indeed the duty, of the coalitions of main exporters to meet their treaty obligations by acting in concert. But there is a fine line between discouragement of illicit trafficking and discrimination against selected State parties despite their right to assured supply. The challenge is how to relate effec-tively the group efforts with the international process for procure-ment control. It will have to involve more systematic and more rapid reporting of all relevant transactions, and not just of licences denied. If reporting is universal, uniform and automatic, objections based on trade secrets might become less relevant, with the possible additional benefit of reducing the cost of the information systems. Such improve-ment would greatly assist the international verification organizations in their work, would facilitate harmonization and possibly future consolidation.

We can say in the end that, despite formidable political challenges, the IAEA, the OPCW and the CTBTO have demonstrated that they can effectively verify compliance by State parties with their non-proliferation and disarmament obligations, if the Member States provide them with sufficient political and financial support. The onset of unilat-eralism in US policy in recent years has aggravated the already existing difficulties stemming from inconsistent support, at a time when the integrity of the established regimes was being threatened by some State and non-State actors. There is now reason to hope in the post-Iraq environment that the admission of past mistakes will restore the faith in multilateral solutions, on pragmatic grounds of common interest. With this expectation, at least in the medium term, we hope that it will be possible to resume the further development of the WMD control regime.

To achieve this goal, intensive effort is required at many levels. The important role of diplomatic dialogue has already been stressed, but the struggle for human survival cannot be left only to government officials, often constrained by short-term or narrow national interests. This complex field involving highly technical issues of vital importance to the future of peace and security is too important to leave to governments alone. The role of thinkers and experts is important in analyzing the issues in order to indicate sensible directions. In this regard it is most significant that Secretary-General Kofi Annan has taken a major initiative for fundamental reform of the United Nations. The recommendations of his High-Level Panel of Governmental Experts on Threats, Challenges and Change deserve serious consideration by member States (UN document A/59/565, 29 November 2004). Equally important is the work done so far by non-governmental research institutions and advocacy groups. As their perspectives and proposals are diverse, their purpose is to generate a dialogue on issues. Another purpose is to inform and educate the broader public whose interest governments are expected to advance. The role of the responsible media is obviously important in laying out the issues. Since, often, groups of national legislators as well as people in the executive branches of the most influential governments are obstacles to disarmament, it is important to make the case before them as well. Historically, the role of public opinion has been effective in urging political leaders and legislators to adopt policies towards peace and disarmament. If fully aware of the present dangers and of the opportunities, the public is capable of influencing the direction of policies on disarmament. When common sense is lacking, it is essential to rely on sensible public opinion to hold the people's representatives accountable.

Notes

Preface

1. John Bolton, 'Remarks to the 5th Biological Weapons Convention RevCon Meeting', Geneva, Switzerland, 19 November 2001, http://www.state.gov/t/us/rm/janjuly/6231.htm

1 The Structure and Logic of the WMD Ban Regime

1. The concept of a 'poor man's atom bomb' comes from the fact that a biological weapon is cheap to produce, easy to deliver and can cause mass casualties, especially if it unleashes a contagious disease.
2. Graham S. Pearson, *The UNSCOM Saga: Chemical and Biological Weapons Non-Proliferation* (London and New York: Macmillan Press, 1999), p. 65.
3. The debate between scholars espousing realism (including neorealism) and those questioning or opposing it has been long and voluminous. One summary of the issues is found in John G. Ruggie, *Constructing the World Polity: Essays on International Institutionalization* (London and New York, 1998).
4. Reprinted in Stephen D. Krasner (ed.), *International Regimes* (Ithaca and London: Cornell University Press, 1983), p. 2.
5. Strange found five grounds for criticizing the approach: it might be a passing fad, it was imprecise, it was value-loaded and implied things that should not be taken for granted, it was too static a view of things and, finally, it was too state-centred. She argued that 'regime was yet one more woolly concept' that is a fertile source of discussion simply because people mean different things when they use it. Susan Strange, '*Cave hic dragones*: A Critique of Regime Analysis', in Krasner, *International Regimes*, pp. 338–51.
6. Joseph Cirincione (ed.), *Repairing the Regime: Preventing the Spread of Weapons of Mass Destruction* (New York and London: Routledge, 2000), p. 3; and Joseph Cirincione with Jon B. Wolfsthal and Miriam Rajkumar, *Deadly Arsenals: Tracking Weapons of Mass Destruction* (Washington, DC: Carnegie for International Peace, 2002), p. 25.
7. To ensure effectiveness, the CTBT was designed so that it could not go into effect until the 44 States that were deemed to have a theoretical capability to obtain or develop nuclear weapons became parties to the Treaty. These were listed in Annex II of the Treaty.
8. J. Samuel Barkin, 'Realist Constructivism', *International Studies Review*, 5 (2003), pp. 325–42.
9. Ian Hurd, 'Legitimacy and Authority in International Politics', *International Organization*, 53 (1999), p. 379.
10. Thomas Franck, *The Power of Legitimacy Among Nations* (New York: Oxford University Press, 1990) p. 16.

11. *Ibid.*, p. 19.
12. John Bolton, ' "Legitimacy" in International Affairs: The American Perspective in Theory and Operation', Remarks to the Federalist Society, Washington, DC, 13 November 2003, |http://www.state.gov/t/us/ rm/26413.htm
13. Franck, p. 49.
14. *Ibid.*, pp. 150–1.
15. *Ibid.*, p. 52.
16. *Ibid.*, p. 61.
17. United Nations, *The Role of the United Nations in the Field of Verification: Report of the Secretary-General* (New York, 1991), p. 4.
18. UNIDIR and VERTIC, *Coming to Terms with Security: A Handbook on Verification and Compliance* (Geneva and London: United Nations Institute for Disarmament Research and the Verification Research, Training and Information Centre, 2003), p. 1.
19. See David Fischer, *History of the International Atomic Energy Agency: The First Forty Years* (Vienna: IAEA, 1997), pp. 273–87; and Pearson, pp. 216–17
20. Frances Williams and Richard Wolff elaborate the problems in the July 26, 2001 issue of *Financial Times*, as follows:

> At the heart of the US opposition is the belief that it is impossible to construct an effective inspections regime to detect biological weapons. Laboratories developing and producing such weapons look no different from facilities producing legitimate products such as vaccines. The US says the proposed inspection regime would give ample time for those guilty of pursuing biological warfare to destroy the evidence and mask their activities. 'You could produce biological weapons in this office and you could get rid of the evidence in five minutes,' said one administration official.
>
> To underline their concerns, US officials point to the failure of United Nations weapons inspectors in Iraq to detect Saddam Hussein's biological weapons operations.
>
> Against that, the Bush administration says the proposed inspections would undermine its own biotech and drugs industries. By imposing regular site visits, it says, trade secrets would be compromised under the guise of arms control. Officials also claim inspections would compromise US efforts to defend itself against a biological attack, as US defence facilities would come under scrutiny. However, other countries have taken the view that while the draft protocol would be no guarantee against cheating, it would enhance security by acting as a further deterrent to the use or production of biological weapons.
>
> Disarmament campaigners point out that many of the deficiencies in the inspection regime were put there at the insistence of the US, concerned to protect military and commercial secrets.

The problem is that, without some international institution to do the verification, the problems noted will never be overcome. The US, the article continues, suggests as an alternative, a voluntary code of conduct.

2 Evolution of the WMD Control Regime

1. This description elaborates on the standard definition of verification adopted by the United Nations in 1991 (cited in note 17 of Chapter 1).

2. Thomas C. Schelling and Morton Halperin, *Strategy and Arms Control*, 2nd edn (Washington, DC: Pergamon-Brassey, 1985), p. 2.
3. Patrick M. Morgan, 'On Strategic Arms Control and International Security', in Edward A. Kolodziej and Patrick M. Morgan (eds), *Security and Arms Control, Vol.2: A Guide to International Policymaking* (New York, Westport and London: Greenwood Press, 1989), p. 301.
4. Hans Blix, 'International Law Relating to Disarmament and Arms Control, with Special Focus on Verification', in F. Kalshoven (ed.), *The Centennial of the First International Peace Conference* (The Netherlands: Kluwer Law International, 2000), pp. 44–5, 50–2.
5. Leland M. Goodrich and Edvard Hambro, *Charter of the United Nations: Commentary and Documents*, 2nd and rev.edn (Boston: World Peace Foundation, 1949), pp. 165–8, 209–13.
6. United Nations, *The United Nations and Disarmament, 1945–1970* (New York, 1970), p. 107.
7. A perceptive analysis is made in various articles in James Brown (ed.), *Challenges in Arms Control for the 1990s* (Amsterdam: VU University Press, 1992), especially by: Michael O. Wheeler on 'Verification in the 21st Century: A Strategic Perspective', pp. 3–14; Ronald F. Lehman II on 'Issues and Challenges of Verification', pp. 15–20; and Michael Moodie on 'Multilateral Arms Control: Challenges and Opportunities', pp. 71–80.
8. These phases largely correspond with the stages identified by Timothy J. Pounds in his article entitled 'Proposals for On-Site Inspection over the Years: From the Baruch Plan to the Reagan Initiatives', in L.A. Dunn (ed.) with A.E. Gordon, *Arms Control Verification and the New Role of On-Site Inspection* (Toronto: D.C. Heath, 1990), pp. 75–6.
9. Bernard M. Baruch, *Baruch: The Public Years* (New York: Holt, Rinehart & Winston, 1960), pp. 370–1; *The United Nations and Disarmament, 1945–1970* pp. 12–13.
10. Leland M. Goodrich, *The United Nations* (New York: Thomas Y. Cromwell, 1959), p. 226.
11. *The United Nations and Disarmament, 1945–1985*, p. 2.
12. The USSR's 'Draft Treaty on General and Complete Disarmament under Strict International Control' and the US proposal 'Outline of Basic Provisions of a Treaty on General and Complete Disarmament'.
13. Berhanykun Andemicael, 'The Non-Aligned States and International Organization: Participation in Disarmament Negotiations, 1960–1970', unpublished Doctoral Dissertation, Columbia University, New York, 1975, pp. 221–7, 424–5.
14. The full titles are Treaty on Principles Governing the Activities of States in the Exploration and Use of Outer Space, including the Moon and Other Celestial Bodies; and Treaty on the Prohibition of the Emplacement of Nuclear Weapons and Other Weapons of Mass Destruction on the Sea-Bed and the Ocean floor and in the Sub-soil Thereof.
15. The Final Document is reproduced in United Nations, *The United Nations and Non-Proliferation* (New York: UNDPI, 1995), pp. 124–30. Subsequent elaborations are quoted in *The United Nations and Disarmament, 1945–1985*, pp. 21–7.
16. *Ibid.*, pp. 123–4.

17. Frances FitzGerald, *Way Out There in the Blue: Reagan and Star Wars and the End of the Cold War* (New York, London, Toronto, Sydney, Singapore: Simon & Schuster, 2000), pp. 299–300.
18. Blix 'International Law Relating to Disarmament', pp. 63–4, 67–9.
19. Timothy J. Pounds, 'Proposals for On-Site Inspection', pp. 88–9.
20. Michael Moodie, 'Multilateral Arms Control' in Brown (ed.), *Challenges in Arms Control*, pp. 71–4.
21. UN Security Council document S/23500, 31 January 1992, United Nations, *The United Nations and Nuclear Non-Proliferation* (New York, 1995), p. 168.
22. Rolf Ekeus, 'Arms Control and the New Security Structures', in Brown (ed.), *Challenges in Arms Control*, p. 24.
23. United Nations, *The Evolution of IAEA Safeguards, International Nuclear Verification Series, No.2* (Vienna: IAEA, 1998), pp. 24–7.
24. OPCW, *Chemical Disarmament: Basic Facts* (The Hague: OPCW, 1999), p. 11; Robert J. Matthews, 'Chemical Disarmament: Advent and Performance of the OPCW', in Trevor Findlay (ed.), *VERTIC Verification Yearbook, 2000* (London: VERTIC), pp. 71–2.
25. Nicholas Sims, 'Verifying Biological Disarmament: Towards a Protocol and Organisation', in Trevor Findlay (ed.), ibid., pp. 93–5.
26. Provisional Technical Secretariat, Preparatory Commission for the CTBTO, *Comprehensive Test-Ban Treaty, Text and Annexes* (Vienna, 1999); Oliver Meier, 'Nuclear Test-Ban Verification: Work in Progress', in Trevor Findlay (ed.), *Verification Yearbook 2000*, pp. 32–4; VERTIC Secretariat, Independent Commission on the Verifiability of the CTBT, *Final Report* (London: VERTIC, 2001), pp. 2–8.

3 Baseline Information: Declarations and Data Collection

1. For a useful question and answer handbook, see Amy E. Smithson (ed.), *The Chemical Weapons Convention Handbook* (Washington, DC: The Henry L Stimson Center, 1993), especially pp. 3 and 9–12.
2. Alexander Kelle, 'Overview of the First Four Years', in Jonathan B. Tucker (ed.), *The Chemical Weapons Convention: Implementation Challenges and Solutions* (Washington, DC: Monterey Institute of International Studies, 2001), p. 12.
3. Daniel Feakes, 'Evaluating the CWC Verification System', *Disarmament Forum* (UNIDIR, Geneva, 2002), p. 15.
4. *Ibid.*
5. Kelle, 'Overview', p. 12; and Richard H. Burgess, 'Chemical Industry and the CWC', in Tucker (ed.), *Chemical Weapons Convention*, p. 40.
6. *Ibid*; and Feakes, 'Evaluating the CWC' p. 16.
7. The IAEA may, at the request of a State Party, exempt small amounts of nuclear material from safeguards, as follows: a total of one kilogram of special fissionable material, including plutonium, highly-enriched uranium and/or low-enriched uranium: ten tons of natural uranium and twenty tons of depleted uranium or thorium. Also exempted are nuclear materials used irreversibly in non-nuclear processes (e.g. alloys or ceramics) and gram quantities of fissile material used in sensing instruments and proliferation safe isotopes of plutonium (paragraphs 36 and 37 of INFCIRC/153).

8. This section is based on a more detailed explanation of the strengthened safeguards system given by one of its architects, in Richard Hooper, 'The Changing Nature of Safeguards', *IAEA Bulletin*, vol. 45, no. 1, June 2003, pp. 7–11.
9. Amy Sands and Jason Pate, 'CWC Compliance Issues', in Jonathan B. Tucker (ed.), *The Chemical Weapons Convention: Implementation Challenges and Solutions* (Monterey Institute of International Studies, 2001), pp. 19–20.
10. Reports of the Director General of the IAEA to the Board of Governors, doc. GOV/2003/40, 6 June 2003, GOV/2003/63, 26 August 2003, and GOV/2003/75, 10 November 2003.

4 Technical Monitoring

1. International Atomic Energy Agency, *Safeguards Report 2003*, http://www.iaea.org/OurWork/SV/Safeguards/es2003.

5 Controlling Supply: Procurement and Import/Export Monitoring

1. Mohammed ElBaradei, 'Saving Ourselves From Self-Destruction', *New York Times*, 12 February 2004.
2. International Atomic Energy Agency, 'The Nuclear Suppliers Group: Its Origins, Role and Activities', Attachment to Communication Received from the Permanent Mission of the Netherlands on Behalf of the Member States of the Nuclear Suppliers Group (INFCIRC/539/Rev.1 (Corrected)), 29 November 2000, para. 10.
3. *Ibid.*
4. Fritz W. Schmidt, 'The Zangger Committee: Its History and Future Role', *Non-Proliferation Review*, vol. 2, no. 1, Fall, 1994, pp. 41–2.
5. Fritz W. Schmidt, 'NPT Export Controls and the Zangger Committee', *Non-Proliferation Review*, vol. 7, no. 3, Fall–Winter, 2000.
6. http://www.nuclearsuppliersgroup.org/history.htm
7. International Atomic Energy Agency, INFCIRC/539, Rev. 1 (Corrected), 19 November 2000.
8. *Ibid.*, para. 15.
9. *Ibid.*, para. 19.
10. Wassenaar Arrangement on Export Controls for Conventional Arms and Dual-Use Goods and Technologies, 'Purposes, Guidelines & Procedures, including the Initial Elements (as amended and updated by the Plenary of December 2003)' http://www.wassenaar.org/2003Plenary/initial_elements2003.htm
11. *Ibid.*
12. Richard T. Cupitt, *Multilateral Nonproliferation Export Control Arrangements in 2000: Achievements, Challenges, and Reforms*, The Henry L. Stimson center, Study Group on Enhancing Multilateral Export Controls for US National Security, Working Paper No. 1, April 2001, p. 21.
13. Vladimir A. Orlov, 'Export Controls in Russia: Policies and Practices', *Non-Proliferation Review*, Fall, 1999, pp. 145–9.
14. Victor Zaborsky, 'Brazil's Export Control System', *Non-Proliferation Review*, Summer, 2003, pp. 123–35.

15. United States General Accounting Office, *Nonproliferation: Strategy Needed to Strengthen Multilateral Export Control Regimes*, Report No. GAO-03-43, October 2002.
16. Mohammed El-Baradei, Statement to the IAEA Board of Governors, 8 March 2004 (http://www.iaea.org/NewsCenter/Statements/2004/ebsp 2004n002.html).
17. http://www.australiagroup.net/releases/background.htm
18. Australia Group, Guidelines For Transfers of Sensitive Chemical or Biological Items, 2000 (http://www.australiagroup.net/en/guidelines.html).
19. General Accounting Office, 2002, p. 2.
20. United States of America, *Export Controls and the Chemical Weapons Convention*, Conference of the States Parties, Fourth Session (C-IV/NAT.2), 29 April 1999.

6   Verification by On-Site Inspection

1. Ben Sanders, 'IAEA Historical Background', in David Fischer, Ben Sanders, Lawrence Scheinman and George Bunn, *A New Nuclear Triad: The Non-Proliferation of Nuclear Weapons, International Verification and the International Atomic Energy Agency*, PPNN Study Three, p. 3.
2. Lawrence Scheinman, 'The Current Status of IAEA Safeguards', *ibid.*, pp. 14–16.
3. A succinct account of the history of IAEA safeguards is given in IAEA, *The Evolution of IAEA Safeguards*, International Nuclear Verification Series, no. 2, Vienna, 1998, pp. 9–29; David Fischer, *History of the International Atomic Energy Agency: The First Forty Years* (Vienna: IAEA, 1997), pp. 243–324.
4. For a long time, Argentina, Brazil and Cuba had stayed away from the NPT and from full commitments to the Treaty for the Prohibition of Nuclear Weapons in Latin America (Tlatelolco Treaty), but they eventually acceded and accepted comprehensive IAEA safeguards. In Africa the main holdout was South Africa which had actually developed nuclear weapons under the apartheid minority regime but disposed of them as it handed over power to an African majority government and acceded to the NPT. In the Far East, however, North Korea, a former member of the IAEA, has openly embarked on a nuclear-weapon programme following its withdrawal from IAEA membership and recently also from the NPT.
5. Lawrence Scheinman, *The Nonproliferation Role of the International Atomic Energy Agency: A Critical Assessment* (Washington, DC: Resources for the Future, 1985), pp. 15–17; David Fischer and Paul Szasz, edited by Jozef Goldblat, *Safeguarding the Atom; A Critical Appraisal* (London and Philadelphia: Taylor & Francis (SIPRI study), 1985), pp. 17–18.
6. INFCIRC/153, para. 28.
7. Nuclear material refers mainly to natural uranium, low-enriched uranium, highly enriched uranium, plutonium and mixed oxides of plutonium and uranium. At present the IAEA uses the following criteria for significant quantity and for timely detection of diversion of nuclear material: an SQ of direct-use material is equivalent to 8 kg of plutonium or 25 kg of highly enriched uranium-235 (enriched to 20% or more); an SQ of indirect-use material is 75 kg of low-enriched uranium-235 (enriched to less than 20%) and 10 tons of natural uranium, or 20 tons of depleted uranium and thorium. Timely

detection refers to the estimated conversion time within which diversion of a significant quantity must be detected: thus, within one month for fresh nuclear fuel containing separated highly enriched uranium, plutonium or mixed oxides of plutonium and uranium; and within three month for irradiated fuel containing highly enriched uranium or plutonium; or irradiated fuel containing highly enriched uranium or plutonium.

8. INFCIRC/153, para, 19.
9. This was reflected in the statements of Mohammed ElBaradei and Hans Blix to the Security Council on 27 January 2003.
10. David Kay, as Head of the US Iraq Survey Group reported on 2 October 2003 to US Congressional Committees that his group had found no weapons of mass destruction, except for 'dozens of WMD-related program activities and significant amounts of equipment that Iraq had concealed'. After he resigned in January 2004, Kay stated further that the US Administration was almost certainly wrong in its pre-war belief that Iraq had any significant stockpiles of illicit weapons. See Washington Press Conference with Senators Pat Roberts and John D. Rockefeller and Congressman Porter Gross (2 October) and report on interviews with the media, *New York Times*, 26 January 2004.
11. Hans Blix, *Disarming Iraq* (New York: Pantheon Books, 2004), pp. 271–4.
12. Lynn R. Sykes, 'False and Misleading Claims about Verification during the Senate Debate on the Comprehensive Test-Ban Treaty', *Journal of the Federation of American Scientists*, May/June, 2000.
13. 'Findings and Recommendations Concerning the Comprehensive Test-Ban Treaty', General John M. Shalikashvili, Special Adviser to the President of the United States and the Secretary of State, 4 January 2001; 'Final Report of the Independent Commission on the Verifiability of the CTBT', reported by Trevor Findlay under the auspices of VERTIC, November 2000.
14. In the 1990s, the US suspected the following countries as being of proliferation concern: China (and Taiwan), Egypt, India, Iran, Iraq, Israel, Libya, Myanmar, North Korea, Pakistan, Russia, South Korea, Syria and Vietnam.
15. Thirteen States have declared current or past chemical weapon production facilities: of these, six declared current stocks of chemical weapons or chemical warfare agents – the US, Russia, Albania, India, Libya and South Korea; the remaining seven have declared having only former CW production facilities – China, France, the UK, Japan, Iran, Bosnia and Herzegovina, and Federal Republic of Yugoslavia. Five additional States – Belgium, Canada, Germany, Italy and Slovenia – have declared they were old possessors of chemical weapons. We may add Iraq as another former possessor that was disarmed by the UN Security Council. See Alexander Kelle, The First CWC Review Conference: Taking Stock and Paving the Way Ahead; Disarmament Forum, UNIDIR, no. 4 (2002), p. 4.
16. Amy E. Smithson, 'U.S. Implementation of the CWC', in Jonathan B. Tucker (ed.), *The Chemical Weapons Convention: Implementing Challenges and Solutions* (Monterey Institute of International Studies, 2001), p. 25.
17. Amy E. Smithson, *Rudderless: The Chemical Weapons Convention at 1 1/2* (Washington, DC: The Henry L. Stimson Center, 1998), pp. 27–32.
18. OPCW, 'Review Document, Approved by the First Special Session of the Conference of the State Parties to Review the Operation of the Chemical Weapons Convention', The Hague, 9 May 2003.

19. Richard S. Burgess, 'Chemical Industry and the CWC', in Tucker (ed.), *Chemical Weapons Convention*, p. 41; Amy E. Smithson, 'U.S. Implementation of the CWC', in Tucker (ed.), *ibid.*, pp. 25–8.
20. Burgess, 'Chemical Industry', p. 43.
21. Smithson, *Rudderless*, pp. 8–10; Amy Sands and Jason Pate, 'CWC Compliance Issues', in John B. Tucker (ed.), *Chemical Weapons Convention*, pp. 18–19.
22. Jonathan B. Tucker, 'Introduction', in Tucker (ed.), *Chemical Weapons Convention*, pp. 4–5.

7 Compliance Issues and Recourse

1. UNIDIR and VERTIC, *Coming to Terms with Security: A Handbook on Verification and Compliance* (Geneva: UNIDIR/2000/10), pp. 33–43.
2. Definition adapted from Amy Sands and Jason Pate, 'CWC Compliance Issues', in Jonathan B. Tucker (ed.), *The Chemical Weapons Convention: Implementation Challenges and Solutions*' (Monterey Institute of International Studies, 2001), p. 19.
3. Statement on the status of inspections in Iraq made before the UN Security Council on 27 January 2003 by Hans Blix, Executive Chairman of UNMOVIC, and by Mohamed ElBaradei, Director General of the IAEA. The verification and compliance issues and the political context within the Council, both in various capitals and in Iraq itself, are analyzed in Hans Blix, *Disarming Iraq* (New York: Pantheon Books, 2004), pp. 127–44.
4. Alexander A. Pikayev, 'Russian Implementation of the CWC', in Tucker (ed.), *Chemical Weapons Convention*, pp. 35–7.
5. Amy E. W Smithson, 'U.S. Implementation of the CWC', in Tucker (ed.), *Chemical Weapons Convention*, p. 25.
6. *Ibid.*, p. 21.
7. Statement by John A. Lauder, Director, NCI Nonproliferation Center, to the U.S. Senate Committee on Foreign Relations, October 5, 2000, as quoted in Sands and Pate, '*CWC Compliance Issues*', p. 19.
8. *Ibid.*, p. 20.

8 Building an Effective WMD Control Regime

1. Lewis A Dunn, Peter R. Lavoy and Scott D, Sagan, 'Conclusions: Planning the Unthinkable', in Peter R. Lavoy, Scott D. Sagan and James J. Wirtz, *Planning the Unthinkable: How New Powers Will Use Nuclear, Biological, and Chemical Weapons* (Ithaca and London: Cornell University Press, 2000), pp. 239–40.
2. George Perkovich, Joseph Cirincione, Rose Gottemoeller, Jon B. Wolfsthal and Jessica T. Mathews, *Universal Compliance: A Strategy for Nuclear Security* (Washington, DC, 2004), pp. 9–13.
3. Sam Nunn, Keynote Address at the Carnegie International Nonproliferation Conference, Washington, DC, 21 June 2004.
4. Perkovich, Cirincione, Gottemoeller, Wolfsthal and Mathews, *Universal Compliance*, pp. 15–22.
5. Hans Blix, 'International Law Relating to Disarmament and Arms Control; with Special Focus on Verification and Compliance', in F. Kalshoven (ed.), *The Centennial of the First International Peace Conference* (Kluwer Law International,

2000), pp. 128–9; also Keynote Address by Hans Blix to the Carnegie International Nonproliferation Conference, Washington, DC; 21 June 2004.

6. Mohamed ElBaradei, 'Nuclear Non-Proliferation: Global Security in a Rapidly Changing World', Keynote Address, Carnegie International Nonproliferation Conference, Washington, D.C., 21 June 2004. Many of the ideas were officially presented to the IAEA Board of Governors in his statement on 8 March 2004.

7. John Simpson, 'The Nuclear Non-Proliferation Regime: Back to the Future?', *Disarmament Forum*, no. 1, 2004, p. 14.

8. Jonathan B. Tucker, 'Introduction', in Jonathan B. Tucker (ed.), *The Chemical Weapons Convention: Implementation Challenges and Solutions* (Monterey Institute of International Studies, 2001), p. 5.

9. OPCW. Conference of States Parties 'Report of the First Special Session of the Conference of the States Parties to Review the Operation of the Chemical Weapons Convention, 28 April–9 May 2003, Doc. RC-1/5.

10. For analyses of the trends, see Malcolm Dando, 'Scientific and Technological Change and the Future of the CWC: The Problem of the Non-Lethal Weapons', *Disarmament Forum*, UNIDIR, vol. 4, 2002, pp. 33–44; and George W. Parshall, 'Scientific and Technical Developments and the CWC', in Tucker (ed.), *Chemical Weapons Convention*, pp. 53–8.

11. Michael L. Moodie, 'Issues for the First CWC Review Conference', in Tucker (ed.), *ibid.*, pp. 62–3.

12. See Perkovich, Cirincione, Gottemoeller, Wolfstal and Mathews, *Universal Compliance*, pp. 63–9 on US nuclear policy, and pp. 18–19, 73–6 on South Asia.

13. UN Security Council, Thirteenth Quarterly Report of the Executive Chairman of UNMOVIC to the United Nations Security Council, doc. S/2003/580, 30 May 2003.

14. Robert Kirk, 'A Comprehensive Test Ban Treaty: A New Verification Role for the International Atomic Energy Agency', Occasional Paper Series, The Atlantic Council of the United States, Washington, DC, May 1995, pp. 1–18.

15. For a detailed account of the background and significance of those principles and objectives, see Berhanykun Andemicael, Merle Opelz and Jan Priest, 'Measure for Measure: The NPT and the Road Ahead', *IAEA Bulletin*, vol. 37, no. 3, 1995, pp. 30–8.

16. Perkovich, Cirincione, Gottemoeller, Wolfsthal and Mathews, *Universal Compliance*, pp. 63–72.

17. The idea of circumventing the veto is not new but deserves serious consideration in the light of current threats. As regards WMD control, Richard Butler had proposed after the end of his assignment as Executive Chairman of UNSCOM acceptance of what he called the 'principle of the exception', i.e. agreement in advance by the five permanent members of the Security Council not to exercise their veto power in a case identified by a credible report to involve a violation of a specified treaty – especially one concerning weapons of mass destruction. See Richard Butler, *The Greatest Threat: Iraq. Weapons of Mass Destruction, and the Growing Crisis of Global Security* (New York: BBS Public Affairs, 2000), pp. 238–41.

9 Building Effective Management for the Regime

1. Andrew Clapham, 'Creating the High Commissioner for Human Rights: The Outside Story', *European Journal of International Law*, vol. 5, no. 4, 1995, p. 567.

2. *Ibid.*, p. 567.
3. Jose Bustani, 'Statement by Jose Bustani, Director General of the Organization on the Prohibition of Chemical Weapons', *Global Policy Forum*, 21 April 2002. (http://www.globalpolicy.org/wtc/analysis/2002/0421bustani.htm).
4. *Ibid.*
5. Robert Matthews, 'The OPCW at Five: Balancing Verification in Evolving Circumstances', in *Verification Yearbook 2002* (London: VERTIC, 2002) (http://www.vertic.org/publications/verification%20yearbook.html).
6. The incident is described by Hans Blix in *Disarming Iraq*, pp. 36–7.
7. Report of the External Auditor on the Audit of the Accounts of the International Atomic Energy Agency for the Year Ended 31 December 1997 (GC42-6, Part 1), para. 70.
8. Amy E. Smithson, 'Recharging the Chemical Weapons Convention', *Arms Control Today*, March 2004, http://www.armscontrol.org/act/2004 03/Smithson.asp
9. Maurizio Barbeschi, 'Organizational Culture of the OPCW Secretariat', *Disarmament Forum*, 4 (2002), p. 51.
10. Report of the Second Special Session of the Conference of the States Parties C-SS-2/3, 30 April 2003.
11. Rogelio Pfirter, Opening Statement by the Director General to the First Special Session of the Conference of the States Parties to Review the Operation of the Chemical Weapons Convention, RC-1/DG.3, 28 April 2003.
12. Smithson, 'Recharging the Chemical Weapons Convention'.
13. Report of Working Group A to the Fifth Session of the Preparatory Commission for the Comprehensive Nuclear-Test-Ban Treaty Organization, as Amended by the Preparatory Commission, CTBT/PC-5/1/Add.1,15 April 1998.
14. The United States fiscal year runs from October to September. This was changed from July in the mid-1970s, in response to the fact that the Congress was unable to approve a budget within the time allotted. When this was done, the United States in effect skipped a year in budgeting for assessments.
15. The initial decision of the Conference of States Parties (C-I/DEC.75 of 23 May 1997) on the scale of assessment stated: 'This assessment is based on the percentage of the Scale of Assessments of the United Nations adjusted for the fact that the total for such percentages relating to those States which are States Parties to the Convention amounts to 91.23 percent. Hence the formula used for arriving at the assessed amount for a given State Party is as follows: Assessment of State Party Y equal to UN percentage of State Y multiplied by the total amount of the 1997 assessed budget of the OPCW divided by 91.23 and multiplied by 100.'
16. Peacekeeping operations are funded by a separate assessment, but the major cost is that of paying for national military contingents. Payment for these can and often is delayed.
17. This practice has been resisted by major contributors because the borrowing increases the budget due to the need to pay interest.

Index